GWR GOODS SERVICES

PART 2A

GOODS DEPOTS AND THEIR OPERATION

by
TONY ATKINS

WILD SWAN PUBLICATIONS

ISBN 978-1-905184-33-0

Designed by Paul Karau
Printed by Amadeus Press Ltd., Cleckheaton

Published by
WILD SWAN PUBLICATIONS LTD.
1-3 Hagbourne Road, Didcot, Oxon, OX11 8DP

CONTENTS

Wootton Bassett station, pictured in the last quarter of the 19th century with mixed-gauge bridge-rail main line, looking towards Swindon. The wood and brick-built goods shed was located very near to the station, for ease of access, with the loading gauge in the far doorway of the shed, and the cattle dock beyond. The period is emphasised by the round-topped broad gauge wagon. A shunting horse and dumb-buffered open wagon (with 4-link couplings) are seen in front of the goods shed on the Up Main.

CHAPTER ONE

THE DEPOTS AND THEIR WORK

IN the early days of railways, it was usual to have the goods shed or yard as near as possible to the passenger station so that the stationmaster and his staff could cover both goods and passenger work. This arrangement continued at many smaller stations throughout the GWR's existence, where the stationmaster personally superintended the work of every member of staff – passenger and goods – and, at the smallest places, even performed a large part of the work himself. At large centres, however, separate goods depots were established as business increased, and more elaborate accommodation was provided for handling all kinds of traffic. With increased traffic in towns, new passenger stations were sometimes provided, and goods activities were established in the old, vacated buildings, Paddington being the prime example, but also at Gloucester. Similarly, on absorbing other companies, redundant passenger stations became goods depots, as at Barton (Hereford); Dock Street and Mill Street (Newport); and Oswestry.

As the goods services grew in size and complexity, it became necessary to have Goods Agents (superintendents, the equivalent of a stationmaster) in charge of such depots, with separate staffs; some also had control of outlying depots and sidings. The general rules laid down for the guidance of stationmasters and goods agents were the same at all stations, whether small or large. Their responsibilities consisted not only of ensuring that the rail and cartage sides of the depot operation ran efficiently, but they were also expected to secure the greatest possible amount of goods traffic by rail into and out of their areas. This meant visiting traders in town, 'selling' the GWR and canvassing for new traffic, and so on. In pre-grouping days, there was competition from the many other railways which had alternative routes to the same destinations. After the 1914–18 war there was, in addition, growing competition from road hauliers; by the 1930s, competition between railways had almost disappeared, the greater threat being from road transport. To keep ahead of all the competition, the aim of the GW goods staff was to collect and deliver goods faster, and more reliably, than anyone else. In 1936, for example, canvassers attached to Goods District Offices were supplied with motor cars in order to seek out traffic in remoter areas.

THE GOODS FACILITIES

The facilities provided at places along the line for dealing with freight varied in size according to the traffic, and to the requirements of the locality. In the countryside, a few short sidings could deal with everything and the stationmaster could often be found superintending the shunting and marshalling of trains; the proper sheeting, loading, unloading and checking of goods traffic; prompt delivery and collection of goods and parcels from the town; clearance

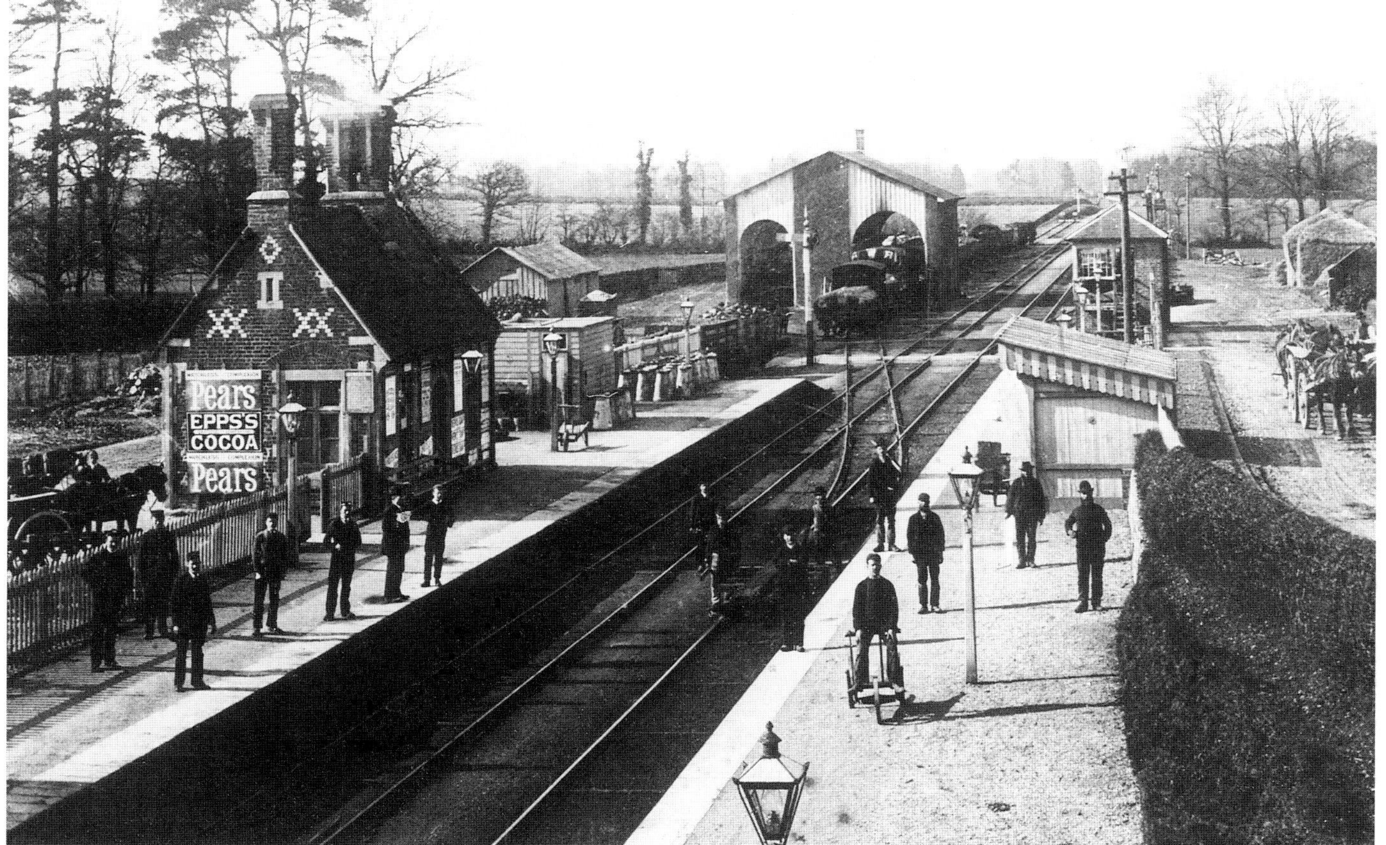

A typical country goods shed at Woodborough station c.1900, providing covered accommodation for both railway wagons and cartage vehicles. Tilley lamps are seen on the station platforms, and probably provided illumination within the shed, too. Smoke marks over the archway of the shed are evidence of locomotives passing through.

Hullavington goods yard in February 1928, looking east, showing, on the left, a cart (road) weighbridge, with a capacity of 12 tons, occupied by a cart-load of hay, a cut-up tree on the ground, just beyond, and a Mileage Siding nearby. A white-painted cattle dock is prominent, with a notice indicating how close traction engines could approach. Just beyond the cattle pens, the yard crane (1½ ton capacity) may just be seen, with small lock-up goods shed and platform beyond it, possibly being serviced by the local ('pickup') goods that can be seen on the headshunt (with the remainder of its train on the siding on the far side of the running lines). A horse-box is seen at the buffers of the end-loading dock, with a barrow of milk churns outside a 'Siphon' beyond, and a further collection of churns on the ground against the cattle pens.

NATIONAL RAILWAY MUSEUM

VENTILATED
96444
NOTICE
10

Oxford, South End goods shed and yard, looking south in the late 1920s with the running lines on the far right. Due to its hard usage, an access road of granite setts had been provided. The gasometers in the distance usually indicated another railway connection to service them with coal and to remove any by-products, and the Oxford gas company was connected by sidings from the running loop beyond the goods yard. The 10-ton crane on the left had an unusual built-up platform, with a horse lorry adjacent, loaded with pipes, whilst beyond, a rail-mounted crane can be seen on the left-hand siding of the pair in the centre. The cart weighbridge features in the foreground, centre right, whilst horse lorries and tilts are seen backed up to the goods shed on the right, with a pointer to the future being indicated by the motor lorry beyond.

C. L. MOWAT

The outer (west) side of Oxford goods shed, seen from the running lines, with de Glehn No. 102 La France *on a down express in the 1920s. A shed road ran the length of the near side of the buildings, being outside the structure at the south end but inside at the north, as seen in this picture. There were additional roads between the shed and running lines, for storage.*

R. GRIEFFENHAGEN

and despatch of goods and coal wagons; all the goods accounts work; answering enquiries as to rates; settlement of claims and disputes; all the goods correspondence, and so on (all by himself at the smallest places) as well as all the passenger duties.

In big towns, the agent had specialist staff to help him. There were large, covered depots devoted to 'C & D' (collection and delivery, or 'smalls' traffic), with separate depots (open 'mileage yards') for minerals and other heavy traffic. The railway also built warehouses for the storage of goods, especially in towns chosen by firms to be their distribution centres, using local road transport, which often ran to fixed schedules. Special facilities might also be provided for dealing with fish, milk, cattle, etc. where needed. Separate sheds for 'returned empties' traffic were also provided in manufacturing areas. At docks, ample provision had to be made for warehousing goods (particularly foodstuffs) which might not be immediately conveyed away by rail after they had been landed. Similar accommodation was provided for the storage of export traffic.

Before the advent of the 'common user' scheme for wagons, and before the grouping, a special type of depot called the 'Transfer Shed' could be found in some places, where traffic for a given district was received from foreign lines for re-loading

Another view of the large depot at Oxford, this time looking north from the public footbridge in the late 1920s. The passenger station may be seen in the distance, to the right of the signal cabin, on the far side of the Botley Road level crossing (and the later underbridge). The LMS company had its terminus on the far side of Botley Road, alongside the Great Western passenger station, and its goods shed can be seen in the middle distance (immediately to the left of the signal post in the foreground) with H. Tuckwell & Sons' shed (builders merchants, located in the LMS yard) to the left of that. Many loaded opens are apparent in the Great Western yard to the right, sheeted in many instances to protect the loads.

C. L. MOWAT

The northern section of Oxford South End yard area, showing the Becket Street yard (which ran alongside that road at this point), with Botley Road beyond the buffer stops, probably in the early 1920s, with indications of L&NWR rather than LMS. The Tuckwell building was unlettered. A newly-painted 'Mex' cattle wagon with large 'GW' on its sides (the change to smaller lettering was made in 1922) can be seen on the extreme right, with a rake of whitewashed cattle trucks (the disinfectant was altered from lime in 1923) on the pens road.

The transhipment shed at Reading c.1900, for the sorting of small consignments of goods from company and foreign lines, mainly to destinations on the GWR in the district, ranging from West Drayton to Basingstoke, Thatcham and Cholsey, but also for the Southern Railway and more distant locations. The notice above the platform to the left specified 'Northern Stations', with 'Up Road Stations' on the right, and 'Wolverhampton' beyond. Returned empty crates can be seen on the left, with a wide variety of goods in barrels, bales, sacks, and boxes elsewhere on the platforms. The use of open wagons as low as two planks for the merchandise is evident. Cranes were in fixed positions along the near platform.

NATIONAL RAILWAY MUSEUM

into GW wagons and then forwarded to destination. The wagons from other companies were returned as soon as possible to their own lines, to avoid payment of demurrage – see our *Introduction* volume, page 41.

There were also 'Transhipment Depots' for GWR traffic, where goods for local stations would arrive as mixed-up loads in wagons from various places, and would be sorted at the depot into branch and station order. Then, depending on wagon usage, consignments were reloaded in sequence before being sent out on the appropriate local train services.

Of course, the change of gauge had brought its own transhipment problems in earlier days on the GWR. Exeter, for example, was for many years the transfer point for all traffic going west, and broad- and standard-gauge goods trains were positioned on opposite sides of a platform in a shed, across which the goods were transferred. Didcot and Gloucester provided other examples.

The gradual establishment of Railhead Delivery Services by road motor vehicles, and the Country Lorry services in the 1920s and 30s, both of which covered wider areas than could horse-drawn collection and delivery, eliminated many of the rail wagon transhipments that had occurred previously. By the 1930s, in GWR documents, what had been called 'transhipment' in earlier times was being referred to as 'transfer'. The previous use of 'transfer' (reloading of goods from foreign wagons into GW wagons) became defunct after the grouping.

Patterns of operation at goods depots did not change very much over the years,

The 'change-of-gauge' transfer shed at Didcot, looking west, with the wider archway for the broad gauge line originally on the left. This shed was not erected until the late 1860s, when the removal of the broad gauge between Oxford and Wolverhampton was envisaged, and a transfer depot for traffic conveyed by broad gauge wagons was required. After its closure as a transfer shed, the standard gauge line became a bay, ending at an office at the far end of the shed, thus permitting road access to the platform for consignment traffic. Much of the provender stores for the company's numerous horses were prepared at and dispatched from Didcot, and the substantial Provender Stores may be seen here in the background, together with storage barns. The processes, involving hay, straw, oats, beans and maize, were driven by electric power from 1901. A. F. CARPENTER

A view from the interior of the old Didcot transfer shed, looking east. Didcot had originally been provided with a goods shed immediately to the west of the main passenger buildings, on the Down side of the main lines, but the transfer shed was adapted for use as a goods shed during 1883, with access from Foxhall Road. This allowed development of the old site alongside the station. A. F. CARPENTER

Slough in April 1892, looking towards London, with the down 'narrow' gauge 'Zulu' on the mixed gauge main line. The goods shed and mileage yard are seen on the left; by this time, it was entirely to the 'narrow' gauge, as were the adjacent Relief lines. Various coal merchants' pitches ('wharfage') to the left were again served only by standard gauge trackwork. The Windsor triangle features on the right, and only one line of the west curve contained broad gauge track. The evolution of goods yard facilities at Slough are portrayed in the following photographs. TAUNT COLLECTION

Slough goods shed and yard, looking west, probably in the 1920s. A rather basic road entrance to the yard was from the right, in front of the 'Iron Mink', and probably originated on Stoke Road, but a more formal access was situated at the western end, off Stoke Poges Lane. Goods facilities at Slough at this time were quite limited. The original castellated Horlicks tower and chimney – such a landmark in the area – can be seen to the right. NATIONAL RAILWAY MUSEUM

Slough, Farnham Road Jct., looking east in the 1920s. The sidings at this time comprised the long loop around the back of the shed, and a dead-end siding terminating to the west of the goods shed. A goods loop line ran alongside the Up Relief, and in front of the goods shed. A considerable number of wagons can be seen occupying these three roads. The yard crane on the left can be seen lifting a large ring-shaped load, with a train being shunted on the yard loop behind. The Horlicks factory subsidiary buildings with a 'Horlicks Malted Milk' sign are seen to the rear (left) of the yard.

L&GRP

An aerial view of Slough Goods, looking east over the Stoke Poges Lane overbridge, probably in the early 1930s. In 1935, the goods shed was reported as being given an additional 100ft extension at its west end, whilst other improvements notified at around this time included a new siding for coal traffic, an extension to the cart road, and new wharfage. The original yard extension to the west of the Stoke Poges Lane bridge is seen at the bottom of the picture; this comprised just a pair of sidings in 1897, but had expanded to four by the end of the Great War. However, the area was modified considerably around 1919/20 with the opening of the Trading Estate nearby; it had started life in the Great War as the repair depot and clearance site for Army road vehicles. The new western extension to the Horlicks factory is also apparent here.

Slough extension mileage yard, to the west of Stoke Poges bridge, looking west in December 1929, soon after completion; these would soon be expanded with an additional siding on each side. Coal factors' storage bins were made of old sleepers, whilst grounded coach and goods van bodies were provided for use as offices, one of which (No. 37469 of 1885 in the centre foreground) still had 'Sales List' stencilled on. The coal sacks were draped over its white roof to dry out. Coal merchants Booth Brothers' horse lorry is seen near the left siding, whilst one of the same firm's wagons is visible on the right. On the left in the distance we can see the Estates sidings, which by this time also incorporated the original extension sidings to Slough Goods yard.

NATIONAL RAILWAY MUSEUM

G W
DODD & SON
SLOUGH
BLOXSOME
BOOTH BROTHERS
BLOXSOME
199
SLOUGH
G W
SALES LIST
37469

From the late 1920s, Slough goods shed was subject to many alterations. The new corrugated extension built onto the west end of the goods shed at Slough is seen here in 1929, with a deep canopy over the road vehicle bays on the left-hand side of the structure. The original brick-built depot is seen beyond, with what appears to have been an additional extension to the original offices at the far end. The cosmopolitan use of wagons and sheets is illustrated by the GWR 'Open' on the right with an L&NE tarpaulin. The shed cartage road was unpaved, as were the great majority of the roadways in yards. The shed received an additional extension in the mid-1930s, whilst just before the outbreak of war, a large warehouse system was built over the old shed, providing two additional floors. NATIONAL RAILWAY MUSEUM

A look now at facilities at another large yard, this time Reading. The sorting yard for the large low-level goods shed at Kings Meadow, north of the main line and east of the Vastern Road crossing, is seen here, looking east in World War 1. A 2-ton crane is seen to the left, on the dock platform at the east end of the goods shed. The line curving around at the right-hand edge of the photograph ran underneath the main lines and connected to the exchange sidings with the SE&CR, and to that company's line to Redhill.

NATIONAL RAILWAY MUSEUM

The bridge carrying the Great Western main line that permitted the connection between Kings Meadow yard and the Southern Railway/Region on the far (south) side. This was originally a double track connection, but was latterly reduced to one, with a dead-end siding. Gas lamps are of a different design from the previous picture, indicating the passage of time. Huntley & Palmer's biscuit factory buildings can be seen in the distance, above the wagons; access to the H & P factory was further up the yard towards London, through a brick arch under the main line. P. KARAU

Reading's low-level 'Goods and Coal Depot' at Kings Meadow is identified by the lettering above the roof, facing the main line, no doubt to impress travellers. The shed was opened in 1896, and photographed here looking east (from near the Vastern Road crossing) in the early 20th century, showing the cartage side of the building. The 'General and Enquiry Offices' were up the steps and through the door in the right-hand section of the building. A traction engine, covered and open cartage trailers of 'C & G Ayres, GWR Agents, Reading' may be seen at various places along its length. NATIONAL RAILWAY MUSEUM

A later view of Kings Meadow goods shed and yard at Reading, looking west towards the Vastern Road which passed under the main lines just to the east of the passenger station. The large Vastern Road mileage yard was beyond. The siding in the foreground was a recent addition, being absent in the earlier picture showing the cartage side, whilst a platform to serve the rail vehicles had been built under the awnings. Gas lamps (also absent before) are seen cantilevered out from corrugated walls of the lift shafts. Inclined loading chutes down to the platform had also been added since the former picture. The period is defined by the Dia V14 'Mink A' No. 89954, dating from 1913. The unpaved cartage road was showing signs of wear. NATIONAL RAILWAY MUSEUM

Kings Meadow goods shed, looking towards Paddington, probably in the same period as that on page 15 (top) – after 1905, as the large 'GW' had been painted on a few wagons. A clear view is given of the two shed roads, suitably spaced for sufficient access to the wagons, whilst the inclined access line from the main lines above may be seen to the right of the shed, set into the embankment. Another Ayres' traction engine and trailer features alongside the wagons to the left of centre in the foreground, whilst another, horse-drawn, vehicle probably belonging to a trader, is seen to the right. A grey-painted (goods) 'Mica' meat van can be seen at bottom centre.

NATIONAL RAILWAY MUSEUM

Vastern Road, Reading, the dividing line between Kings Meadow and Vastern Road yards, looking south-west in 1948. The low-level yard was to the left of the photographer, with Vastern Road yard to the right, beyond the railings. The connecting track between the two, and its level crossing, may just be seen in front of the bridge under the main line, to the left and then passing in front of the hydraulic power house tower. The passenger station can be seen on the embankment, to the right of the water tower above the vans. NATIONAL RAILWAY MUSEUM

The south-eastern corner of Vastern Road yard, looking east, back towards the level crossing and Kings Meadow goods depot, in 1948. The power house may be seen to the right, at the foot of the embankment. NATIONAL RAILWAY MUSEUM

A panoramic view of Vastern Road mileage yard (opened 1896), looking west, illustrating the considerable number of coal and mineral wagons that were typically to be found in the yard. The Dia O2/10 seven-plank opens at the buffer stops to the right of the large crane date the picture as after 1905. Many of the vehicles are seen with their doors open in the process of being unloaded, including some of the wagon-load general merchandise vehicles along the back of the yard, against the continuation of Vastern Road. The pair of lines on the left, together with one from the Signal Works (seen on the left-hand edge of the picture) converged to form the single-line crossing over Vastern Road to Kings Meadow. Each of the two yards had its own independent connection to the main lines above, and the incline for the Vastern Road yard can be seen on the left in the middle distance. Other pointers to the period include the dumb-buffered coal wagons (one Wyken, one Messers) to the right of the crane. The cylindrical tank wagon, above and to the right of the corrugated shed, appears to have had a dedicated siding.
NATIONAL RAILWAY MUSEUM

WYKEN
WYKEN
441
COLLIERY CO
COVENTRY
C&G. AYRES
G.W.R. AGENTS
READING.
T. SIMMONS & SON
99
READING
G.W.R.
MESSERS
GEORGE
COAL
2
WEST
MERCHANT
READING

The western end of Vastern Road yard, showing the exit into Caversham Road, seen in April 1943. The open door of the LMS covered wagon on the right shows boxes which were in the process of either being loaded for transit, or offloaded.

NATIONAL RAILWAY MUSEUM

except for the gradual introduction of labour-saving devices in the between-the-wars period, and again (particularly) just before nationalisation in 1948. In the post-war era, the whole procedure for loading 'outwards' traffic at large depots was changed, goods then being loaded directly from cartage vehicles parked alongside the outwards wagons rather than being off-loaded onto platform trolleys and moved to wagons, as was to be found in the traditional type of goods shed.

The usual accommodation and facilities provided at goods stations could include:

Covered Sheds, where the bulk of the general merchandise ('smalls') traffic was handled, i.e. traffic collected and delivered by GWR cartage and, possibly, also by outside agents.
Warehouses and Cellars, where traffic, not immediately deliverable, was stored awaiting forwarding instructions.
Ramps, for end loading of wheeled traffic.
Cattle Docks & Pens, for transfer of livestock.
Sidings, in the open,
(a) accessible to road vehicles (for 'mileage traffic' such as coal for town use, coke, hay and straw, grain, sand, salt, timber, slates, tiles, and building materials etc,) and
(b) not approachable by road vehicles, for wagon storage where inwards wagons waited to be berthed for unloading, and where outwards wagons waited to be marshalled into transfer trains, or to be picked up en route by long-distance trains.
Stables and Garages for accommodation of horses and road motor vehicles.
Weighbridges for carts and wagons, and platform weighing machines.
Cranes, whose lifting capacities varied according to the requirements of the traffic: 20–30 cwt cranes in the shed; 2, 3, 6, 12 or 20-ton in the yard. They may have been worked by hand, steam, hydraulic or electric power. From the 1920s, portable petrol-electric cranes, fork-lift trucks and other labour-saving devices were employed in increasing numbers.

The use of horses for cartage and shunting work at stations required the provision of stabling, and the old stable building at Faringdon is seen here, as later converted to a road motor garage. The sign 'Motor Spirit Store. Smoking, striking matches or the use of lights in or near this store is dangerous and is strictly forbidden. By order' illustrates the new order. A. ATTEWELL

A cart weighbridge, at the entrance to Paddington goods depot is seen here in the early years of the 20th century with a two-horse covered lorry posed across the end of the office. The animals were kept in beautiful condition, great efforts being made by both the staff and the company to ensure that the horses were in the best of health, and in 'good working order'. NRM

The wagon weighbridge at Slough, seen in 1936; this was situated at the east end of the yard, by the roadway leading down from Stoke Road.
NATIONAL RAILWAY MUSEUM

Another cart weighbridge, this time in the yard at Hungerford in later years. Even the more modest yards had such facilities, which were utilized by both company vehicles and those of private concerns who would pay for the privilege. A. ATTEWELL

Right: *The outdoor goods weighing machine at Witney, the mechanism of which was protected by a wooden cover and sacking. The inscription on the cast platform reads 'To weigh 20 cwt Henry Pooley & Sons Ltd Birmingham & London'.* A. ATTEWELL

Far right: *A smaller capacity weighing machine on the platform at Bromyard station, probably used for parcels traffic.* A. ATTEWELL

An example of a mobile weighing machine at Morris Cowley, similar to those above, but mounted on wheels. Wooden chocks had been placed under the wheels. The Dia V14 'Mink A' dates from 1925, but the weighing machine appears to have been around for many more years; the photograph was probably taken late in 1929. NATIONAL RAILWAY MUSEUM

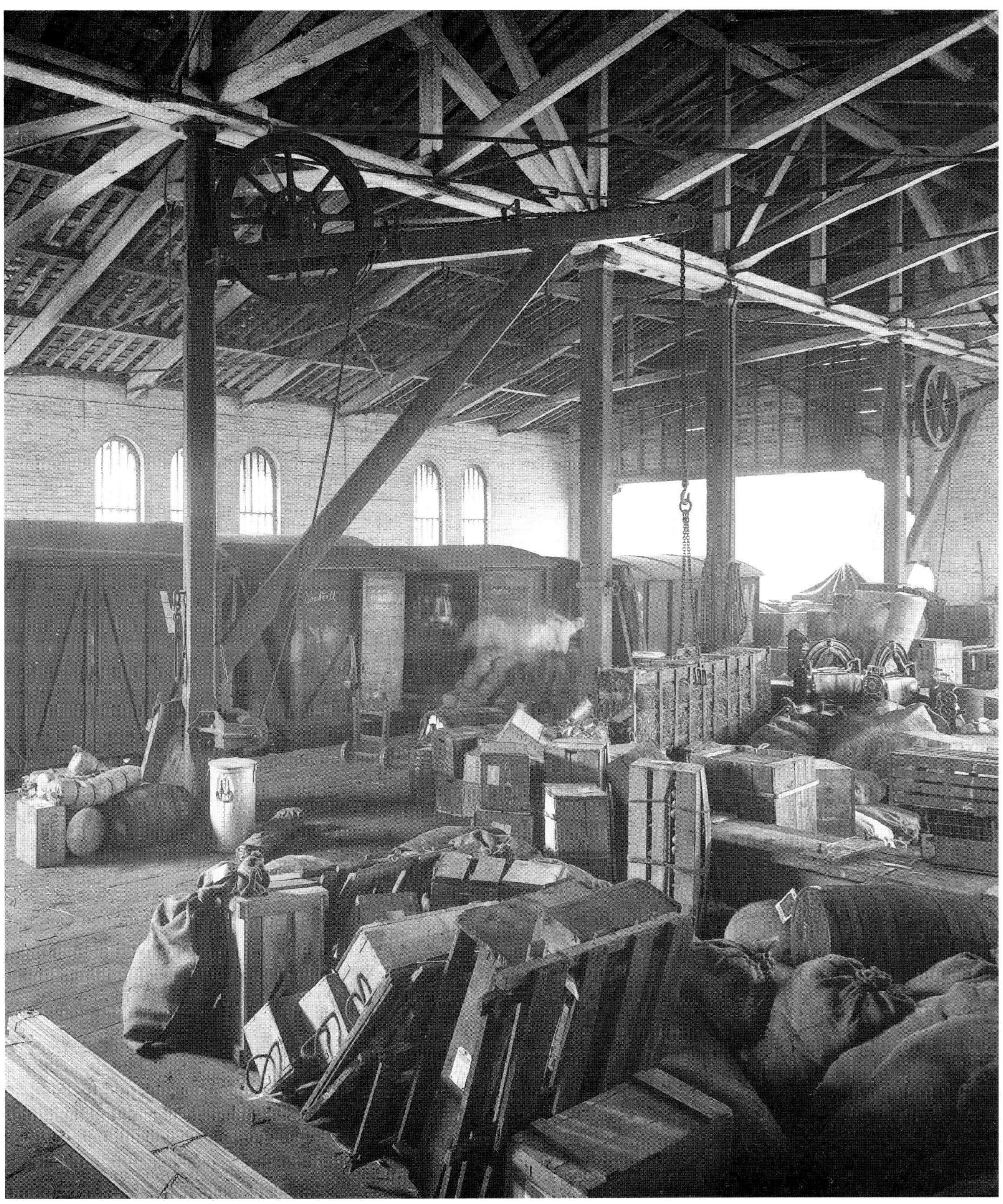

There were numerous designs of yard and shed cranes throughout the Great Western system, and the few illustrated here and over the following pages are examples only. This simple 1½ to 2 cwt shed version was photographed at Newbury before the First World War, had a timber frame, and swivelled on its centre post; such a design was generally quite adequate for the limited weights encountered within the confines of the goods shed. Notice the wide selection of traffic in the shed, ranging from fruit in crates to machine mangles. NATIONAL RAILWAY MUSEUM

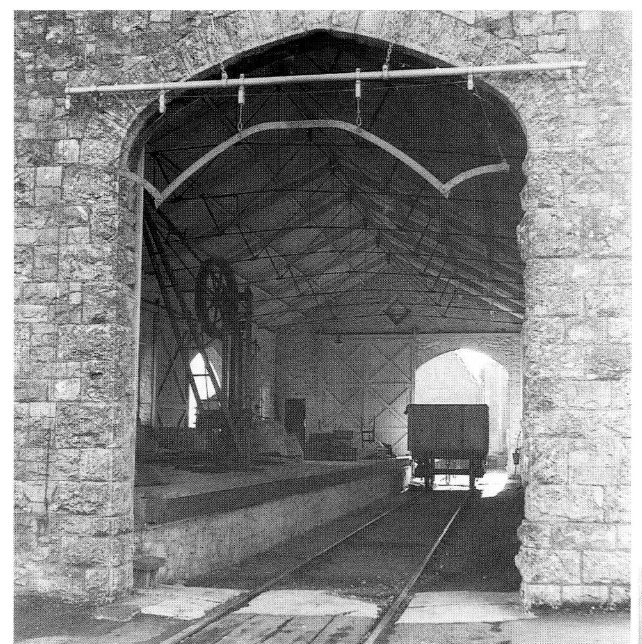

Looking into the stone-built shed at Cheddar where an iron crane stood inside on the goods platform, and a loading gauge hung on the entrance outside wall. J. H. MOSS

Below: *Another view of the Cheddar shed crane, possibly in wrought iron, seen from the cartage loading bay side (on the left of the picture above). The fire buckets on the wall were an ever-present reminder of the combustible materials carried by the railways.* J. H. MOSS

The yard crane (specified for 6 tons) at Badminton encompassed the goods siding, the lock-up platform and the cartage road. The 'J'-shaped jib was designed to be able to slew over the tops of high-sided wagons.
ROYE ENGLAND

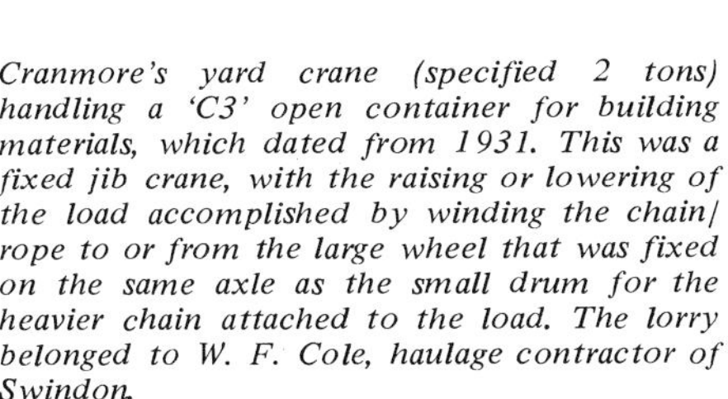

Cranmore's yard crane (specified 2 tons) handling a 'C3' open container for building materials, which dated from 1931. This was a fixed jib crane, with the raising or lowering of the load accomplished by winding the chain/rope to or from the large wheel that was fixed on the same axle as the small drum for the heavier chain attached to the load. The lorry belonged to W. F. Cole, haulage contractor of Swindon.
NATIONAL RAILWAY MUSEUM

A much larger type of yard crane in the process of transferring a container between a Bedford low loader and a rail vehicle. One man is seen at the hand crank with his compatriot on the brake (far side) and a third man on top of the container to attach the hook for lifting. The location is believed to have been in wartime at Swansea – hence the blacked-out offside headlamp.
STEAM PICTURE LIBRARY

A yard crane at an unidentified location, seen in the 1950s.
A. ATTEWELL

Pipework being unloaded from a Dia J4 'Macaw B', in November 1942, at Theale and probably for construction of the rail-connected Ministry of Fuel & Power aviation fuel depot at Padworth (Asiatic Petrol Co).
NATIONAL RAILWAY MUSEUM

A more modern yard crane at Barbers Bridge on the Dymock branch, notified as rated at 2½ tons, and mounted on a brick base. J. H. MOSS

A 3-ton yard crane at Looe.

Paddington goods depot just before the Great War, where the 'old' and 'new' sheds joined together (with different roof patterns). Yet another design of shed crane can be seen here with the operator using a lever to control the hoist, having loaded a barrel into the 5-plank open wagon with slings. Slewing of the crane seems to be by a rope attached to the top of the jib, in the hands of the porter on the left. A porter is seen trolleying some Wm. Vernon sacks, which look as if they contained potatoes or items of a similar dimension.
NATIONAL RAILWAY MUSEUM

Incoming goods delicately balanced on a sack truck (with two boxes marked 'Vermorel Villefranche') by a goods porter wearing an ostler-type waistcoat and apron. Another small shed crane can be seen behind.
NATIONAL RAILWAY MUSEUM

Then, of course, there were the staff under the control of the goods agent, who were divided into 'outdoor' and 'indoor' (office) staff, and included:

The carman, who collected and delivered the bulk of the smalls traffic.
The cartage staff, generally (after 1922, under the separate Road Transport Department).
The porter, who unloaded the inwards traffic from the incoming loaded wagons, hand-trolleyed it to road carts or lorries, there to load it; and vice-versa for outwards traffic.

Separate 'Stowers' were sometimes responsible for loading up outwards railway wagons in large depots. The 'Caller-off' called out particulars of the goods coming out of, or being loaded into, railway wagons to enable the 'Checker' to compare the details with the consignment note (outwards traffic) or invoice (inwards) as the case may have been. Other grades employed included Number Takers, Shunters, Weighbridge men or boys, Warehousemen, Policemen, Watchmen and others. Foremen supervised different sections of work, and Cartage-, Shed-, Yard-, Docks-Inspectors exercised general supervision. They were directly responsible to the goods depot agent for efficient loading and unloading of wagons, and collection and delivery; in the case of mileage traffic, they ensured that trucks were conveniently placed for traders; and it was their responsibility that wagons leaving a depot or yard were properly loaded, sheeted and roped and generally fit to travel safely.

Two pictures of small vehicles positioning heavy loads into vans. In the upper view, a Ransomes mobile crane with elevating jib was employed to get a load through the van door and into place; the lower picture shows a post-World War II fork-lift truck with a crane attachment performing a similar task. The advantage of these shed mobile cranes are self-evident, and Ransomes & Rapier produced standard vehicles for use up to 6 or 7 tons.

(318)

G.W.R. PARTICULARS OF DUTIES. SOLIHULL Station.

No. of Turn.	Grade	Hours of Duty. From	Hours of Duty. To	Interval. From	Interval. To	Details.
2.	Goods Clerk.	8.0am.	5.30pm	12.0n'n.	1.0pm.	Prepare forwarded goods invoices, and obtain signatures forx goods delivered.
		8.0am.	1.30pm	(S.O.)		Enter all outwards and inwards P.T.F. invoices in P.T.F. register daily and report all P.T.F.
						Advise M.G.O. and R.C.H. of any goods on hand unaddressed, unclaimed or unentered.
						Prepare goods monthly accounts, statistical returns etc. in connection therewith.
						Make alterations and additions in Goods route Book.
						Attend to general correspondence and testing of weights and charges.
						Prepare Goods weekly revenue return.
						Enter rates in rate book.
						Prepare rebate form where necessary.
						Check all charges on inwards invoices.
						Collect cash from carman and checker, also weighbridge receipts. Enter same in cash book and pay over to Station Master at intervals during the day, entering same in subsidiary cash books.
						Record warehouse and split delivery charges in books provided.
						Obtain signatures and carriage on "smalls" delivered at Goods shed.
						Prepare general returns for Chief and District Goods Manager.
						Report Goods in bad order.
						Raise delivery charges on S.to S. and out of boundary traffic.
						Recharge all foreign ropes etc.
						Deal with route advice circulars.
						Enter rates and charges on outward consignment notes for invoicing purposes.
						Check all charges on outward invoices.
						Record Demurrage and Siding rent charges and bring them promptly to debit
						Assist generally as instructed by Station Master.
						SIGN ON AND OFF DUTY DAILY AND BE IN POSSESSION OF RULE BOOK.

5,000 9.35 2Gp—P.O. S.

First and foremost of the 'indoor' staff at the larger depots was the Chief Clerk who was the Agent's right-hand man and understudy. Then came the Clerks-in-Charge of the various sections into which the work of large goods stations had to be divided. Specialised books have been written on goods station commercial and clerical work: the topic embraced invoicing, accounts, insurance, cartage, claims, rates, demurrage, siding rent, correspondence, wages and personnel matters, etc.

In the collection of charges, carmen would cash-in daily at the depot, but many firms had 'Ledger' or monthly credit accounts with the railway while others had 'Accommodation' or short credit accounts. There were also credits and debits to be recorded between different goods depots on the whole railway system for ropes, packing, etc not returned within 14 days. Rates and Route books had to be kept up to date and freely available to the public (Regulation of Railways Act, 1873).

Much trouble could be caused when goods arrived at a station without invoices, and an important job of the office staff was to ensure that the proper paperwork accompanied the goods on the same train, or was sent by passenger train to the receiving station.

When porters and cartage men were on bonus schemes (introduced at some stations by the GW in 1900), the weight of goods each man moved daily had to be recorded. There were many statistical records to be kept by the office staff such as the tonnage handled and carted by the company (Arrival and Despatch Books).

There were also *Wagon Books*, in which were recorded every loaded wagon arriving at, and departing from, the station. From these, siding rent charges for private-owner wagons not unloaded within the stipulated time could be assessed. Similarly demurrage charges, for railway-owned wagons conveying station-to-station (S-to-S) mileage traffic not promptly unloaded by traders, could be calculated.

Statistics were kept relating to detentions (wagons kept in depot under load for more than 48 hours); average loading weights of wagons; loading to transfer stations; daily weight of traffic from principal stations; punctuality of trains; number of wagons forwarded daily of different descriptions; number of horses working daily and weights hauled per man per day; absences of staff; stock of road vehicles, barrows, chains, cranes, weighing machines; stages; yard and siding capacities; warehouse space, etc. All these data related to the preparation of 'Half Yearly Certificates' which had to be sent by District Goods Managers (DGM) to the Chief Goods Manager at Paddington.

In addition, there were teams of auditors, reporting to the Chief Accountant, who travelled (unannounced) round the system checking up on documentation and accounting procedures.

AUTHORISED STAFF ESTABLISHMENT.

GOODS DEPARTMENT.

Conciliation Grades. STATEMENT "A"

GRADE.	Office or District.																	Total.
	C.C.M.O.	London.	Reading.	Bristol.	Exeter.	Plymouth.	Gloucester.	Cardiff.	Cardiff Valleys.	Swansea.	Worcester.	Birmingham	Shrewsbury.	Central Wales.	Liverpool.	Manchester.	Ireland.	
Callers Off	6	142	21	35	10	9	3	41	11	14	20	24	—	—	32	—	—	368
Capstanmen	—	66	3	7	—	—	—	5	3	—	—	28	—	—	—	—	—	112
Carters, Leading	—	1	1	2	2	—	—	—	—	—	—	1	—	—	2	—	—	9
Carters	—	532	17	258	12	35	32	98	—	—	22	385	12	—	27	62	—	1,492
Chain Horse Drivers*	—	47	—	—	—	—	—	—	—	—	—	—	—	—	—	—	—	47
Checkers	4	271	40	192	30	26	28	101	46	74	26	173	15	—	76	—	16	1,118
Checkers, Senior	—	33	—	—	—	—	—	4	4	—	—	—	—	—	5	—	—	46
Cooper and Repairer	—	1	—	—	—	—	—	—	—	—	—	—	—	—	—	—	—	1
Cranemen	—	1	2	—	—	—	—	—	—	—	—	—	—	—	2	—	—	5
Foremen, Bookroom	—	1	—	—	—	—	—	—	—	—	—	—	—	—	—	—	—	1
,, Working	—	24	4	2	1	1	3	6	5	1	3	1	—	—	1	—	—	52
,, Yard	—	1	—	5	—	—	—	—	—	—	—	2	1	—	—	—	—	9
Gatemen	—	—	—	—	—	—	2	—	—	3	—	—	—	—	1	—	—	6
Loaders	—	232	9	56	1	—	9	41	4	15	—	35	—	—	38	7	—	447
Messengers, Lad	—	73	4	21	5	2	2	20	7	10	8	28	1	—	17	9	2	209
Motor Drivers	—	89	1	30	8	4	2	20	—	—	8	74	—	—	23	10	—	269
Numbertakers, Adult	—	12	2	2	—	—	—	7	—	16	—	9	—	—	1	—	—	49
,, Junior	—	3	—	3	2	3	—	2	4	14	1	12	—	—	3	—	—	47
Officemen	1	27	3	10	—	2	—	5	—	2	—	11	—	—	3	2	—	66
Porters, Adult	—	641	95	213	70	43	48	176	55	85	56	328	30	1	225	1	31	2,098
,, Junior	—	69	16	26	8	3	15	21	1	15	7	19	3	—	34	1	1	239
Road Motor Attendants	—	—	—	—	2	2	—	—	—	—	—	4	—	—	—	7	—	15
Rope Splicers	—	2	—	—	—	—	—	—	—	—	—	—	—	—	—	—	—	2
Sheeters and Ropers	—	4	—	33	—	—	5	29	11	—	—	—	—	—	—	—	—	82
Shunters, Class 1	—	27	—	23	—	—	4	—	—	—	—	23	3	—	7	—	—	87
,, ,, 2	—	—	—	—	—	—	—	—	—	—	—	19	—	—	—	—	—	19
,, ,, 3	—	36	—	31	—	—	4	—	—	—	—	18	5	—	7	—	—	101
,, ,, 4	—	—	—	2	—	—	—	—	—	—	—	15	—	—	2	—	—	19
Shunt Horse Drivers	—	1	—	—	3	—	2	—	—	—	10	8	2	—	12	—	—	38
Slipper Boys	—	—	—	—	5	—	—	1	—	—	4	7	—	—	10	—	—	27
Timekeepers	—	9	—	6	—	—	—	—	—	—	—	3	—	—	3	2	—	23
Tracers	4	12	—	8	—	1	—	1	—	—	—	3	—	—	—	—	—	29
Vanguards	—	600	—	32	5	—	—	18	—	—	—	100	1	—	—	34	—	790
Vansetters	—	—	—	—	—	—	—	—	—	—	—	—	—	—	—	10	—	10
Watchmen	—	—	—	—	—	—	—	1	—	—	1	5	—	—	—	—	—	7
Weighbridgemen	—	21	—	10	1	—	—	3	—	6	—	2	1	—	3	—	—	47
Totals { Adults	15	2,233	198	925	142	126	142	556	139	216	146	1,171	69	1	470	91	47	6,687
Totals { Juniors	—	745	20	82	23	5	17	44	12	39	20	166	5	—	64	54	3	1,299
Totals { Adults and Juniors ..	15	2,978	218	1,007	165	131	159	600	151	255	166	1,337	74	1	534	145	50	7,986

Shop and Miscellaneous Staff. STATEMENT "B"

GRADE.	C.C.M.O.	London.	Reading.	Bristol.	Exeter.	Plymouth.	Gloucester.	Cardiff.	Cardiff Valleys.	Swansea.	Worcester.	Birmingham	Shrewsbury.	Central Wales.	Liverpool.	Manchester.	Ireland.	Total.
Shop Staff (Sheet Dept.) Male ..	—	—	—	—	—	—	—	—	—	—	—	—	—	—	—	—	—	291
,, ,, Female ..	—	—	—	—	—	—	—	—	—	—	—	—	—	—	—	—	—	14
Boatmen	—	—	—	—	—	—	—	—	—	—	—	7	—	—	—	—	3	10
Dock Gatemen	—	1	—	—	—	—	—	—	—	2	—	—	—	—	—	—	—	3
,, Leading	—	1	—	—	—	—	—	—	—	—	—	—	—	—	—	—	—	1
Firemen	—	2	—	—	—	—	—	—	—	—	—	—	—	—	—	—	—	2
,, Leading	—	1	—	—	—	—	—	—	—	—	—	—	—	—	—	—	—	1
Messengers, Adult	4	1	—	1	—	—	—	—	—	—	—	—	—	—	—	—	—	6
,, Junior	12	3	2	1	—	1	2	4	2	4	1	1	1	—	2	1	1	38
Totals	16	9	2	2	—	1	2	4	2	6	1	8	1	—	2	1	4	366

HOW GOODS WERE HANDLED

Let us trace consignments of goods through a typical depot. 'Outwards' or 'Forwarded' traffic would be collected by the carman at the sender's premises. A consignment note accompanied the goods, containing: the date; names and addresses of sender and consignee; number of packages with marks and descriptions; gross weight; station to which the goods were to be sent; who paid the carriage. The carman signed for the goods, having satisfied himself that the goods were as described, and that they were safely packed. This would be repeated at all the firms he called at. Alternatively, a firm could make their own arrangements to convey their consignments to the goods depot, in which case the paperwork was done on arrival at the depot.

Two 'forward control' lorries loading up for town distribution, with every cubic inch of capacity being utilised. These were photographed just after nationalisation – the left-hand vehicle was in BR livery whilst the right-hand one retained a GW roundel. A checker is seen in the foreground with his clip board.

A set of more modern platform scales with a dial readout; these slowly came to replace the traditional arm and counterweight design at many locations, and had the advantage of an instant display to an inexperienced operator. The load, a long crate, probably protected semi-fragile contents.
NATIONAL RAILWAY MUSEUM

Arriving at the depot, the carman's vehicle would be passed over the weighbridge and, having registered the consignment notes in a book with the indoor staff, he would then go on to the goods shed. He would back his vehicle against the loading platform and, if appropriate, remove the horse or mechanical tractor. The consignment notes would be handed over to the Checker who, as the goods were being unloaded, compared the actual items with what was on the invoice, noting any discrepancies and defects. During unloading, the goods were weighed individually on the platform machine for charging purposes, although in busy depots the weights given by the senders on the consignment notes were taken 'as-read' (but the railway made spot checks). There were also spot checks on following days for about 10% of a previous day's charging calculations.

Empty wagons for outwards traffic would have been berthed, and prepared by being swept out and, where necessary, littered with straw, sawdust or other similar material to prevent damage to goods by damp, etc. Destinations were provisionally chalked on the wagons by the Outwards Shed Foreman, and they were then ready for loading. Goods were now trolleyed or carried by hand to the trucks at which time the checker inserted on the relevant consignment note the number of the wagon into which the goods were placed. He then initialled, dated and timed it, and passed it to the office for preparation of the invoice. Heavy goods may have required crane assistance from road vehicle to truck.

A porter in the process of loading up a sheeted wagon at Paddington Goods with the help of a sack truck now confronted with the lip of the lowered wagon door. The crate was marked 'British Grown Pure India Tea'. To his right is what appears to have been a protective case for a set of scales, whilst a checker's table can be seen in front of it, laying on the floor.
NATIONAL RAILWAY MUSEUM

This picture shows the ever-present problems of wheeling sack trucks into open wagons from goods platforms, with 2½in 'bumps' (the thickness of wagon timbers) at top and bottom of drop doors. The door of this LNER wagon had a tapered top edge to allow loading and unloading, but this was evidently still too steep for the fragility of the load, and a steel ramp plate had been placed over it. The crates were 'returnables', the property of United Glass.
NATIONAL RAILWAY MUSEUM

Loading a large barrel into an 'Open A' in the 1920s. A wooden ramp with tapered ends had been placed over the side door to allow a smooth movement from the platform, as the door did not have any top chamfering. Most GWR wagons built after 1920 had a projecting lower-plank 'sack truck' drop door to give a level connection into the wagon. NATIONAL RAILWAY MUSEUM

A selection of wagon labels, indicating origin, destination, wagon number, class number to help the guard calculate the weight of the train, and other details. Note this 'class number' had nothing to do with the classification of goods (see Introductory volume).

During the making-up of the wagon load, and before the wagon was finally closed down, the staff stowing wagons were to ensure that goods were positioned safely, so that nothing was likely to fall from an open wagon during the journey, or during shunting. Articles were so arranged that they could not damage each other by movement or pressure, i.e. heavier articles were to be at the bottom, lighter at the top; and, in mixed consignments to a given destination, bales and trusses containing carpets, drapery, etc. or foodstuffs should be so loaded that they were not likely to be damaged by liquids leaking from barrels, drums or cans.

When loading was complete, the vehicle was ticketed on both sides with labels showing the date of forwarding, destination station and railway company, route, name of consignee and contents (with 'Class 1', '2', or '3' overprinted numerals, to help the guard to calculate the operational weight of his train en route). In the meantime, the invoices for the goods would have been prepared, sent down from the office, and placed in racks or clips on the wagons or, in early days, nailed to the body of the wagon itself. Open wagons were commonly used for C & D traffic right up to the end of the 1920s, and these would be carefully sheeted; usually, covered goods wagons (vans) did not require this extra precaution, although if a van was known to leak, an old or sub-standard tarpaulin would be put over the roof and lashed down after the doors had been closed. Loaded vehicles would then be drawn out of the shed (often by capstan or horse), particulars of wagon and sheet numbers, destinations, etc. being recorded by the Number Taker.

At this juncture, the work of the Goods Department was now complete as far as outwards traffic was concerned, and the wagons became the responsibility of the Traffic Department, whose staff marshalled them into the necessary order for outgoing trains. The goods department staff, by continually 'dressing' the shed sidings in big depots as they moved fresh wagons in for loading, were able to keep the shunting of loaded wagons to a minimum.

For Inwards or Received traffic, the operations were repeated, but in reverse order. As the incoming trains put off wagons in the reception sidings, the Number Taker noted wagon and sheet numbers, the origins of Station Trucks, the date, time, and train by which they had

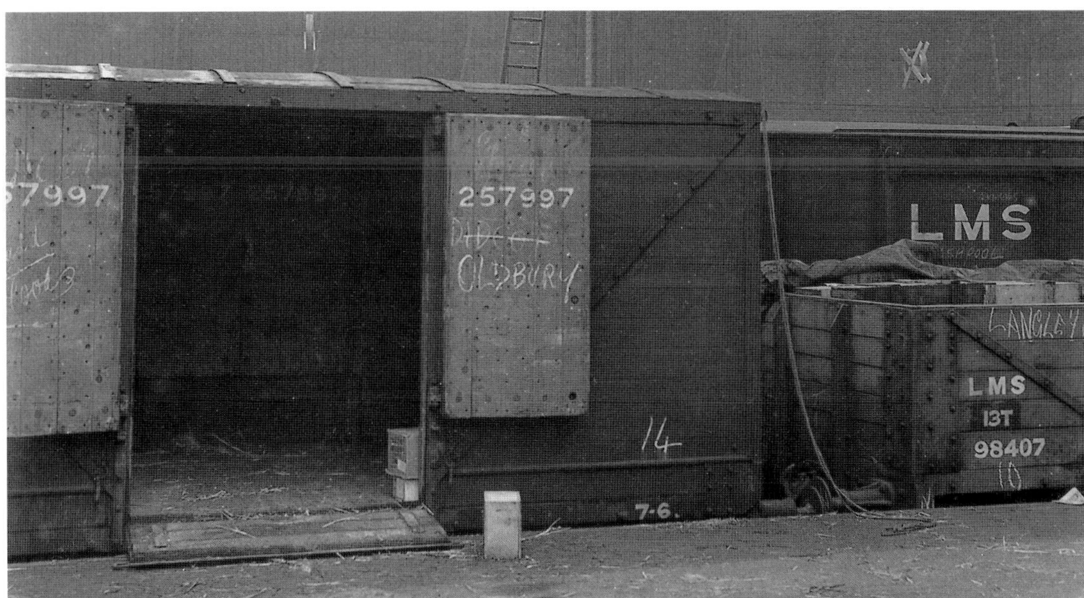

The interior of Hockley depot in 1941. Nearly all vans required ramp bridges from platform to interior floor if the goods were to be trolleyed in; however, this 'foreign' van (ex-LNWR) had an unusual lower drop door to form a ramp, and upper swing doors. The destinations for loading were often chalked on wagons, inside and/or out. What appear to be defunct overhead clock faces on the platform to the rear are seen covered by an 'X'. NATIONAL RAILWAY MUSEUM

Loading of a van at Paddington soon after nationalisation. Inside, a motor device was being manoeuvred into position by two men, and located at a convenient point for its order in the offloading sequence. Outside, cardboard boxes of Vacco glassware on a sack truck were awaiting loading (note the crude numbering of the truck), whilst tyres, crates and other boxes were also positioned in readiness. Many boxes of Shippam's paste may be seen stacked behind. The checker was using a clipboard at this point, rather than a lectern/desk. NATIONAL RAILWAY MUSEUM

PRIVATE AND NOT FOR PUBLICATION.

GREAT WESTERN RAILWAY

Circular No. 1174.A.
W.A. 30456.

CHIEF GOODS MANAGER'S OFFICE,
PADDINGTON STATION,
LONDON, W.2.
1st March, 1940.

DEMURRAGE, INTERNAL USER and SIDING RENT CHARGES

Detention by the Public of Railway Companies' Wagons, Containers and Sheets, and Private Owners' requisitioned Wagons, and retention of Private Owners' Wagons, not requisitioned, on Railway Companies' Lines.

The following charges, free periods and regulations, will operate on and from Friday, 1st March, 1940. (The instructions contained in Circulars No. 1174 of 1st May, 1926, and No. 1273 of 1st May, 1936, and amendments dated 1st October, 1937, are hereby superseded).

1. Scale of Demurrage Charges and Free Periods on Railway Companies' Wagons (including **Private Owners' Requisitioned Wagons) excluding Wagons used for the conveyance of Coal, Coke or Patent Fuel; or of Iron Ore, Ironstone, Lime or Limestone for Blast Furnaces and Steel Works**— (**see Clause 2**).

(i) **Charges.**

	Per Wagon. For each day or part thereof after the expiration of the free period. £ s. d.
WAGONS OTHER THAN THOSE SPECIFIED BELOW	6 0
HIGH CAPACITY WAGONS	
Above 16 and not exceeding 20 tons	8 0
Above 20 and not exceeding 30 tons	12 0
Above 30 tons	1 1 0
SPECIALLY CONSTRUCTED WAGONS	
Above 15 and under 20 tons	12 0
20 tons and under 30 tons	1 5 0
30 tons and up to 60 tons	2 2 0
Over 60 tons	By special arrangement.
REFRIGERATOR & INSULATED VANS	1 5 0

* **Specially Constructed Wagons are those built for carrying a special class of traffic, such as Machinery, Boilers or Heavy or Bulky Articles.**

NOTES.—

(a) The above charges must be raised in all cases where the Trader is responsible for the detention of the Company's Wagons.

(b) If a Wagon is used for a load which could be conveyed on a wagon of less carrying capacity the charge must be regulated by the weight of the load.

(c) When, owing to the bulk or dimensions of the load, it is necessary for a specially constructed wagon to be used, the minimum charge per day is 12s., although the weight of the load may not exceed 15 tons.

(d) If a Wagon is used for a load which, if ordinary Wagons had been utilised, would require two or more vehicles for its conveyance, the charge to be not less than would be made on such number of ordinary Wagons.

(e) When Refrigerator and Insulated Vans are used for ordinary goods traffic, the free period allowed and charges are those applicable to ordinary Goods Wagons.

(ii) **Free Periods**—(See Clause 8).

BEFORE CONVEYANCE.

At Stations, Depots, Private Sidings, Ports, Docks and Wharves.	1 day (a)

AFTER CONVEYANCE.

At Stations and Depots.	1 day (b)
At Ports (Shipment Traffic).	1 day (c)
At Private Sidings, Docks and Wharves	1 day (a) if returned empty. 2 days (a) if returned loaded.

arrived. The shed foreman then instructed the shunters which wagons were to be shunted into the open yard for unloading, and which were to be berthed in the shed. Those for unloading in the open would generally contain station-to-station traffic such as: truck loads of returned empties (sometimes there would be a special empties shed); perhaps meat or vegetable traffic for one consignee; road vans on wheels; 'lift vans' (i.e. containers), carts, carriages and so on; that is, all traffic in truck loads which consignees carted themselves, or which otherwise required ramps or large-capacity cranes to handle. 'Mileage' traffic also included coal, minerals and building materials in bulk, not dealt with 'through the shed'.

The newly-opened coal yard at Thorney Mill Sidings, on the Staines branch near West Drayton, pictured on 17th August 1943 looking north, with a coal merchant (London Co-op) sacking-up his coal in the wagon and loading down onto the flat bed of his lorry. To deter coal merchants from breaking railway rules, yards would have cast-iron notices proclaiming 'Great Western Railway. Warning is given against the dangerous practice of propping up the doors of merchandise trucks for the support of coal weighing machines, for loading or unloading traffic, or for any other purpose. The Great Western Railway Company give notice that such practice is prohibited, and any person disregarding this caution will be held responsible for injury or damage that may result. James Milne. General Manager Mar 1922'. The merchant here was heeding the warning, though many didn't.
NATIONAL RAILWAY MUSEUM

Sacks of potatoes being unloaded from a sheeted GWR 4-planker on to a Great Western horse lorry. The levels of the wagon floor and trailer bed were convenient, minimising the amount of lifting required by the staff. A white-painted 'Mica B' meat van can be seen to the right of the carter, probably delivering a load of meat to a larger trader in the area. NATIONAL RAILWAY MUSEUM

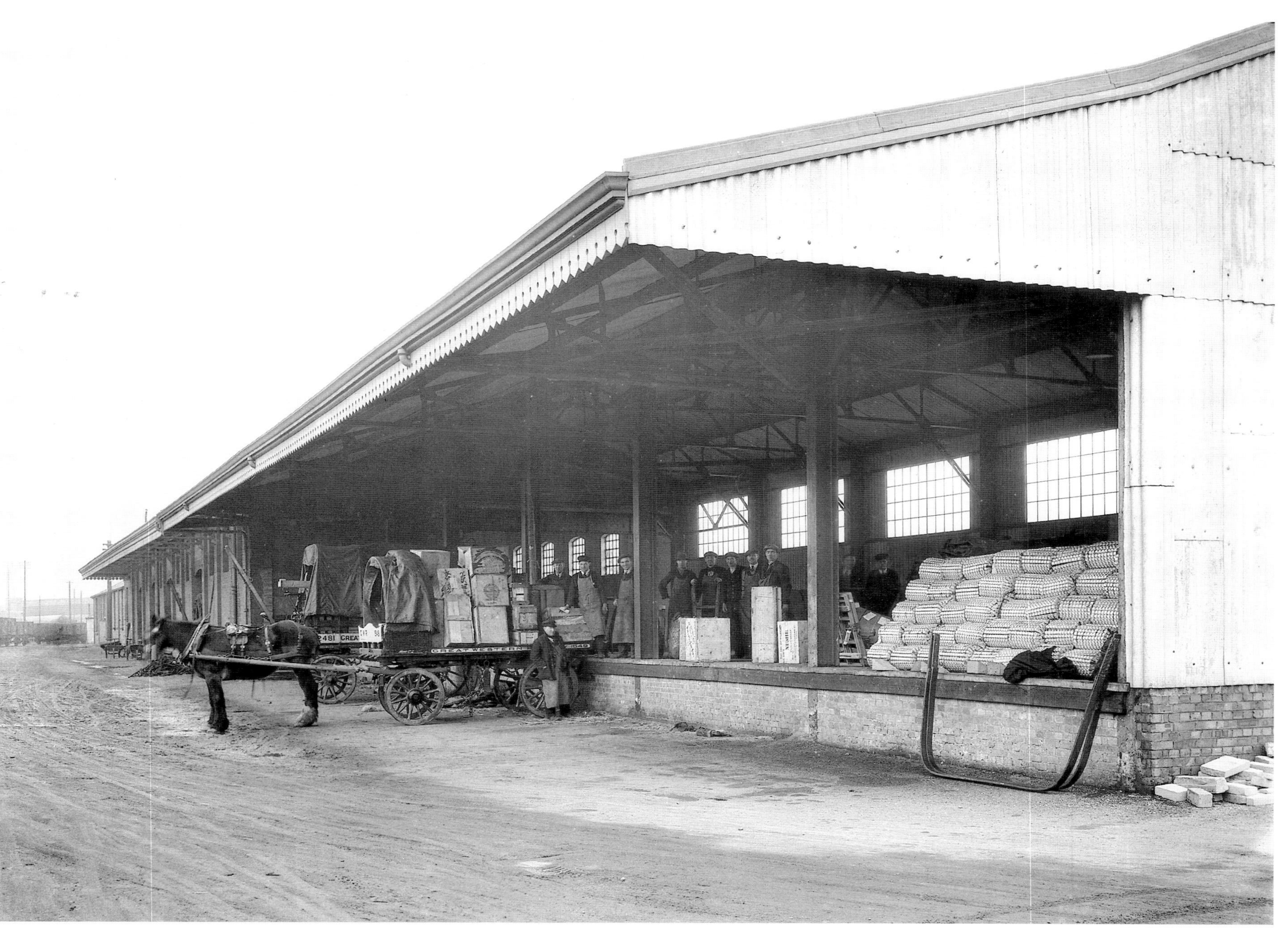

The newly-opened first extension of the goods shed at Slough, seen in 1929, with eight goods porters posing on the cartage platform, and the carter standing in front of the rear wheel of his vehicle. The weather sheet appears to have been rolled back over the driver's box to permit loading, and would doubtless have been repositioned over the load if rain was imminent. The wagon behind was a fully-covered horse van, with a high seat for the driver.

NATIONAL RAILWAY MUSEUM

Wagons put into the shed were dealt with by an unloading gang in charge of a Checker, who saw that articles called-off from the wagon corresponded exactly with the invoice from the sending station; if not, discrepancies or defects were noted down. Practice varied in different parts of the system, but, strictly speaking, all invoices should have been taken into the office for entry into the *Arrival Book*, to be numbered up, charges checked, under-charges and overcharges dealt with, *before* the wagons were unloaded. Outstations invoicing traffic to Paddington in the 1930s produced a delivery sheet for each item of entry, so that the documents could be passed more quickly through Checker to Carter.

The Checker and Caller-off were usually experienced men on the permanent staff of the station, whilst the rest of the gang was made up of men (and sometimes women), often casual workers, whose job was to convey goods from the wagons either to appointed pitches on the platform set apart for particular districts, or direct to waiting road vehicles.

Sometimes it was found that articles entered on the invoice were not on the wagon, or that goods were received for which no entries could be found on the invoice. Such instances gave rise to entries in the *Not to Hand* and *Unentered* books respectively, and required the clerical staff to sort matters out by telegraphing the sending station, etc. The 'Missing and Tracing' category was long and detailed in the *Telegraph Code Book*. The following codes might have been used :

'*Pike*': 'Following missing. Have you any trace? If so, send to...'.
'*Servia*': 'Certainly sent you; have further search made, and wire result.'
'*Fungus*': 'No trace of forwarding the following.'
'*Rudd*': 'Following missing from train named, said last seen your station. Send to...'
'*Cygnet*': 'Following invoiced from you not to hand. Wire date, train, truck and to what point sent, and trace forward.'
'*Dove*': 'Wagon number given below, from station named sent away as empty, contains the following. If with you, dispose of as follows and reply.'
'*Notlab*': 'Following wagon (or wagons) on hand without labels. Are you short of it, or can you trace forwarding from your district?'
'*Chutney*': 'If any trace, wire reply. If no trace, reply by Urgent Train Message.'
'*Heron*': 'Ascertain from Guard of undermentioned train the destination of vehicles of the description and numbers given below, put off here without label on date named.'

When a wagon had been completely unloaded, the invoices were passed to the delivery office for preparation of cartage delivery sheets, which determined how the Cartage Loaders packed road vehicles for particular destinations or delivery rounds in towns. One cartage loader may have been responsible for simultaneously filling up half-a-dozen or more vehicles receiving goods from a variety of different men on trolleys. During the Second World War, consignments were carried 'paid', which simplified documentation and obviated invoicing.

The carman who had been selected by the cartage foreman for a particular duty would obtain the delivery sheets and charge notes from the office, and proceed on his round, driving his vehicle over the weighbridge on his way from the depot. Having delivered all consignments, obtained signatures in receipt and collected moneys due, the carman returned to the station, where he parked his vehicle (or stabled his horse) and 'cashed-in' with the delivery sheets to the office. All the carmen's takings formed part of the depot's daily cash remittance. At Bridgwater, for example, this was taken at the close of day to the passenger station, made up, put in a wallet and placed into the travelling safe on the scheduled stopping train to Bristol, to be banked or otherwise disposed of.

Some C & D traffic might be dealt with in the yard using the same book-keeping procedures as for the goods shed traffic, but in the case of the majority of goods unloaded in the yard (station-to-station mileage traffic), consignees were advised of the arrival of their goods on a special form so that they could make arrangements to collect the items or load addressed to them. When they picked up their consignments, signatures were obtained in the *Yard Delivery Book* and charges paid or credit given. Other important duties dealt with by the yard staff were receipt and dispatch of livestock: this will be discussed in a later volume in the series. Wherever railway wagons were accessible to road vehicles, a company rule determined that the road vehicles had to be parked at least 6 feet away from the nearest line or siding when not in the process of loading or unloading, in order to avert danger when wagons were moved.

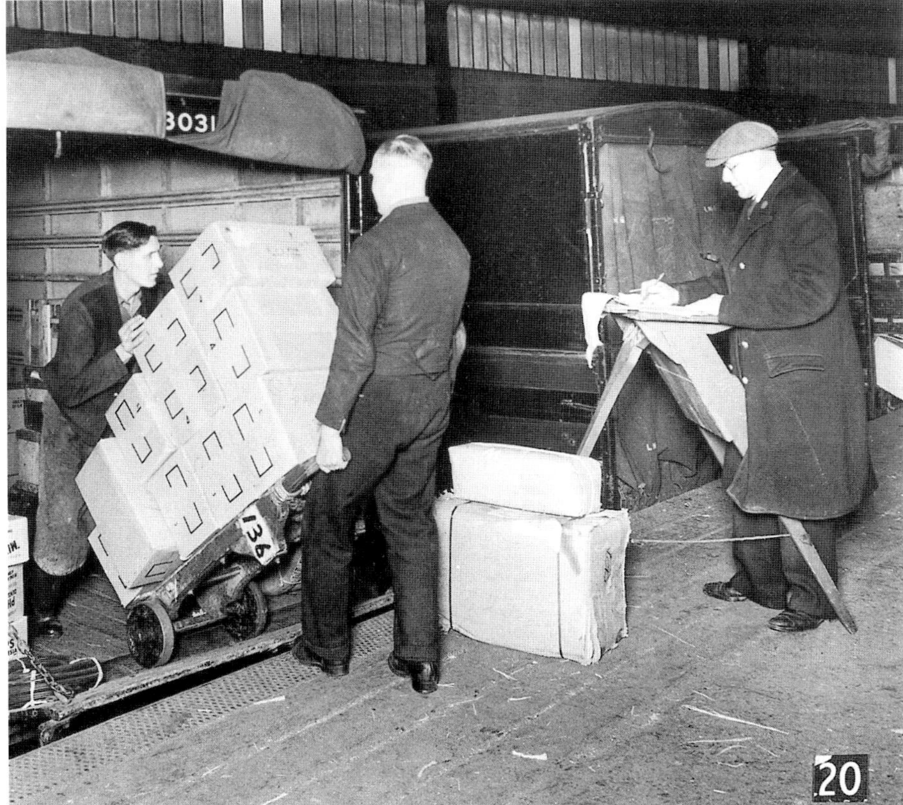

This checker (still wearing a GWR overcoat) was using a portable 3-legged desk at Paddington as a cartage van was being loaded, just after nationalisation. Boxes of Milk of Magnesia and Phillips' Dental Magnesia, and a coil of hose are seen at the bottom corner of the van, with another sack truck of boxes being manhandled onto the vehicle. The tailboard of the van sloped up to the goods platform in this instance, and was held in position by chains.
NATIONAL RAILWAY MUSEUM

All large goods depots handled so-called 'order traffic', i.e. grain, flour, butter, bacon, eggs, cheese, cattle and poultry food, fertilizers, oils, etc., which were invoiced to the station to be warehoused, pending instructions on disposal from the trader. Particulars of all such goods were entered into a register called the *Wait Order Book*. Other miscellaneous goods were dealt with in the warehouse including:

1. Goods invoiced 'to be called for' (such as personal luggage, household furniture, etc.).
2. Goods refused by the customer as 'not ordered' or 'in excess of order' (the latter, it was said, the result of commercial travellers booking more goods than ordered on the chance that the customer would hesitate to refuse delivery from the railway!).
3. Goods for consignees residing outside the recognised free delivery limits.
4. Goods for consignees unknown and/or at untraceable addresses.
5. Goods refused through damage, alleged delay, or on account of charges.

It is appropriate to comment here on the practice, by some British traders, of despatching their goods 'under mark' in late-Victorian/Edwardian days. Instead of providing a full address on packages, items were merely marked or branded with letters, numbers or hieroglyphics (such as the figure 27 within a diamond) without the name of the destination station being obvious. The aim of this practice was to prevent rival traders from learning the names and addresses of their customers and suppliers (it was also said that some firms sent under mark simply to avoid the expense and trouble of addressing each and every package with the full name and address of the consignees). While the name and address of the consignee was, of course, on the consignor's consignment note to the railway, the practice of sending goods under mark was a great nuisance to the operation of cartage and goods depots. It was also sometimes done with 'returned empties'. There was, needless to say, a great likelihood of delays, incorrect despatching, wrong delivering and so on, for which the railways were invariably blamed. Since railway companies wanted to keep such traffic, they tended to put up with all the inconveniences rather than persuade the manufacturers to be more helpful, or simply attempt to charge them for the

Many of the larger goods facilities had a warehouse attached (or nearby) to provide a storage area that was often rented out to traders, and/or from which the goods could be gradually distributed. In this view, the upper storey grain store at Brentford docks is seen in 1925, containing cattle cake. NATIONAL RAILWAY MUSEUM

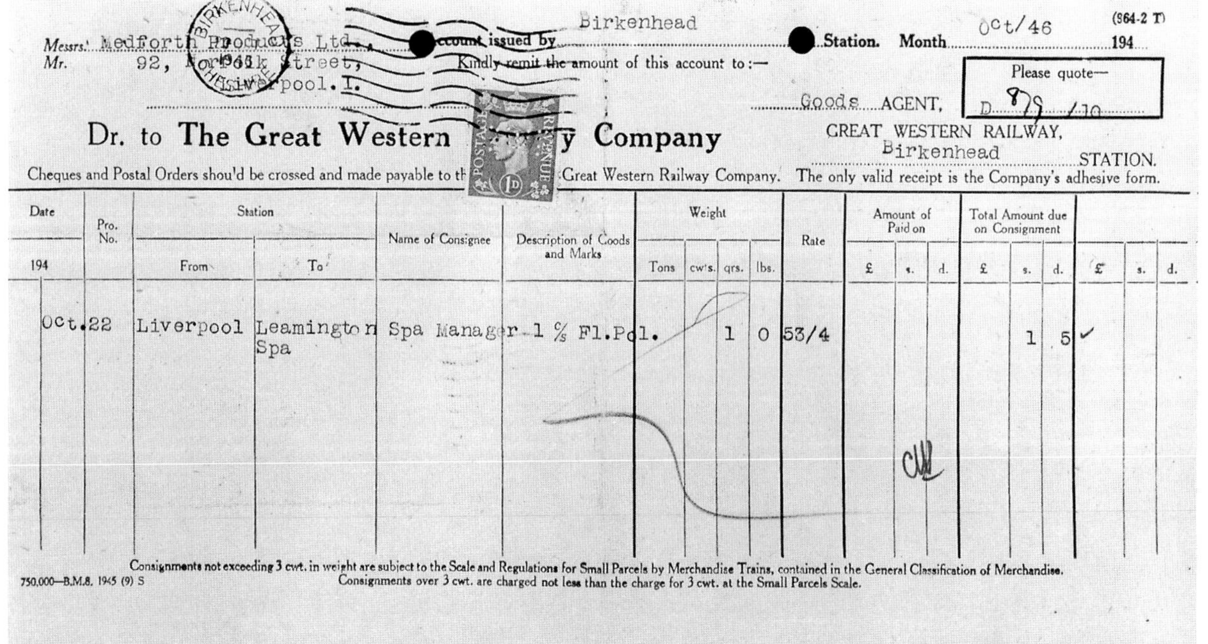

(964-2 T)

Messrs. / Mr. Medforth Products Ltd., 92, Norfolk Street, Liverpool. I.

Account issued by Birkenhead Station. Month Oct/46 194

Kindly remit the amount of this account to:—

Goods AGENT, GREAT WESTERN RAILWAY, Birkenhead STATION.

Please quote— D 879/10

Dr. to The Great Western Railway Company

Cheques and Postal Orders shou'd be crossed and made payable to the Great Western Railway Company. The only valid receipt is the Company's adhesive form.

Date 194	Pro. No.	Station From	Station To	Name of Consignee	Description of Goods and Marks	Weight Tons	Weight cwts.	Weight qrs.	Weight lbs.	Rate	Amount of Paid on £	s.	d.	Total Amount due on Consignment £	s.	d.	£	s.	d.
Oct.22		Liverpool	Leamington Spa	Spa Manager	1 % Fl.Pol.			1	0	53/4					1	5 ✓			

Consignments not exceeding 3 cwt. in weight are subject to the Scale and Regulations for Small Parcels by Merchandise Trains, contained in the General Classification of Merchandise.
Consignments over 3 cwt. are charged not less than the charge for 3 cwt. at the Small Parcels Scale.

750,000—B.M.8. 1945 (9) S

An immense amount of paperwork was generated by the goods service daily, and the larger depots required dedicated offices to handle it. Here, the Mileage Office at Hockley, with its female staff, can be seen in 1935. Various types of early mechanical adding machines are on view. NATIONAL RAILWAY MUSEUM

privilege. In 1906, however, the GWR took a stance and started to attach sticky labels, on which the name and address of the consignee had been copied, to all goods sent under mark, thus removing the anonymity. Evidently the extra cost to the company was deemed worth it. Even so, the system of sending goods under mark did not disappear, and the problems remained. The streamlining of goods procedures during the First World War helped to abolish the system.

CHARGING, WAYBILLING & INTER-WAR ECONOMICS

To arrive at the rate to be charged for the carriage of a consignment of goods from one station to another, two books had to be consulted: the first was the *Classification,* and the second was the *Rate Book.* As already discussed in the introductory volume to this series, the group into which an item was classified in the 'common carrier' scheme for railways depended on the comparative value and the care or expense necessary for safe conveyance. The *Rate Book* was of greater size than the *General Railway Classification of Goods by Merchandise Trains.*

From the early days of railways, a copy of the *Rate Book* had, by law, to be supplied to every goods station, and a duplicate copy retained in the Rates Office at railway headquarters. Each book contained a full list of goods stations of all companies in England and Wales, alongside which were a succession of columns. In each column was entered the rates per ton for

EXTRANEOUS CHARGES BOOK

Ref.	From	Truck No.	Name	Goods	Weight T	C	qrs	lbs	From To Period	Rate	Rent £	s.	d.	Handling £	s.	d.	Miscell. £	s.	d.
CM 291 (3/142)	Exeter	13579	Jones-Smith, Bristol	200 Bags Kibbled Linseed Cake	10	–	–	–	Aug 2—Aug 8	4d.	–	3	4						
				120	6	–	–	–	Handl Aug 5 and 8 order nos. 125 and 132	8d.				–	4	–			
									Shooting 40 sks Aug 5	2d.							–	6	8
CM 278 (2/135)	Humphries & B.	—	Hughes & Co. Bristol	40 Bags Sharps	3	–	–	–	Deld. Jones lorry, Aug 6 order no. 377										
				Into Warehouse					Apr 22	8d.				–	2	–			
									Apr 22—Apr 28	2d.	–	–	6						
									Apr 29—Aug 4 14 weeks @ minimum	2d. 9d.	–	10	6						
									Aug 5—Aug 11	2d.	–	–	6						
				Out of Warehouse	3	–	–	–	Aug 6	8d.				–	2	–			

1/544/4.

GREAT WESTERN RLY.—From WOLVERHAMPTON. to Church Stretton
(2503)
Undercharge Advice you enter to us July 31 1894.
Waterlow & Sons Limited, Printers, London Wall, London.

Invoice Date	No.	Consignee		Article	Weight T. C. Q. lbs.	Rate.	Paid on.	Paid.	To Pay.	Undercharge Paid.	To Pay.
July 26	21/216	[illegible]	Charged	89 Lard.	6 6 1.	10/10	4		3 14 9		
			Should be			13/4	6 4		4 10 6		15 9
			Charged								
			Should be								
			Charged			Enter up for July [illegible]					
			Should be								

50,000—10-93.

Please send to pay Invoice for 15/9 immediately.

Mr.

Yours truly, J. Farrant

(2853)

PRO. No. OF THIS NOTE.

CONSIGNMENT NOTE FOR THE CARRIAGE OF MERCHANDISE (Other than Dangerous Goods and Merchandise for which Terms and Conditions are specially provided) BY MERCHANDISE TRAIN subject to the Standard Terms and Conditions of Carriage.

To the GREAT WESTERN RAILWAY COMPANY. .... *Station,* .... *194*....

Receive and forward the undermentioned Merchandise.

Full Name of Sender .... *Full Address* ....

In certain instances alternative Company's Risk and Owner's Risk rates are available. In such cases state whether the Merchandise is to be carried at the Company's Risk Rate or Owner's Risk rate ....

	These columns to be filled in by Sender.						For use of Railway Company's Staff only.			
Owner and Wagon No.	To what Station and Railway to be sent and if to wait order, so state.	Consignee. Full Name and Full Address.	No. of Packages.	Description of Merchandise and Marks.	Weight (inclusive of packing). T. c. q. lbs.	State if charges are payable by Sender or Consignee.	Rate per Ton.	Paid on. £ s. d.	Paid. £ s. d.	To Pay. £ s. d.

12,000 bks., 150 lvs.—
B.M. 12. 1945. (2) S.

Traders are requested when consigning goods **"Carriage Paid"** to endorse the address labels or tallies **"Carriage Paid"** or **"Carriage Paid Home."**

Name of Company's Carman .... *Van No.* .... *Received by* .... *Loaded by* ....

the different classes referred to, together with any special and exceptional figures which may have been arranged from time to time for particular types of traffic. There were, before the grouping, other books, arranged slightly differently, for rates to Scottish stations.

Where there were 'competitive routes' to a given destination over different companies, the figure usually agreed was based upon the shortest route. When new railway lines were built, it was advantageous to get 'through rates' agreed. Thus, there was increased traffic over the Didcot, Newbury & Southampton Railway once the GW and L & SW had agreed to what should be charged for the conveyance of the different classes of goods.

When goods were handed into a station for transit, and a rate for the journey existed in the *Rate Book*, the invoicing clerk was able to send on an invoice at the same time as the goods, with the charges entered as 'paid' or 'to pay', whichever the sender required, as shown on the consignment note. If rates for traffic to the destination station did not exist in the *Rate Book*, the goods could still be put on a train, but the clerk had to send a 'PTF' ('particulars to follow') invoice to the destination station. At the same time, the clerk applied to Paddington for a figure, giving details of the traffic. The Great Western Rates Office would communicate with the other railway companies concerned suggesting, as circumstances may have required, one of three things: a set of rates for all classes of goods between the sending and receiving stations; a figure for the particular lot of goods under notice; or an exceptional rate with specific conditions. On agreement, the two stations were informed, and when it was intended to make the rate a permanent one, the figure would be entered in the station *Rate Book* (and in the duplicate book at Paddington).

In addition to arranging rates for goods actually carried, for which figures had not previously been in force, the Rates Office was constantly being approached for rates for 'prospective' traffic to enable traders to tender for the supply of materials, etc. to a particular destination. In respect of charges, both 'owners' risk' (OR) and 'company's risk' (CR) rates were quoted, each relating to claims for loss, damage or delay in transit. In 'OR' contracts the trader took the risk, and paid a lower amount than with the 'CR' rate. He could also save money in the expense of protect-

A cast notice at Hungerford goods yard, giving opening times. A. ATTEWELL

MERCHANDISE TRAFFIC.

769. The **Instructions** for compiling **Merchandise Accounts** as shown herein are intended to be **supplementary** to, and not in lieu of, the **Book of General Directions** to Agents and Members of their Staffs with regard to the Management of Stations and Conveyance of **Merchandise Traffic.** *Instructions for compiling Merchandise Accounts.*

770. The term "Merchandise" Traffic is used to denote the following descriptions of traffic :— *Merchandise.*

(*a*) Goods Traffic of four kinds, viz. :— *Goods.*

1. "Collected" .. .. Goods collected by the Company, but not delivered by them.
2. "Delivered" .. .. Goods not collected by the Company, but delivered by them.
3. "Collected and Delivered" Goods collected and delivered by the Company.
4. "Not Carted" .. .. Goods not collected and not delivered by the Company.

(*b*) Coal Class Traffic embracing— *Coal.*

Coal.
Patent Fuel (Coal).
Cannel.
Culm.
Fuel consisting of Coal, Peat and Pitch compressed into blocks.
Slack or Smudge for Fuel.
Coke.
Coal Cinders or Coke Breeze for Fuel.
Carbo.
Coalite.
Coalexld.

(*c*) Other Minerals embracing all traffic in Classes 1 to 6 of the General Railway Classification. *Other Minerals.*

(*d*) Live Stock Traffic, embracing Cattle, Calves, Pigs, Sheep (including Lambs and Goats), Horses (including Ponies, Mules, and Asses) n Cattle Trucks, carried by Cattle or Goods Trains. *Live Stock*

DEFINITION OF TERMS AND FORMS.

771. A "Consignment" is any quantity of traffic sent at one time by ne person or firm addressed to one person or firm at one Station. *Consignment.*

772. "Consignor" signifies the sender of a consignment. The name should be given on the Invoice in the sender's column, unless instructions to the contrary are held. *Consignor.*

773. "Consignee" is the person to whom the consignment is sent, whose name is to be given in the "Consignee" column of Invoice. *Consignee.*

Invoice. 774. An "Invoice" is the form used by Stations on which particulars of Merchandise conveyed from one Station to another are entered. The particulars include the destination Station, the consignors' and consignees' names, the numbers and owners of the wagons in which the traffic is carried, the route by which it is sent, and also a full description of its nature, weight, and charges generally.

Paid On. 775. "Paid On" signifies that a sum so entered has been or is to be paid out to some person or Company for services rendered, such as a Carrier's charges for conveyance of a consignment to a Railway Station, or railway charges for prior conveyance when not booked through from end to end, etc. A "Paid On" may also represent an amount due to the Great Western Company for services rendered.

"Paid On" credit to forwarding Station. 776. A "Paid On" is always a credit to the Forwarding Station.

"Paid." 777. "Paid" signifies that the sum entered has been or is to be collected from Consignor, and is a debit to the Forwarding Station.

"To Pay." 778. "To Pay" signifies that the amount so entered is charged forward and is payable at the Station to which the consignment is entered, and is to be collected either from the Consignee, or some Company or person to whom it is to be handed for future conveyance. The amount to be entered in this column by the forwarding Station is the authorised charge between the Station entered from and the Station entered to, but if a "Paid On" has been incurred the amount thereof is to be added to the amount of the "To Pay" charge; by this means the entering Company is reimbursed.

Recharge. 779. A "Recharge Invoice" is one not representing goods (except in the case of Ropes, Chains, etc., the property of a Railway Company), and is issued for the purpose of transferring a debit from one station to another. It shows the same amount in the "Paid On" and "To Pay" columns.

"Paid Through" or "Pay Through." 780. "Paid Through" or "Pay Through" entered on an invoice signifies that the Forwarding Station has the authority of the Sender to pay through the carriage of goods to their ultimate destination. On all goods so entered the receiving Station should pay the carriage to destination, and recharge the amount thereof to the sending Station.

Local Traffic. 781. Traffic between any two Stations on the Great Western system, *i.e.*, accounted for to the Great Western Company at both ends, is Local, with the exception of certain cases where it is carried over other Companies' lines.

Foreign Traffic. 782. Traffic not accounted for to the Great Western Railway at both ends is Foreign.

Abstract. 783. An "Abstract" contains on each line the total of each separate Invoice of Goods Traffic one way between one pair of stations only, with the monthly total at foot. Abstracts, when posted, are to be carefully added up and checked, and the totals carried to the Summaries.

The interior of the goods office at Pershore, looking towards the shed, a decade or so after nationalisation, but very much still GWR in character, including the First Aid cabinet. This office became exceptionally busy in season with the distribution of vegetables and fruit by goods train, and additional staff were required to keep on top of demands. J. H. MOSS

The other end of the Pershore office, showing the amount of desk space required to deal with the consignments' paperwork. Telephones can be seen on the walls, including one at the far end with a separate earpiece and mouthpiece 'on the hook', probably still on the company's district 'omnibus' circuit. A stool appears to be covered in GWR carriage seat rep. The old gas lighting had now been replaced by electric. J. H. MOSS

ing the goods, with a lesser degree of packing required than for 'CR' (which in turn often made the consignment weigh less). With 'OR', the railway would only admit liability for 'wilful misconduct' on the part of its staff. There was a Claims Department within the CGM's Office, and, in 1920, a new post of 'Claims and Salvage Agent' was created by the GWR; the first incumbent was Mr. John Johnson, who had started his career at Warrington in 1892.

The process of arriving at a rate involved a variety of factors, such as the distances carried over various railways, the services rendered at the forwarding and receiving ends, loading and unloading, collection and delivery, covering and uncovering, station accommodation, alternative routes, competing stations, and other aspects. In certain special cases where short sections of line were particularly expensive to construct, it was agreed by Act of Parliament that railways could be reimbursed accordingly. On the GWR, the Severn Tunnel was a case in point, and the company had the right to charge traffic passing through the tunnel as if it were 12 miles long instead of the actual 4¼ miles. The Talerddig Cutting on the Cambrian Railways was between Carno and Llanbrynmair stations, 5½ miles apart, but the railway was authorised to charge as if the distance were 11 miles. The North British company were permitted to charge for traffic over the Forth Bridge as if it were 23 miles long.

During World War I, various changes in traffic patterns occurred, and with them the need for rates for goods between stations that had never carried such traffic before. Pitwood was one example: in peacetime, this had been imported mainly from Norway and Russia, the flow of which was much reduced or even stopped during the conflict, and the shortfall had to be made up by timber from home sources. Thus, rates had to be worked out from a large number of country stations to the mines. Similarly, the manufacture of new items of goods in the UK – which had previously been imported – required new rates. Of goods formerly imported from Germany, glass insulators, china dolls and toys figured strongly, in addition to larger and more costly items. Moreover, the large quantities of materials supplied by contractors for the War Office and the Admiralty needed new rates (and sometimes special terms).

The most far-reaching development in railway rates offices during World War I was the curtailment of competitive rates to encourage traffic onto the line; the Railway Executive Committee had removed the need for inter-company settlements, since the Board of Trade had agreed to provide the 1913 'standard revenue' to all companies. Experience of this restriction brought home the benefits of unity of control to the companies and the government.

In normal times, a railway could please itself how it recorded and checked goods in transit when passing from one of its own stations to another. For 'foreign' traffic, however, there had to be a system common to all companies. Three factors had to be satisfied:

1. Linking of the charges with the particular goods.
2. An independent record of foreign traffic by the stations of each company at the beginning and end of the journey.
3. An easy and effective method of checking station accounts.

The paperwork of inter-company transactions for goods and parcels was aided by the introduction of the 'waybilling' (invoicing) system in mid-Victorian times. When consignments were handed in at a railway station for conveyance, the names of the sender and the consignee were entered on a waybill, as was the weight and the amount of the carriage charges. Items collected at receiving offices in towns were transferred to the railway's forwarding station with similar particulars entered upon a sheet or cart-bill, from which the waybills were made out by the parcels booking clerk; this was also the case for goods sent in to goods depots by firms, the particulars being entered on the firm's 'consignment note'. A label was then stuck on the parcel showing the name of the forwarding station, and whether the charges were prepaid by the sender or to be paid on delivery by the consignee. On receipt at the destination station, the parcels would be checked with the particulars shown on the waybill, and a signature obtained from the consignee to an entry on the delivery sheet.

Duplicate copies of the waybills were made by the forwarding station, and were each day sorted into station order, checked and totalled, errors in charging identified (overcharges and undercharges), the original waybills undergoing a similar process at the receiving stations. At the end of the month these totals were entered on summaries, tabulated on forms called *Abstracts*, and forwarded to the GW Accounts and Audit Offices to check and compare, and prepare *Inaccuracy Sheets* if necessary; and in the case of foreign traffic, to pass on to the Railway Clearing House for division of the receipts between the appropriate companies.

Guards of passenger trains had to check that the entries on the waybill corresponded with the parcels delivered to, or given up, by him. Similar procedures applied to guards of pick-up goods trains conveying 'station trucks', although guards of through goods trains did not – indeed, could not be expected to – do the same for whole freight train loads.

Sometimes, a waybill would be received at a station without the related goods consignment, and vice-versa. Invoices of traffic conveyed by goods train were, for many years, nailed to the side of the wagon with tintacks, and later carried in invoice boxes or clips. Sometimes, when the traffic had a long, cross-country rail journey before it, the invoices were sent by post. When things went wrong, correspondence, telegrams, telephone calls round and about could usually sort matters out, and get the item to the correct destination for delivery.

The arrival of parcels or goods at the wrong station had to be 'booked in' however, and the original waybill dealt with. Credit was given to that station for the trouble and cost of handling the erroneous item and sending it to where it should have gone, and a fresh 're-charge' waybill and voucher system sorted out the accounts at all stations. Similar accounting procedures were in place for errant parcels arriving at a station on a different company to that consigned.

Many book-keeping entries had therefore to be checked every month, and any unresolved situations corrected, as were problems caused by incorrectly-filled waybills. These problems occurred mostly at large stations at times of great pressure. Strictly speaking, all paperwork relating to such difficulties had to go through the headquarters goods office, which slowed the correction process down, but eventually this requirement was by-passed, and goods agents were permitted to clear items up to a certain value between themselves (5s 0d just before World War I). Accounts cleared in the accounts books were summarised each month, and deducted from the total receipts on the balance sheet, vouchers being certified by the relevant goods agents and kept for inspection by auditors. By Edwardian times, over 6 million 'inaccuracy sheets' were being generated annually across the country. The staff who had to operate the system felt that they were in the stranglehold of the Audit Office, and that the system of checking was more costly than it was worth.

The waybill system was introduced not only for purposes of accounts, but also to provide a check on goods during transit. In the case of parcels, the presence or absence of an item, or an indication of damage or pilferage, was indicated on the waybill by the staff en route. Generally speaking, this second objective was very inadequately fulfilled, as the sheer quantity of parcels traffic made a satisfactory check almost impossible to carry out. Furthermore, the concept broke down when waybills, through pressure of work and time, did not accompany the parcels, but were sent forward by a later train.

By the late 19th century, it had come to be accepted that the waybill system was laborious and bulky, and efforts were made to reduce it to a simpler form, more economical in labour and expense. The GWR's L. C. Webber Reed, of Carmarthen, proposed a 'stamp and label' system which was introduced in July 1904 by the company for parcels weighing under 2 cwts. The method was soon adopted by the other large railway companies, at first for traffic on their own lines only. On the GWR, this system was used initially only for 'carriage paid' traffic, waybills being retained for 'to pay' parcels (i.e. carriage paid by recipient). The labels themselves had a face value (2d to 5s od) and additional stamps were not employed. These 'paid' labels were numbered progressively, in the same way as passenger tickets, and this provided a simpler way of balancing the accounts at a station than the checking of sheets of stamps. A daily record was kept at the stations of parcels forwarded and received, the number of parcels, with the amount of charges (both 'paid' and 'to pay') totalled; these daily totals were entered on a summary at the end of the month, and forwarded to the GWR Accountant.

On arrival at the receiving station, the parcels were checked with the particulars shown on the labels. In the event of overcharge or undercharge, the labels were altered, the correct charges collected, and the forwarding station advised accordingly. There were procedures for balancing the books when parcels were received with no labels, or at the wrong station, and so on.

The stamp/label system did not provide a check against loss or theft. However, since parcel traffic received quick transit (unlike ordinary goods traffic before the fast vacuum goods trains were introduced), the consignee would invariably know when something was missing, and promptly make enquiries. This could not be said for transit by ordinary goods train in Victorian days.

Waybilling remained in place for 'to-pay' parcels traffic weighing less than 2cwts until January 1911, when the 'stamp and label' scheme was applied to that category of traffic as well, with the slight difference that, in place of a value stamp, a ticket (known as a docket) was placed on the package showing the stations between which it was passing and the amount of carriage to be collected.

On jointly-owned lines, there may have been alternative routes for goods traffic intended for final destinations off that joint line. In pre-grouping days particularly, individual railway companies preferred routes which gave them the longest carrying mileage. Sometimes, the sender specified the route; but if not, goods from wayside stations on joint lines were sent according to a formula agreed by the joint companies. Thus, on the Birkenhead Railway (joint GWR and L & NWR), special calendars were issued with the days printed alternately in red and black; on 'black' days, goods were sent off the joint line via the L & NW, whilst on 'red' days it was conveyed via the GWR.

The Webber Reed parcels reform scheme of 1904 was adopted by the wartime Railway Executive Committee in 1915 for all railways. The additional wages involved in the adoption of an 8-hour working day for railwaymen had effectively increased the cost of clerical work, especially that involved with the old waybilling methods. Furthermore, many clerks experienced in the intricacies of the old systems had joined the armed forces, so the introduction of accounting reforms which eliminated wasteful office routine and cut costs was essential. The simplification of the Webber Reed method was that, while accounting and abstracting methods remained the same at the sending station, invoices were not abstracted at the receiving station (thus reducing the paperwork by half); furthermore all traffic had to be 'carriage paid'.

After the First World War, matters slowly returned to normal. As times improved, the GWR was gradually able to invest in its infrastructure with a view to keeping things up to date, fighting off road competition, and attracting new traffic to the railway. But times were not easy for the company. During the period of government control in the First World War, rates for goods and mineral traffic had not been permitted to rise, all railways being guaranteed by the government their 'standard revenue', i.e. what they had earned in 1913. Of course, the costs of working the traffic had increased considerably through WWI with the greater cost of coal and the introduction of the 8-hour working day. In 1913, the total traffic expenses of the railways taken over by the Government were £23 million; for the year 1920, the total was £74 million.

One of the first deliberations of the Rates Advisory Committee set up under the new Ministry of Transport in 1919 was to recommend to the Minister that railways should be permitted, from 1920, to double their pre-war goods and mineral rates, docks and canal charges, and wagon demurrage charges. This was by way of an interim measure until, under the Railways Act of 1921, the new 'big four' could work with the new Railway Rates Tribunal (into which the old Railway and Canal Commissions were subsumed) to determine the basis of charging in the future. An 'Appointed Day' was to be identified at which a revised classification of goods, altered standard charges (by rail and cartage), altered methods of charging (revision of consignment notes, etc), revised 'recognised journey distances' (because of company amalgamations) etc. would come into force. The 'Appointed Day' was eventually fixed by the Rates Tribunal as 1st January, 1928; it will be appreciated that the changes took a long time to arrange as the Rates Departments of the railways had a massive task on their hands. The number of distances calculated and exceptional rates examined totalled many millions, and as many as 350 temporary clerks were employed by the GWR in the compilation of the new goods rates books, whilst in 1926 alone, a special staff of over 100 clerks was engaged at Barry (no office space at Paddington being available) to calculate mineral rates. All of this was on top of the regular work of the Rates Department, which was already pretty heavy owing to the fight against road competition. Over half-a-million new and exceptional rates were fixed and offered in 1925, in addition

One of the most damaging industrial disputes that Britain has experienced was the General Strike of 1926. Here, a very quiet Paddington goods depot is seen at 12.30 p.m. on Monday, 10th May 1926 (the tenth day of the strike). The road weighbridges in the foreground were on the road entrance coming from under Bishop's Road bridge and the CGM's office, from the high level alongside the passenger station. The photograph illustrates the depot in the middle of rebuilding (see also later in the book). The high-level coal yard on the right had been cleared, the high-level wagon bridge gone, and part of the new building is visible on the left. Part of the old building with a curved roof had yet to be replaced.
NATIONAL RAILWAY MUSEUM

to the quotation of many thousands of rates already on the books.

For the first six or so years of their new existence, the big four were therefore in a sort of limbo as regards charging, although their outgoings were increasing all the time. Apart from an initial boom immediately after the war, the country's trade was slack, particularly in those heavy industries (coal, iron and steel) served by the railway. In order to stimulate trade and rail traffic, in 1923 the railways voluntarily *reduced* the higher charges they had just been allowed to levy, first to 60%, then to 50% over pre-war levels. To stimulate the shipment coal trade, these reductions were applied to dock dues, tipping charges, etc, and there was a special scheme to encourage the use of the more efficient 20-ton 'Pole' mineral wagons. The reductions applied also to canal tolls, warehouse rents, wharfage and other charges.

Unfortunately, the hoped-for revival in trade did not materialise, and matters came to a head after the coal and general strikes of 1926, which intensified the overall depression and lack of confidence. Together with the problems caused by growing road competition, it had become imperative by 1927 to restore charges to at least 60% over pre-war rates from the prevailing 50%. Firms challenged the railways' right to do this, even though the levels were still voluntarily lower than the permitted increases of 1920; it was all to do with 'exceptional' as opposed to standard rates. A test case (*Tate & Lyle v. LMS and LNE Rlys*) went all the way to the House of Lords, where it was decided that the railways did have the authority to do so under the transitory provisions of the 1921 Act. The 'Appointed Day' with all its new and permanent arrangements had yet to be declared, so that, in some ways, the railways were still in transition from the government control of the war years. The increase back to the 60% over pre-war rates enabled the GWR to maintain estimated gross receipts on goods traffic at roughly 8½ % above the 1923 figures.

After the 1926 strikes, there was a short-lived increase in activity as industries worked through the backlog and caught up, but then conditions reverted to their previous depressed state, particularly in the coal, and the heavy iron and steel industries in South Wales, served by the Great Western. At the end of 1930, over forty pits connected with the Great Western system were closed, while eighteen pits were working short time. At the same time, the slump in shipping resulted in a substantial reduction in the need for coal for bunkering.

To give assistance to basic industries, the government began the Railway Freight

De-Rating Scheme in 1928–29 under the Local Government Act, whereby there was a 75% remission on local rates on freight transport buildings and facilities. The whole of the relief – about £3 million per annum – was passed on by the railways in terms of reduced charges for conveyance of specific traffics. Selected goods were coal for export; timber, iron and steel for pit props and shoring purposes in mines; coal, ores, limestone and other raw materials delivered to iron and steel works; and certain agricultural traffic such as manure, fertiliser, feedstuffs, potatoes, milk and livestock. The South Wales Coal Marketing Scheme, introduced in 1930, was designed to prevent unnecessary competition in prices within the trade, and to stabilise the market. Similarly, the Coal & Mines Act of 1930 introduced a quota system for coal production among the different collieries; this had a side effect of requiring the GWR to stable considerable numbers of empty PO coal wagons once a mine had produced its quota, until a new quota period began. The Freight Rebate Scheme continued in the 1930s but the railways were later assessed for rates on buildings at lower values than previously, so that by 1937 they had collectively oversubscribed some £10 million to the fund. Having had this sum returned, there was less money available for subsidy of goods charges, so the rebate scheme at the end of that decade became limited to only milk and livestock traffic, and coal for export.

There had been considerable imports of iron and steel in the 1920s, increased tonnages of which during the 1926 strikes caused an abnormal shortage of wagons at the ports. A few works, such as at Ebbw Vale, were closed for a period due to the depression in trade. Later, in 1935, the country reached an agreement through the International Steel Cartel which limited iron and steel imports to just over half-a-million tons (which was about 50% of imports in previous years); this resulted in increased business for British iron and steel works and, consequentially, for the railways, particularly in terms of raw materials traffic to the works.

To deal with unemployment generally (and not only in the coal and steel industries), the government passed the 1929 Loans & Grants Act, the intention of which was to give impetus to trade throughout the country by extensive new building works. The Great Western took advantage of the scheme with the construction of new loco depots, stations, and re-equipment of various facilities all over the system. Another source of funds for this sort of work came from a duty paid on first class fares, remitted in 1929 so that the money could be used for improvements. The GWR had paid £30,000 duty in 1928 which, when capitalised, became £700,000. By 1931, direct government grants to the GWR amounted to £8.5 million. When the 1929 Act was passed, all the plans authorised by the GWR Directors in 1923–25 for rebuilding and modernising the goods stations at Paddington and Bristol had just been completed, but further alterations and improvements were then put in place at both places under the aegis of the government scheme. By far the major scheme was at Paddington, Bishops Road, to accompany the extensive improvements to the passenger accommodation.

The effect of growing road competition also featured prominently in the lowering of receipts from goods train traffic in the 1920s and 1930s, especially in general merchandise. Apart from reducing railway rates and charges (including quotation of special rates, and the introduction of 'flat' rates per ton or per package), the railway took other measures to combat this form of competition, including:

1. Improved and enlarged terminal facilities and warehouse accommodation
2. The speeding-up of transit of small consignments
3. Increased stock of road-rail containers
4. Augmentation of country lorry services
5. Additional rail-head distribution facilities
6. Provision of an increased number of cartage vehicles
7. Private siding rail connections to factories and works of all sorts.

A major problem for the railways (not addressed until the 1930 Road Traffic Act and the 1933 Road-Rail Traffic Act) was that road hauliers were unregulated, and could not only undercut the railway charges but also agree deals with individual firms (see 'undue preference' in the *Introduction* volume of this series).

After the introduction in 1928 of revised standard charges, aimed to restore the earnings of the railway companies to their pre-war levels, the Railway Rates Tribunal performed annual reviews to see whether changes could usefully be made to help the railways if the targets were not being met. It regularly concluded that '...no modifications [to the 1928 scheme] would enable the railways to earn their respective standard revenues...'! Nevertheless, the 1933 report by the GW on its Goods Department opened with the observation that '... the outstanding feature of 1933 was the fact that the continued decrease in revenue since 1929 was arrested in the second half of the year, and a small but gratifying increase in receipts over 1932 was recorded ....' That improvement, particularly in merchandise traffic, continued more or less for the rest of the decade. Nevertheless, in 1936 the Rates Tribunal, reviewing the performance of the railways during 1935, agreed with the railway companies that '... any increase in charges would not be expedient nor would it enable the railways more nearly to approach their standard revenue ... the world state of trade and intensive transport competition were responsible ... the railways were being run on the most economic and efficient lines ...'. The following year, an application was made to increase standard charges, since costs of materials and working were increasing, and it was felt that the trade of the country had improved sufficiently (the GWR's net revenue was £2 million below its 1913 standard revenue). In the event only a small, inadequate, increase was authorised.

In 1929, a system of 'Registered Transits' was inaugurated, which guaranteed the time of arrival of 'smalls' traffic (see page 19 of the *Introduction* volume). For a payment of 2s 6d, the registered item of goods was followed through to destination, the transit being controlled from point to point to ensure delivery by the time quoted (subject to fog and other unavoidable risks). In 1931, some 16,000 consignments were dealt with under this scheme and by 1933, over 30,000 intra-GWR consignments and 6,000 'foreign' consignments were registered, the latter being possible since the other railway companies adopted the scheme during that year. By the mid 1930s, the number of consignments conveyed 'under the sign of the Green Arrow' had risen to over 115,000 per annum. A demand also grew for registered transits where delivery was required on the *second* day after dispatch (often for traffic where one wagon transhipment en route was involved).

Also in 1929, the COD (cash on delivery) system, which had already been functioning for Post Office deliveries in Britain, was applied to railway goods traffic. For a small fee, varying with the value of the goods, the 'COD' amount was collected by the railway from the consignee and paid to the sender of the goods. In

1934, the service applied to consignments not exceeding £40 in value. The scheme applied throughout Britain and to several Continental ports, and embraced all traffic with the exception of livestock, wet fish and ice, explosive and dangerous goods and (for the Continent only) highly-perishable goods.

During 1931, the big four railway companies introduced a scheme whereby urgent freight and parcels for destinations on any air route operated by Imperial Airways Ltd. could be handed in at nominated railway stations and forwarded at an inclusive charge. Goods went by express train to London and thence by air freighter to the Continent, Egypt, Iraq, India and Central and Southern Africa. A similar joint scheme operated in reverse.

An improvement in the paperwork was the introduction of triplicate consignment notes in the early 1930s, whereby the drudgery of copying forms was eliminated. In a similar vein, special typewriters where the paper was fed continuously from a roll, were installed in some depots for the preparation of delivery sheets. When the new offices for the Newport Goods District were opened in 1929, '... in their layout and equipment they embody the latest ideas of modern office practice. With the exception of the district officer, his assistant, and chief clerk, the whole of the district staff will be accommodated in one large room ....'

The Road Traffic Act of 1933 officially empowered railways to quote firms for the conveyance of the whole of their goods traffic on the basis of a flat rate per ton, or per package, irrespective of distance (so-called 'Agreed Charges') as an alternative to the charging scheme embodied in the General Classification of Goods (as modified in 1928). Road hauliers had been doing this for years, but the railways had not been permitted to do so, and consequently had – unfairly – lost a considerable amount of traffic to the roads. Traders wanted this uncomplicated method as it simplified costing and reduced to a minimum the work of checking transport charges. The agreed charge was the average of the firm's payments to the Great Western for the whole of their traffic during two representative months. By 1935, applications from over 500 firms to the GWR were awaiting the sanction of the Railway Rates Tribunal. By the late 1930s, there were nearly 500 firms using this facility, and negotiations with a further 1,000 companies in progress. The goods involved were mainly from light industry or foodstuffs.

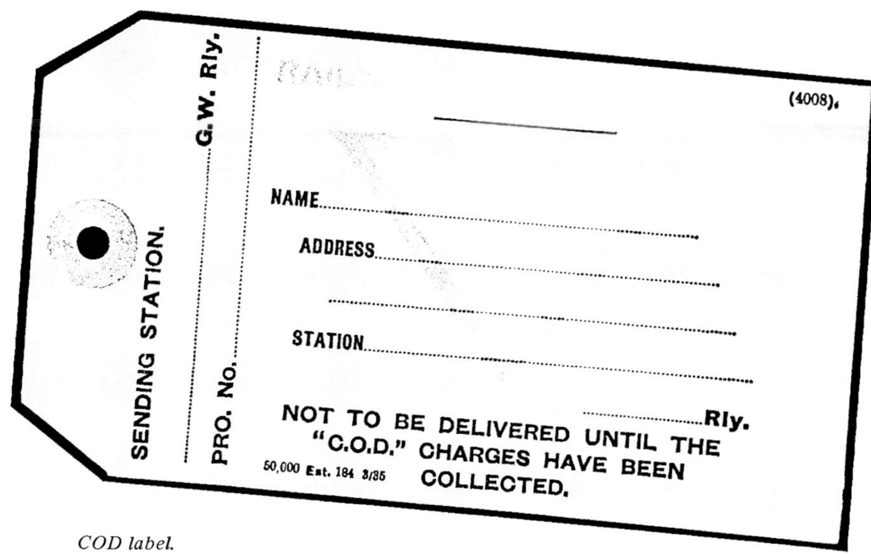

COD label.

The Second World War brought many of the same sort of difficulties on the clerical side of goods working as had occurred in WWI. To simplify procedures, the 'Weight Only' system of invoicing and accountancy was introduced in the Autumn of 1940; during 1942, this system had been extended to 319 Great Western stations. To push clerical economy to its utmost extent, a complementary 'Carriage Paid' system was put in place in 1943 for all traffic carried by goods train. Furthermore, flat rates for the charging of British and Canadian Government traffic were agreed, together with a combined form of consignment note, invoice and account, resulting in still further economies. The 'addressing of goods' campaign, and the work of claims prevention inspectors and mobile claims investigators, also proved their worth.

The introduction of the Zonal collection and delivery scheme at the end of WWII had its effect on invoicing and accounting. As against 1,100 goods stations dealing with 'smalls traffic' before the introduction of the scheme, all traffic was now concentrated into approximately 148 railheads and sub-railheads, to which the whole of the invoicing formerly done at the 'absorbed' depots was transferred (see our *Cartage* volume in this series). Special arrangements were put into effect at the same time to ensure that invoices would be available at destinations in advance of the traffic. The 'Transit of Invoices' scheme was inaugurated in January 1947; invoices were conveyed in special canvas wallets by nominated night passenger train services between thirteen sorting centres, known as District Concentration Offices.

Although the company continued to make improvements in the postwar era, austerity and impending nationalisation limited the scope. In 1946, owing to the heavy decline in the volume of services and government traffic, and the increased costs of operating, a deficit at the end of the year was foreshadowed. To provide against this, the Minister of Transport decided that an increase of 25% over prewar rates should be put in place from July, knowing, however, that this measure would not yield the required revenue. After a public inquiry, the Minister of Transport announced that as from 1st October 1947, all rates and charges were to be increased to 55% over the prewar figure.

Then the railways were nationalised.

SACKS, ROPES & SHEETS

For transit by rail, bulky loads had to be secured by ropes, and sometimes by chains, whilst some types of goods in open wagons had to be protected from bad weather by tarpaulins ('sheets' in railway parlance). Some railways hired out sacks to corn merchants, and others for conveyance of grain by rail.

Before the grouping, the Great Western was one of the railways that contracted outside firms for the supply and maintenance of sacks. The GWR employed The West of England Sack Co., and Gospill, Brown & Co., whilst two, later constituent

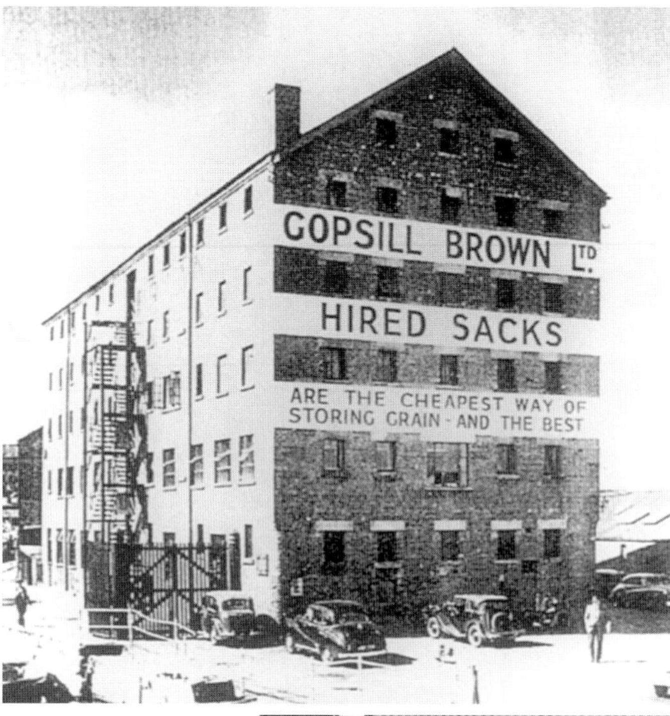

The Gopsill Brown Ltd. sack warehouse at Gloucester docks. A considerable number of sacks were used for grain and foodstuffs offloaded at the docks, and could be hired by traders from a company such as Gopsill Brown rather than purchasing and maintaining their own.

This corrugated iron storage shed at Ross-on-Wye mileage yard was used for Gopsill Brown sacks, and their name-board was fixed to the left of the sliding door.
E. T. RAWLINS

When moving horses in great bulk, it was sometimes necessary to carry the 'lesser' animals in cattle wagons. Here, some of those vehicles were sheeted for horse traffic at the cattle pens on the north side of Paddington goods depot, before rebuilding took place. The view was taken looking southwards towards the excursion/parcels platform 1A (out of picture).
NATIONAL RAILWAY MUSEUM

companies, viz: the Brecon & Merthyr and the Cambrian, employed Garlick & Co. of Liverpool. Stations kept a stock of empty sacks on hand, packed up in twenties (nineteen inside one), each sack holding 4 bushels. In 1904, sacks were let out on hire at the rate of ½d per sack per week, with ¼d per sack per week demurrage if not returned in time to the station from which they were hired. All transactions were carried out in the name of the contractor, not the Great Western. Sacks passing on to foreign lines were traced by the Railway Clearing House (RCH) in ways similar to wagons. Sometimes, an extra charge was paid at the forwarding station when it was known that sacks could be going on to other lines; this was called a 'sack risk' charge.

Ropes were standardised by the RCH: they were 25ft long, made of hemp, and had a ferrule in the middle on which was stamped the number of the rope and the initials of the owning railway, and in some cases the name of the station at which it was kept in stock. Company ropes were also distinguished by details such as different coloured strands: GW ropes had two green and one white strand (but on the Watlington & Princes Risborough branch in 1906, they contained two yellow and one blue strand!). Most Cambrian ropes had one red and one green & white strand. Rhymney Railway ropes had their ends painted green, with the centre red; the M & SWJR had one red and two yellow strands. Unlike sacks, no charge was made when ropes were used, but to ensure their prompt return, a charge of 10s 0d was made to the destination station. Should that station detain a rope for more than 14 days, the forwarding station had only to accept a debit of 5s 0d when the rope was eventually returned; the receiving station could argue the case with the Chief Goods Manager if it wished.

Sheets not only protected goods from rain and snow, but also gave protection to inflammable goods carried in open wagons against sparks from engines. As with ropes, each sheet was numbered and distinguished by company markings. Traders were not charged for the use of sheets, except when used to cover lime, etc, or on cattle wagons used for horse traffic (where, to keep horses from panicking, the open-top sides were sometimes sheeted over) for which a charge of 1s 0d per sheet for each journey was charged. Like sacks, tarpaulins were traced through the RCH. Every station kept a record of arrival and departure

GREAT WESTERN RAILWAY.

(5781)

Station No. 41

THIS RETURN MUST BE WRITTEN IN INK.

DAILY REPORT TO DISTRICT GOODS MANAGER OF POSITION AT 8 A.M. FOR RAILWAY COMPANIES' GOODS ROLLING STOCK, SHEETS AND G.W. ROPES; ALSO TOTAL NUMBER OF RAILWAY COMPANIES' WAGONS AND SHEETS DETAINED UNDER LOAD OVER 48 HOURS.

Date 7/2/1939

At [illegible] Rd Station.

DESCRIPTION (CODE)	INWARDS LOADED. Received since 8.0 a.m. yesterday.	Discharged since 8.0 a.m. yesterday.	On hand 8.0 a.m. to-day.	EMPTY. Received since 8.0 a.m. yesterday.	Forwarded since 8.0 a.m. yesterday.	On hand 8.0 a.m. to-day.	Outwards loaded since 8.0 a.m. yesterday.	Wagons held back.	WAGONS DETAINED UNDER LOAD OVER 48 HOURS. (COLUMN 9) Total No. of Wagons.	Type.	Consignee.	Date of arrival.	(a) Coal.	(b) G.W. Delivery.	(c) Consignees' Cartage.	(d) Warehouse.	(e) O.C.S.	(f) Other Reasons.
	1	2	3	4	5	6	7	8										
†† Opens																		
„ A																		
„ B					2	94	5	94	Stalled									
(1) Total					4	94	5											
One Plank Opens																		
Conflats																		
Serpents																		
Match Trucks																		
(2) Total																		
(3) Opens C																		
Minks	1		1															
Vac. Minks																		
(4) Total	1		1															
Fruits A						9	5											
„ B																		
Micas					1	6												
„ A & B																		
Cones																		
Motor Car Vans																		
(5) Total					1	15	5											
Macaws																		
Macaws A																		
„ B																		
„ C																		
„ D																		
„ E																		
„ F																		
„ G																		
„ H																		
† Mites																		
(6) Total																		
Mex																		
„ B						[illegible]												
(7) Total																		
Loriots																		
Corals																		
Crocodiles																		
Roll Wagons																		
•																		
•																		
(8) Total																		
(9) Sheets				3	2	9												
(10) Ropes (G.W.)																		

1 108

Note.—Col. 6. Must **not** include empty wagons waiting repair, which must be shewn in Col. 8.
Col. 7. Must **not** include partly loaded wagons which must be shewn in Col. 8.
Col. 8. Must include loaded wagons held back, partly loaded wagons and empty wagons awaiting repair.
• Insert Types.
† Twin Timber trucks to be counted as one.
†† Excluding types shewn below.

Signature [illegible]

Station Masters and Goods Agents will be held personally responsible for satisfying themselves that the statement is accurately prepared.

This return must be completed as soon as possible after 8.0 a.m. daily, and despatched to the District Goods Manager by the first available train.

6,000 pads, 100 lvs.—B.M./N.2 1938-9 (2) S.

of all sheets, and weekly returns of all 'foreign' sheets were sent to the RCH. Demurrage of 6d for the first day and 1s od for each day thereafter was charged in 1904. In the First World War, the BoT/REC readjusted the periods allowed to traders before tarpaulins had to be returned, and these changes corresponded to those applied to wagons in order to make more economical use of rolling stock and equipment. Furthermore, failure to comply with the orders (issued under the Defence of the Realm Regulations) was a summary offence. For unloading at stations, the period did not change from before the war (two days, exclusive of day of receipt of the sheeted wagon), but at private sidings the period was shortened from three days to two if the wagon was returned empty, and from five days to three if it was reloaded. Shipment traffic at ports had to be unloaded and the wagon and/or tarpaulin placed at the railway's disposal within three days (exclusive of day of arrival); it had been four days.

Right: *Another need for sheets is illustrated in this example of a typical covered horse-drawn wagon used for C & D services in towns; they generally worked to a distance of 1½ to 3 miles from the depot with general merchandise traffic. This vehicle was photographed in Cardiff Newton depot.*
NATIONAL RAILWAY MUSEUM

Hay bales being loaded into a variety of Great Western open wagons and two MR wagons at the right at Pershore before World War 1. The hay was bulky rather than heavy, so loads could be four or five bales high. This is higher than a sheet supporter, so in consequence most wagons have two overlapping tarpaulins placed across (not along) the wagons and roped accordingly.

188
188. GREAT WESTERN RAIL

A problem with the use of tarpaulins was so-called 'hollow sheeting', i.e. sheets that were merely draped across the top of the open wagon, and would sag down into hollows between the goods inside. In wet weather, rain accumulated in the hollows, and if there were pin-holes in the tarpaulin, rain would damage the goods. Matters were improved when the tarpaulin could be held up over the goods, thus allowing rain to run off. Round-ended open wagons helped somewhat – except that there was no support over the middle of the wagon, and hollows would be produced in slack tarpaulins. The provision of sheet supporters as part of wagon equipment answered all the difficulties: a bar the length of the wagon, and hinged permanently on the ends, could be swung up over the wagon and locked in place to support the tarpaulin like a ridge tent. When not required, the supporter bar rested along the top of one side of the wagon. Supporter bars were generally introduced on GWR 4-plank (later 5- and even 7-plank) wagons in 1902, which were coded 'OPEN A', and 'OPEN B' (vacuum fitted); wagons equipped in this way were built by the Great Western until the mid 1920s. The LMS and LNER were not, however, convinced over the value of sheet supporter bars, and when these GWR wagons began to move around widely off the system in the 'Common User' pool after the grouping, the Great Western decided to stop spending money on the provision of further bars when the other companies did not reciprocate. Furthermore, with growing road competition, there was an increasing preference to use vans for the sort of goods that required protection by tarpaulins in open wagons. By the end of 1928, some 5,000 more GWR goods vans were in traffic than at the grouping, whilst the company's stock of sheets was reduced from 58,000 to 57,000.

GWR sheet factories made new, and repaired old, tarpaulins not only for railway wagons but also for open cartage vehicles. Tarpaulins were made from canvas, impregnated with linseed oil and vegetable

The head of a rake of the first production batch of sheeted opens fitted with the Williams patent sheet supporter (Dia O4 'Open A' with five equal planks, built in 1902, at the time of the cast plate numbering system). The picture shows the pattern of lettering and numbering on GWR sheets at that time.
NATIONAL RAILWAY MUSEUM

Unsupported sheeting on wagons could soon fill with rainwater, as seen at Hockley in February 1940; this might allow water to seep onto any load below through pinholes or other defects in the tarpaulin, and could lead to a claim from the trader whose goods were affected. Lettering and numbering on sheets was now different from the earlier picture above.
NATIONAL RAILWAY MUSEUM

Tarpaulin tilt on a solid-tyred forward-control Thornycroft at Westbourne Park in October 1929. The tarpaulin and supporting hoops could be moved back along the sides to cover the whole vehicle if required. There was no windscreen, and the driver was protected by a small sheet wrapped up around the dashboard above the 'GWR'. Sconces for oil headlamps were on rods coming down from the roof.
NATIONAL RAILWAY MUSEUM

A much later design of sheeted Thornycroft lorry, though with a similar delivery and collection role to the vehicle pictured above.

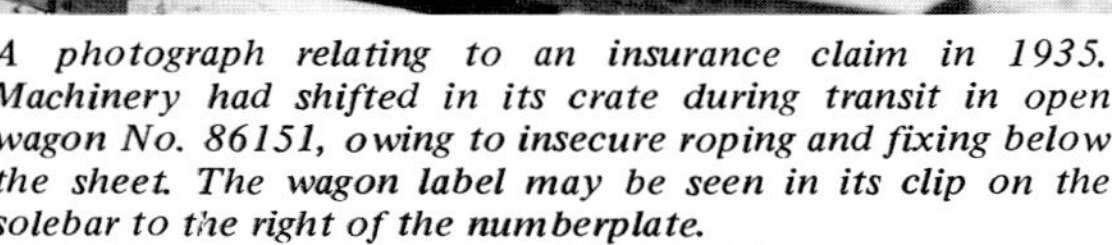

A photograph relating to an insurance claim in 1935. Machinery had shifted in its crate during transit in open wagon No. 86151, owing to insecure roping and fixing below the sheet. The wagon label may be seen in its clip on the solebar to the right of the numberplate.
NATIONAL RAILWAY MUSEUM

Sheeted drays along the cartage road at Hockley in 1941.
NATIONAL RAILWAY MUSEUM

Stencilling sheets in the Worcester Sheet Shop during 1931; a line of paint-stained footprints diagonally across the nearest sheet spoils the appearance, but would not affect its performance. Above, sheets were slung up in the roof for storage.
NATIONAL RAILWAY MUSEUM

A sheet laid out for folding. This had to be done carefully to avoid any crinkling that might later jeopardise the waterproof properties of the sheeting. NATIONAL RAILWAY MUSEUM

black, the resulting material taking on a leathery texture which was still flexible in frost and snow. Tarpaulin manufacture aimed to combine toughness and lightness with durability. New sheets were tacky, and it was recommended that they be used straight away and not left folded. When new, the sheets (21ft x 14ft 4ins) weighed about 75lbs – anything more than about a hundredweight (112lbs) was deemed too heavy to be handled by a railwayman working alone. Tarpaulins had a useful life of about six years.

The sheet factory also made lightweight tarpaulins for station use, to protect parcels on platform trolleys, as well as horse loin cloths, carmen's aprons and so on from canvas offcuts.

Including those inherited from the absorbed companies, there were eight sheet shops on the GWR in the early 1920s from which distribution of sheets around the system took place. With the policy of providing additional covered vans in place of open wagons, three shops (at Paddington, Swansea and Barry) were closed in 1927, and later the Gloucester

G.W.R.

SHEET TRUCK No. 12 No. 2 AREA

Bourne End to WORCESTER SHEET SHOPS

TO SERVE:-

Bourne End	Thame	Charlbury
High Wycombe	Tiddington	Ascott-under-Wychwood
West Wycombe	Wheatley	Shipton
Saunderton	Littlemore	Kingham
Princes Risboro'	Oxford	Adlestrop
Bledlow	Handborough	Moreton-in-Marsh
		Campden

TRAINS:

5-45 p.m. ex Taplow—Bourne End to High Wycombe
3-55 a.m. ex Slough—High Wycombe to Oxford
8-30 a.m. ex Oxford—Oxford to Moreton-in-Marsh
7-25 p.m. ex Moreton-in-Marsh—Moreton-in-Marsh to Worcester

Date____________193__ Truck No.________

500—11/33.

A wagon label for an area sheet-collecting wagon.

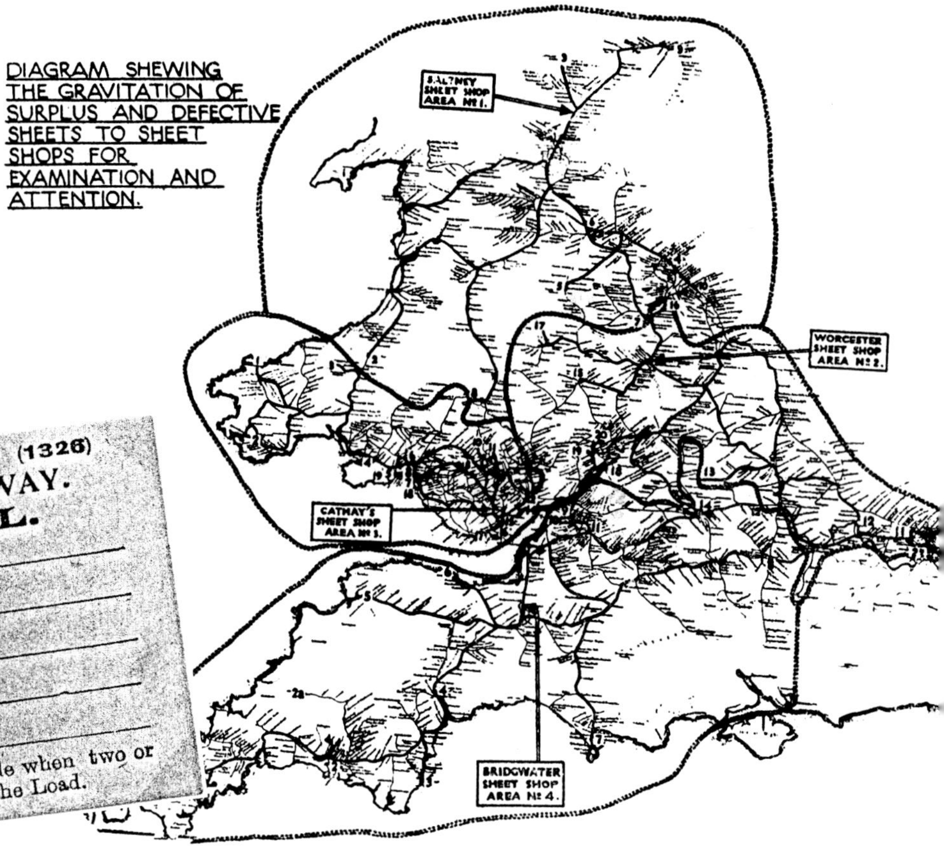

DIAGRAM SHEWING THE GRAVITATION OF SURPLUS AND DEFECTIVE SHEETS TO SHEET SHOPS FOR EXAMINATION AND ATTENTION.

SALTNEY SHEET SHOP AREA No 1.

WORCESTER SHEET SHOP AREA No 2.

CATHAY'S SHEET SHOP AREA No 3.

BRIDGWATER SHEET SHOP AREA No 4.

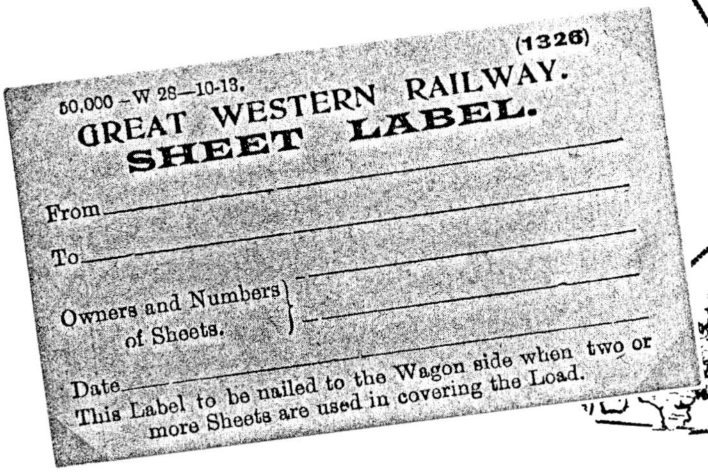

(1326)

50,000—W 28—10-13.

GREAT WESTERN RAILWAY.

SHEET LABEL.

From

To

Owners and Numbers of Sheets.

Date

This Label to be nailed to the Wagon side when two or more Sheets are used in covering the Load.

Llanthony yard shop was closed, leaving the following four sheet shops covering the following assigned areas:

> *No. 1 Area, for Saltney Sheet Shop*: From stations north of a line drawn from Bryn Teify through Llandilo, Torpantau, Craven Arms, Tenbury Wells, Stourport, Brettell Lane, Lye, Henley-in-Arden to Lapworth (inclusive).
> *No. 2 Area, for Worcester Sheet Shop*: From stations south of No. 1 Area and east of a line drawn from Presteign, through Hay, Pontrilas and down the Golden Valley line to Little Mill Junction, all inclusive, and north of and including the main line from Paddington (embracing all London Depots) to Llanwern via Didcot, Swindon and Gloucester but excluding the section between Wantage Road and Swindon.
> *No. 3 Area, for Cathays Sheet Shop*: From stations in South Wales, i.e. south of No. 1 Area and west of No. 2 Area.
> *No. 4 Area, for Bridgwater Sheet Shop*: From stations south of No. 2 Area and east of the River Severn.

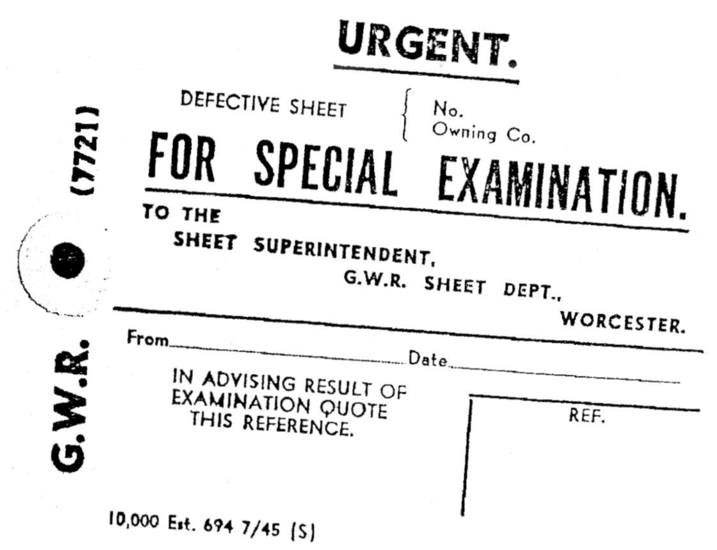

URGENT.

DEFECTIVE SHEET { No. Owning Co.

FOR SPECIAL EXAMINATION.

TO THE SHEET SUPERINTENDENT, G.W.R. SHEET DEPT., WORCESTER.

From ______ Date ______

IN ADVISING RESULT OF EXAMINATION QUOTE THIS REFERENCE.

REF.

G.W.R. (7721)

10,000 Est. 694 7/45 (S)

Management of the sheet shops was transferred to the Stores Superintendent from July 1926.

All sheets were sent periodically to the sheet shops to be overhauled (there were 'sheet trucks' running over various parts of the system). Figures stencilled on the sheets indicated the maintenance date.

There were strict instructions on how to tie down sheets on wagons: various editions of the *Appendix to the Rule Book* had a number of illustrations of recommended methods, though needless to say, they were not always followed. In a 1918 circular from Mr C. Aldington (Superintendent of the Line) and Mr C.A. Roberts (Chief Goods Manager), it was reported that '… a case recently occurred where the ties of a sheet were fastened to the crossbar of the end door of a wagon, … the wind raised the sheet and caused the bar to be lifted with the result that some of the traffic fell out on to the line … All concerned must note that sheet ties must not be fastened to crossbars or catches of tip end doors of wagons ….'

CHAPTER TWO

SMALL CONSIGNMENTS: WAGON CATEGORIES & TRANSFER

BEFORE a radical reorganisation of goods traffic working in 1932, there were five categories of loaded wagon for small consignments, viz:

1. Through (Direct) Wagons
2. Tranship or Transfer Wagons
3. Composite Wagons
4. Station Trucks (Road Vans)
5. Pick-up Wagons

At any given station, the pattern of wagon loading, and the numbers of different categories of wagon used, would clearly depend on the major types of goods normally dealt with. Factors such as the volume of traffic for a given destination and the geographical relation between the forwarding and receiving stations dictated what happened.

Transfer goods labels. The Didcot label would have been placed on a 10-ton ventilated van at the Didcot transfer shed. Marlborough transfer goods opened in 1933 at the closed High Level Marlborough station.

DIRECT, TRANSHIP AND COMPOSITE WAGONS

The major traffic movements along the main routes carried 'full loads' and 'transfer loads'; a full truck load of merchandise between two points formed the ideal loading. But what was a 'full' load? Owing to the peculiarities of the 'common classification of goods' (see the *Introduction* volume in this series), there could be no common basis for charging for complete wagon loads because of the great differences in commodities carried; various goods at diverse rates required widely differing amounts of wagon space. Lists of wagon loadings on the GWR taken at random in the 1920s showed that a single wagon may have contained anything from 94 to 156 separate articles, intended for 26 or so consignees. The average load of the 700 Station Trucks running in 1909 was only 1 ton 2 cwt.

In the face of road competition after the First World War, there was a growing demand for speedy journey times and quick deliveries. A conflict thus arose between economy in the use of wagons (i.e. holding back for full loads) and the amount carried in the wagons (i.e. sending the wagon off partially loaded in order to speed transit). To take advantage of movement in scheduled fast goods trains, 1 ton was regarded as a truck load below which it was desirable not to go for 'through loads'. The average wagon loading for general merchandise in the 1920s was about 3½ tons (cf. the RCH standard wagons were built to carry 12 tons).

When local stations had consignments for a destination of less than 1 ton, they would be sent forward to 'transfer' (or 'tranship') stations. There were over 60 authorised tranship centres on the GWR prior to 1932, together with about 100 small junction stations which served to 'focus' small consignments from many different stations into full wagon loads intended for one destination. These, and other loads of less than 1 ton from other stations, would be reloaded to make up a full wagon load to be sent on to the common destination. (There were sometimes exceptions to the 1 ton lower limit when the traffic was bulky, rather than heavy.)

As traffic originating at big industrial centres required an extensive system of through wagons, it made good sense to send transfer traffic to these points, and also to important junctions serving many branch lines. In only one instance – Pontypool Road – was a station maintained as a tranship point alone. To help station agents, there was the 'GW Transfer Map', which showed the regional loading ability of all the tranship centres, and indicated those stations for which given tranship points were the natural assembling and distributing centres. Later, with the introduction of concentration schemes for both rail and road activities, the number of transfer stations was drastically reduced.

Last was the 'Composite Wagon', which was a truck that contained two separate lots of traffic, each lot weighing less than one ton, destined for two separate, but

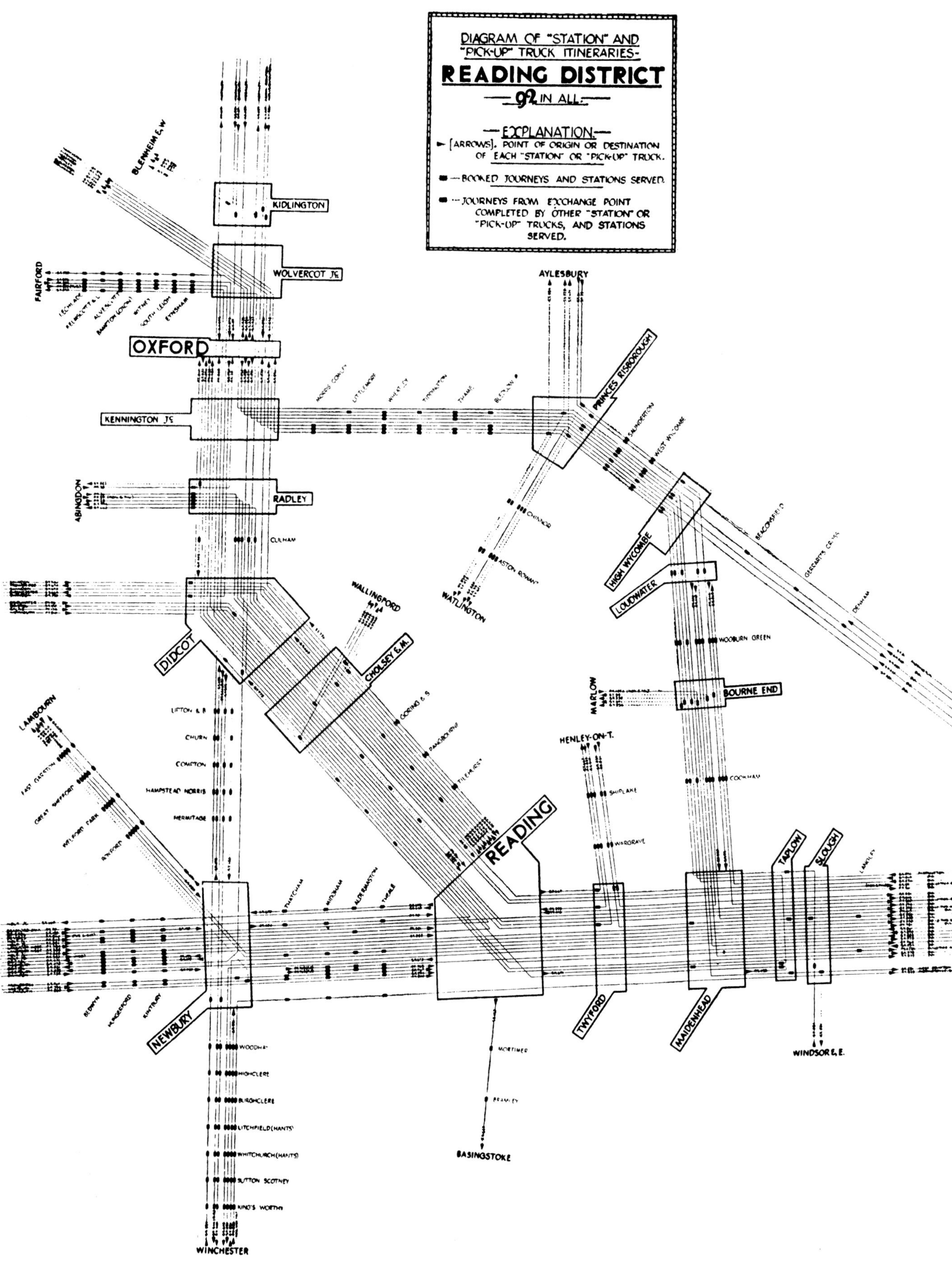
DIAGRAM OF "STATION" AND "PICK-UP" TRUCK ITINERARIES-
READING DISTRICT
-92 IN ALL-
-EXPLANATION-
[ARROWS]. POINT OF ORIGIN OR DESTINATION OF EACH "STATION" OR "PICK-UP" TRUCK.
BOOKED JOURNEYS AND STATIONS SERVED.
JOURNEYS FROM EXCHANGE POINT COMPLETED BY OTHER "STATION" OR "PICK-UP" TRUCKS, AND STATIONS SERVED.
BLENHEIM & W
KIDLINGTON
WOLVERCOT JC
FAIRFORD
LECHLADE
ALVESCOT
BAMPTON (OXON)
WITNEY
SOUTH LEIGH
EYNSHAM
OXFORD
KENNINGTON JC
MORRIS COWLEY
LITTLEMORE
WHEATLEY
TIDDINGTON
THAME
AYLESBURY
PRINCES RISBOROUGH
SAUNDERTON
WEST WYCOMBE
ABINGDON
RADLEY
CULHAM
CHINNOR
ASTON ROWANT
WATLINGTON
HIGH WYCOMBE
BEACONSFIELD
GERRARDS CROSS
DENHAM
LOUDWATER
WALLINGFORD
DIDCOT
CHOLSEY & M.
WOOBURN GREEN
MARLOW
BOURNE END
GORING & S
PANGBOURNE
TILEHURST
CHURN
COMPTON
HAMPSTEAD NORRIS
HERMITAGE
LAMBOURN
EAST GARSTON
GREAT SHEFFORD
WELFORD PARK
BOXFORD
HENLEY-ON-T.
SHIPLAKE
WARGRAVE
COOKHAM
READING
TAPLOW
SLOUGH
LANGLEY
THATCHAM
MIDGHAM
ALDERMASTON
THEALE
BEDWYN
HUNGERFORD
KINTBURY
NEWBURY
TWYFORD
MAIDENHEAD
WINDSOR & E.
MORTIMER
BRAMLEY
BASINGSTOKE
HIGHCLERE
BURGHCLERE
LITCHFIELD (HANTS)
WHITCHURCH (HANTS)
SUTTON SCOTNEY
KING'S WORTHY
WINCHESTER

close, stations. Neither lot alone gave a good load, so both lots sent together to a transfer point would mean the unloading of one at least. Station staffs were therefore given the discretion of sending these two lots together, making a fair wagon load, specially labelled and accompanied by a 'Composite Load Slip', directly to the first of the two stations. Traffic for that destination was removed and the wagon space thus created was used for forward loading of goods originating at the first station and intended for the second.

The stowage and positioning of goods in station trucks was most important in order to allow easy removal and/or addition of consignments at the various stations en route, and the floor plan for this was displayed on the truck label. The numbering of the contents on the photograph of an outside-framed wooden goods van was done to illustrate a 1905 GWR Magazine article on the subject. The Station Truck label can be seen on the van at the bottom left-hand corner, identified by its route number, 527.

STATION & PICK-UP TRUCKS

Stations not on the main routes which had insufficient goods to form a through truck or a transfer wagon would load the consignments into one vehicle, along with articles for other stations in the same direction. Such wagons were called 'Station Trucks'. Their operating routes covered a vast area of cross-country (or 'roadside') working, serving nearly every station or depot on the system, though in general each called at only a few stations; these could be between two main depots on the same line, or perhaps along the length of a branch.

3141 / 282

Great Western Railway.

Station Truck.

Bristol to Dudley

282

Trains-Ex Bristol 11.50 p.m.-ex Worcester 1.10 p.m.

Date__________190 Truck No.__________

Station Truck labels changed in design, route number, and often in route and timings, over the years. The Bristol to Dudley label is from 1905, whilst the loading diagram for the Paddington to St. Ives station truck is from 1936. A full list of ST workings for 1893, 1923 and 1939 is included as an Appendix in Volume 2B of this series.

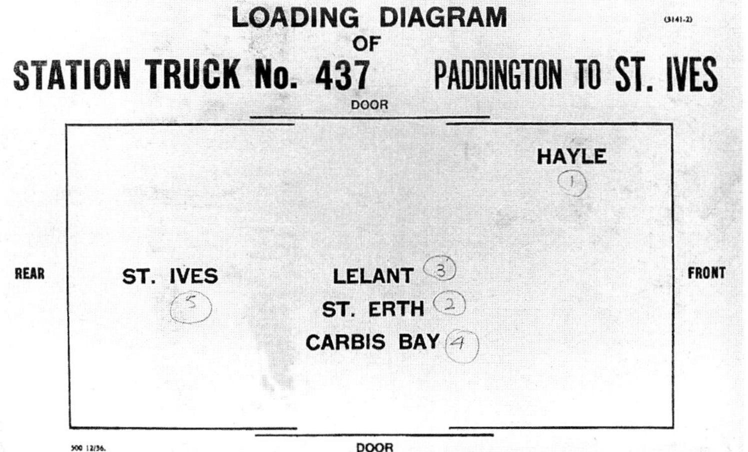

LOADING DIAGRAM OF

STATION TRUCK No. 437 PADDINGTON TO ST. IVES

DOOR

HAYLE (1)

REAR

ST. IVES (5)

LELANT (3)

ST. ERTH (2)

CARBIS BAY (4)

FRONT

DOOR

Those vehicles serving more distant points were conveyed by long-distance trains to a location at or near their starting point. For example, the Paddington to Dolgelly truck was taken by the 9.10 p.m. Paddington as far as Oxley, then by the 2.45 a.m. Oxley on to Ruabon. The truck was then attached to the 5.45 a.m. ex-Ruabon, and commenced its work soon afterwards at stations between Llangollen and Corwen. At Corwen, the truck was transferred to the 9.30 a.m. goods departure for Dolgelly, serving all stations, and thus completing its journey.

There were, in a few instances, more than one ST between two places; for example, in 1893, the 11.40 a.m. and the 11.45 p.m. trains from Oxford each carried a vehicle for Taplow, the former calling at all stations along the Thame branch, whilst the latter served Wheatley, Thame and Princes Risborough only, although both covered all stations on the Wycombe & Maidenhead branch.

Whilst the vast majority of STs served only a particular section of line, in this early period there were examples of some very lengthy routes. Perhaps the best examples were to be found on the 3.0 a.m. Paddington local goods to Gloucester, which carried trucks for Dudley, Hockley, Weymouth, and Gloucester. The train called at all goods stations to Didcot (due 12.10 p.m.), from whence the STs went their own ways: the Dudley vehicle called at most stations thence via the Oxford & Worcester line, the Hockley all stations via Banbury, the Weymouth all stations via Chippenham, whilst the Gloucester on the 3.0 a.m. went on to serve all stations to that city.

Regular station trucks were conveyed on scheduled trains, so that station staff knew when to expect them, and were ready to unload their portion of the goods, often at passenger platforms, so that vans were favoured over sheeted opens. In a few cases, station trucks were taken by passenger or mixed trains, e.g. between Exeter and Dulverton (1886) and between Plymouth and Lifton (1939).

Station trucks were separately numbered, with a large label prominently displaying the numerals being attached to the vehicle. Goods loaded in station trucks were recorded on the *Station Truck List* which the guard of the train carried with him, and the person receiving the goods at various stations signed a receipt on the list for the articles. In a given station truck, packages for as many as 15 stations might be placed, which meant careful positioning

523 R/S

75,000 8/28 Est. B.M. 288 S GREAT WESTERN RAILWAY. (3141)

STATION TRUCK.

From Oxford

Destination FAIRFORD

Route via

CONTAINS GOODS FOR STATIONS

Between and

Truck No. 26657

Train Date 16-6-20

3

(3141)

G.W.R.

STATION TRUCK No.

FROM

STATIONS TO BE SERVED	SPACE FOR RE-INSERTION OF NAMES OF STATIONS TO BE SERVED.	No. OF PACKAGES FOR EACH STATION.
	3	

DATE TRAINS:-

TRUCK No.

70,000—B.M./59 1912 (S).

so that goods to come out last were placed in the van first, and so on. Under the 'Missing and Tracing' subject in the 1939 *Telegraph Code Book*, 'Blackbird' was the codeword for 'The goods are not entered upon Tranship or Road Van List given'. Station trucks were available for conveying small lots of goods from any of the stations which they served; they were not confined to traffic from the depots where they originated. Particulars of goods added to a station truck en route had to be entered on the station truck list, or shown upon a separate list kept by the guard.

The 'Pick-up Wagon', of which there were 205 in 1926, was a 'relief' station truck, and was used where roadside work was heavy. A pick-up wagon would accept loads at several stations in succession, and when full would be sent on to destination, thereby relieving the existing station truck service over the same portion of the line.

In 1926, there were 553 station trucks (in addition to the pick-up wagons), the list of which was contained in the *Book of Standard Instructions for Working Goods in Small Consignments*, commonly known as the 'Station Truck Book'. The label number/destination usage varied over the years, as will be discussed later, and examples of full years are included in the Appendix.

As many as 11 station trucks could be despatched from one station at a time: the 3.10 p.m. goods train from Weymouth to Westbury conveyed Nos. 629 to 639 inclusive: all trucks served the stations at Dorchester, Grimstone & Frampton, Evershot, Yetminster, Marston Magna, Sparkford and Castle Cary, whilst many also called at Bruton, Witham and Frome. But their final destinations differed considerably: for example, No. 629 went to Bristol, No. 630 to Exeter, No. 631 to Hockley, No. 632 to Oxford, Nos. 633 and 634 went to Paddington, and 637 to Smithfield. This latter vehicle would be a 'Mica B' (or such vehicle) conveying meat traffic from many of the branch stations, and only taking on goods (some station trucks were 'pick up' only). The vans for London were picked up by the 'Up Jersey' (6.35 p.m. Weymouth), which called at Witham. No. 636 went to Reading, initially by 'The Searchlight' (2.50 p.m. Penzance) from Westbury to Newbury, then by the 6.30 a.m. Newbury goods on to Reading. No. 638 went to Swindon by the following goods trains: 12.45 a.m. Westbury to Trowbridge; 5.25 a.m.

Trowbridge to Melksham; 6.20 a.m. Bristol (East Depot) from Melksham to Chippenham (for Calne); and by the 8.35 a.m. Bristol (East Depot) from Chippenham to Swindon, calling at Dauntsey (for Malmesbury) and Wootton Basset. No. 639 just served all stations to Westbury. No station, however small, was omitted from the service. A meat van carrying the No. 75 label from distant Bridport, for Smithfield, was put on the first vacuum train (the 'Flying Pig', 4.0 p.m. Exeter to Old Oak Common) at Westbury by way of the 12.50 p.m. Bridport to Maiden Newton, then the 1.40 p.m. Weymouth from Maiden Newton to Westbury. It reached Smithfield by the 1.40 a.m. transfer goods from Old Oak Common. This 'Mica' picked up at stations along the branch line to Maiden Newton and then to Westbury.

Another interesting service in 1934 was the three station trucks from Bristol to Honeybourne – Nos. 102, 103 and 104 – which all took different routes. No.102 (routed via Pontypool Road and Worcester) served Pershore, Fladbury, Evesham, Littleton & Badsey, thence Honeybourne; No. 103 (via Swindon and Oxford) served Handborough, Charlbury, Ascot-Under-Wychwood, Shipston, Kingham, Adlestrop, Moreton-in-Marsh (for Longdon Road, Stretton-on-Fosse, Shipston-on-Stour), Blockley, Campden, then Honeybourne; lastly, No.104 (via Stoke Gifford and Gloucester) served Bishops Cleeve, Gotherington, Winchcombe, Toddington, Weston-Sub-Edge, Broadway and Honeybourne.

The three station trucks numbered 405, 406 and 407, from Paddington to Bristol, also went by different routes: No. 405 ran via Frome, Mells Road, Radstock, Midsomer Norton & Welton, Hallatrow, Clutton, Pensford, Brislington, Bristol (for Camerton, Monkton Combe); No. 406 went via Badminton, calling at Swindon, Wootton Bassett, Brinkworth, Little Somerford, Hullavington, Badminton, Chipping Sodbury (for Winterbourne), Coalpit Heath and Bristol; and No. 407 travelled via Box, calling at Chippenham, Corsham, Box, Keynsham (for Saltford) and Bristol.

A station truck for the M & SWJ was No. 231 from Gloucester (8.10 a.m.) to Swindon Town, calling at Andoversford, Withington, Foss Cross, Cirencester, South Cerney, Cricklade, Blunsdon, Moredon, Rushey Platt and Swindon Town (Swindon); it continued from Swindon Town by the 2.2 p.m. (SX) or 3.5 p.m. (SO) to Ludgershall and served Chiseldon, Ogbourne, Marlborough, Savernake, Grafton, Collingbourne, Ludgershall, (for Weyhill, Andover) and Tidworth.

The numbering of station trucks changed almost yearly; this was due either to the decline in traffic in a certain area, or to the addition of stations needing these services. Hard and fast rules for identification are difficult to make: e.g. in 1909, ST No.282 related to a wagon on the Bristol to Dudley route, but the station truck numbers given for Bristol in 1925 were between 110 and 156; and in 1934 from 78 to 135. Station truck No. 282 in the 1934 lists was for a wagon from Hockley (Birmingham), serving stations between Moreton-in-Marsh and Shipston-on-Stour. Another example of a change was ST No.527 which served stations between Oxford and Leamington in the 1925 lists, but between Shrewsbury and Hereford in 1934.

It has been said that station trucks could be a convenient 'get-out' for unprincipled staff wanting to rid themselves of unlabelled or troublesome items! There was at Park Royal a 'Missing Goods' depot for this sort of thing.

63

Column No. 1.	Column No. 2. Places to which the Stations shewn in Column No. 1 make daily direct wagons.	Column No. 3. Station Trucks and Pick Up Wagons Serving Stations shewn in Column No. 1.	Column No. 4. Places from which direct wagons are daily made to Stations shewn in Column No. 1.
Sarnau ..	.. ..	(132), 198, 199, 205, 209, 406, 440, 465, 505, 506, 602, 603, 729.	
Saundersfoot ..	.. ..	134, 186, 210, 466, 598, 599, 602 to 608, 730, 760, 761, 820.	
Saunderton ..	.. ..	31, 3[illegible], 528 (529), (531), 570, 671, 824.	
Savernake ..	Grafton .. .. Marlborough	129, 242, 347 to 351, 471, 475, 552, 669, 739, 767, 794.	Grafton. Marlborough.
Scorrier	.. ..	(77), (149), 182, 280 (692).	
Seend ..	..	(129), 242, 347, 348, [illegible]51,	
Senghenydd			
Severn Brid[illegible] (S. & W.).			
Severn Tun[illegible] Junction.			
Sharpness			
Shepherds			
Shepton M[illegible]			
Shifnal ..			
Shiplake			
Shipston-o[illegible] Stour.			
Shipton			
Shireham[illegible]			
Sh[illegible]rley			
Shrewsb[illegible]			
Shr[illegible]			
Silv[illegible]			
Sk[illegible]			
Slo[illegible]			

149

NOTE.—Stations, the names of which are shewn in Brackets (from pages 76 to the end), are on a Branch, or are those at which the Train conveying that particular Station Truck does not call.
*Wagons marked with an * PICK UP traffic ONLY at the stations shewn, and must not be used for any other purpose.*
Unless otherwise shewn Station Trucks and Pick-up wagons run daily.

Destination.	Conveyed by: Train.	Conveyed by: From.	Between what Points: From.	Between what Points: To.	Stations served.
From TRAM INN.					
Bristol.	10.25 a.m. 11.50 p.m. 5.45 a.m.	Hereford Abergavenny Pontypool Road	Tram Inn Abergavenny Pontypool Road	Abergavenny Pontypool Road Bristol	St. Devereux, Pontrilas, Pandy, Llanvihangel, Abergavenny, Bristol.
From TROWBRIDGE.					
Bristol.	6. 0 a.m. 8. 5 a.m. 12. 1 p.m. 9.50 a.m.	Trowbridge Holt Hallatrow Salisbury	Trowbridge Holt Camerton Freshford	Holt Camerton Freshford Bristol	Bradford-on-Avon, Freshford, Limpley Stoke, Monkton Combe, Camerton, Bristol.
Leicester. L. & N.E. (G.C.)	2.40 p.m. 10. 5 p.m.	Westbury Bristol (E.D.)	Trowbridge Chippenham	Chippenham Banbury	Holt Jcn., Melksham, Chippenham, Leicester.
Theale.	2.40 p.m. 5. 0 p.m. 6.20 p.m. 7.50 p.m.	Westbury Holt Westbury Newbury	Trowbridge Holt Patney Newbury	Holt Patney Newbury Theale	Holt Junction, Devizes, (Seend), Patney and Chirton, (Lavington, Edington & B.), Woodborough, Pewsey, Savernake, (Marlborough), Bedwyn, Hungerford, Kintbury, Newbury, (Burbage), Thatcham, Midgham, Aldermaston, Theale.
From TRURO.					
Devonport.	3.30 a.m. 12.15 p.m.	Truro Doublebois	Truro Liskeard	Liskeard Devonport	Grampound Rd., Burngullow, (Drinnick Mill), St. Austell, Par, (Fowey, Luxulyan, Bugle, Roche, St. Columb Rd., Newquay), Lostwithiel, Bodmin Rd., (Bodmin, Wadebridge), Doublebois, Liskeard, Menheniot, St. Germans, Saltash, Keyham, Devonport.
Falmouth.	7. 0 a.m.	Truro	Truro	Falmouth	Ferranwell, Penryn, Falmouth.

The two adjacent goods depots at the joint Hereford Barrs Court in 1932, looking south with the L&NWR yard and shed on the left, and the GWR to the right, with its jib crane and gantry. When confronted with the increasing and 'unfair' competition from commercial road transport in this period, the railways frequently pooled their goods facilities and worked closely together in an area to combat the threat, and this had occurred in Hereford during the early 1930s. The traffic diagram for Hereford can be seen on the opposite page.

C. L. MOWAT

WAGON LOADINGS

When loading goods, staff at transfer stations used their own discretion as between a full direct truck, station truck, pick-up wagon, or composite load, and the route taken to the destination, which was governed by the variation in quantity of goods between one day and the next. The following examples serve to show how the scheme worked:

From Cardiff to Ledbury: Cardiff had the alternative of loading goods to Hereford, Gloucester, or Worcester, but they loaded to Gloucester, from where there was a station truck serving Ledbury. *From Slough to Stroud*: Slough was a station where the ability to make full direct wagons varied from day to day. On some days, they could load consignments to Swindon, but more often they were able to load to Gloucester in which case the traffic would be worked back from Gloucester to Stroud. While over-carrying occurred, intermediate transhipment at Reading was cut out.

A more difficult case would be a consignment from Oxford to Lampeter. It would be extremely unlikely that Oxford would be able to load directly to Aberystwyth or Carmarthen, and the loading pamphlet would suggest first to Cardiff, from where the consignment would be loaded to Carmarthen.

Similar principles applied to the routeing of traffic passing through one foreign company's territory on the way to another's. For example, smalls traffic from Bridgwater (GW) to York (LNE) should have been loaded to Bristol (GW) for the direct wagon to York, and not to Crewe (LMS) for transfer.

Transfer arrangements were amended when it seemed sensible to do so. For example, all transfer work formerly performed at Ruabon was transferred to Wrexham after the grouping, whilst that formerly carried out at Truro was (with certain local exceptions) transferred to Plymouth. A major reorganisation of rail

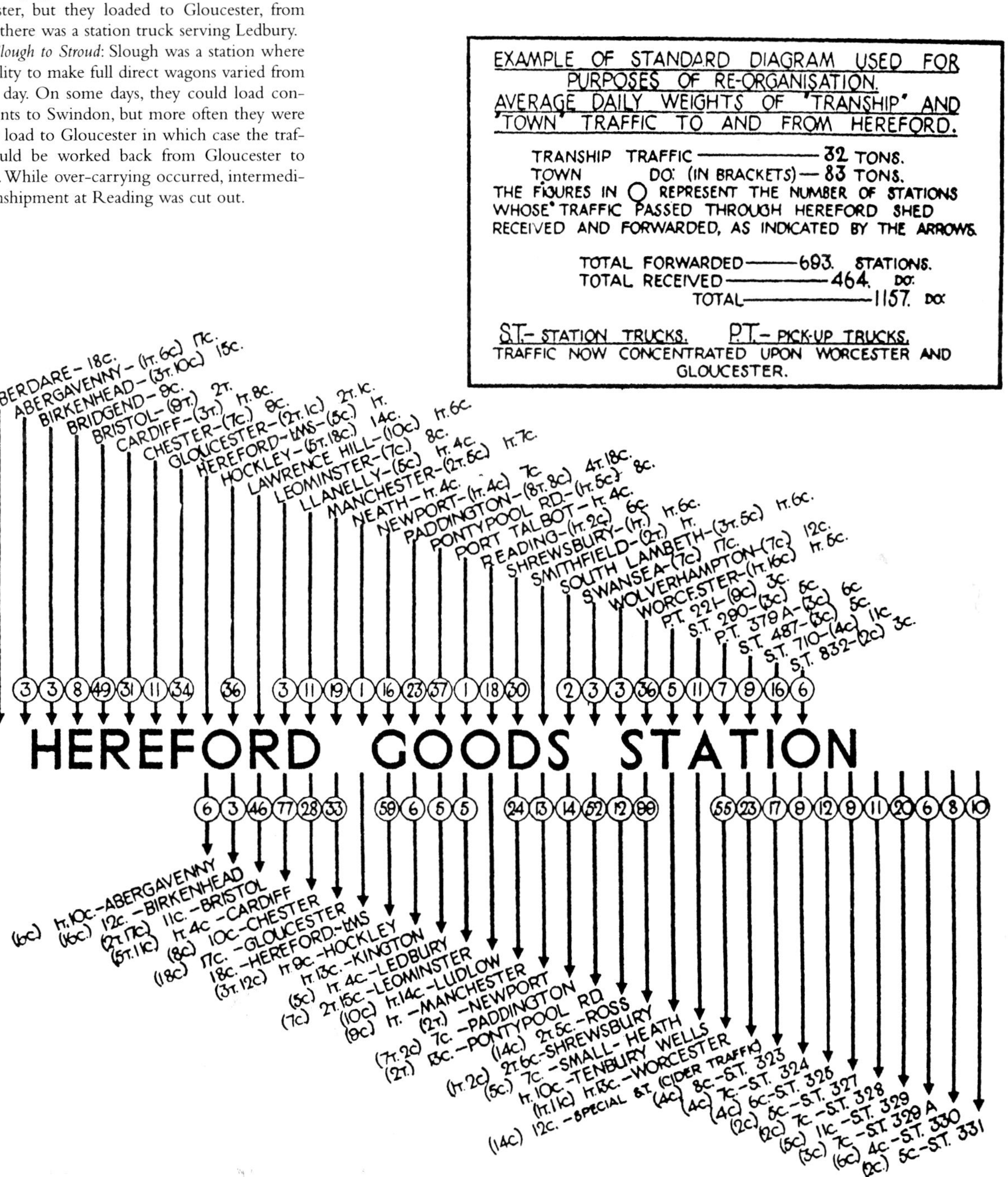

Another view of the transhipment shed at Reading in Edwardian days (see also page 4). Wagons could be unloaded either side, depending on final destination (Up Road stations to the right; Northern stations to the left, with pitch for West of England traffic further down the platform on the left). Sheets were either partially, or completely, removed for the unloading. A checker with his three-legged lectern is seen on the right monitoring and recording the movements of consignments. Shed cranes with J-shaped jibs can be seen on the right (the nearest is 'No. 6 Tested 4.8.01'), whilst a crane with an angled jib is visible further down the shed; both could swing over high-sided wagons. The wide variety of goods being handled demonstrates that, before the Great War, practically everything went by rail. NATIONAL RAILWAY MUSEUM

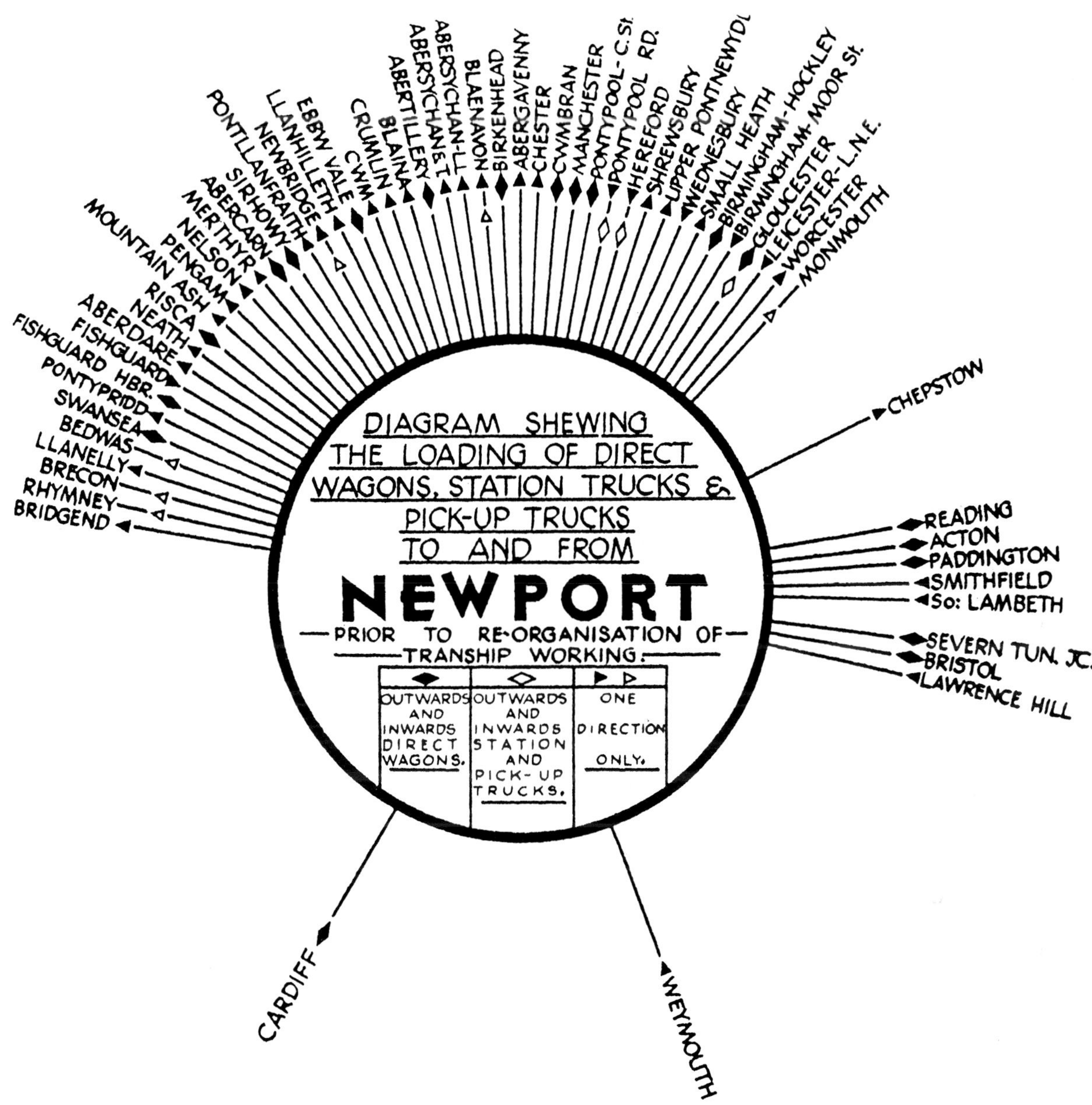

tranship arrangements on the GWR took place in October 1932, after which 'fastest time' became the criterion of efficient transit, not 'least mileage'.

ROAD TRANSPORT IN TRANSHIP

The old geographical basis of goods working regarded over-carrying (i.e. sending goods on a through train to a station beyond the final destination, to be worked back) as something to be avoided. As a result of detailed traffic studies, however, it was realised that a 24-hour delay occurred with each transhipment, and this was simply unacceptable once road competition could provide a better service. The GWR's response was to speed up transit by using motor lorries to deliver the goods from 'Railhead Stations', which covered ever-increasing areas. For example, motors ran out from Birmingham (Hockley) in the morning to 14 stations in the Midlands with goods consigned to them which had been loaded to Hockley for (rail wagon) transhipment. The same lorries and vans returned to Hockley in the evening with goods that could benefit by the superior goods train services from Hockley, rather than be moved by rail from the local station. It was the success of these Birmingham transfer lorries and vans that provided the inspiration for the 'Zonal' collection and delivery scheme introduced immediately after WW II.

In the 1920s, the number of tranship centres began to diminish, leading to the complete reorganisation of 1932. Demand for speedier transits and increased scope for utilisation of direct loading from the bigger stations caused over-carrying to be regarded differently. Afterwards, the fullest advantage was taken of the loading ability of those larger stations which were already tranship points, i.e. the greater the number of goods stations serving a given area, the smaller the tonnage of goods dispatched to each and, hence, the more transhipments necessary to get them there. Instead of following strictly geographical routes, it was better (and in the end quicker) when the journey to and from the tranship stations could be made with fewer interruptions.

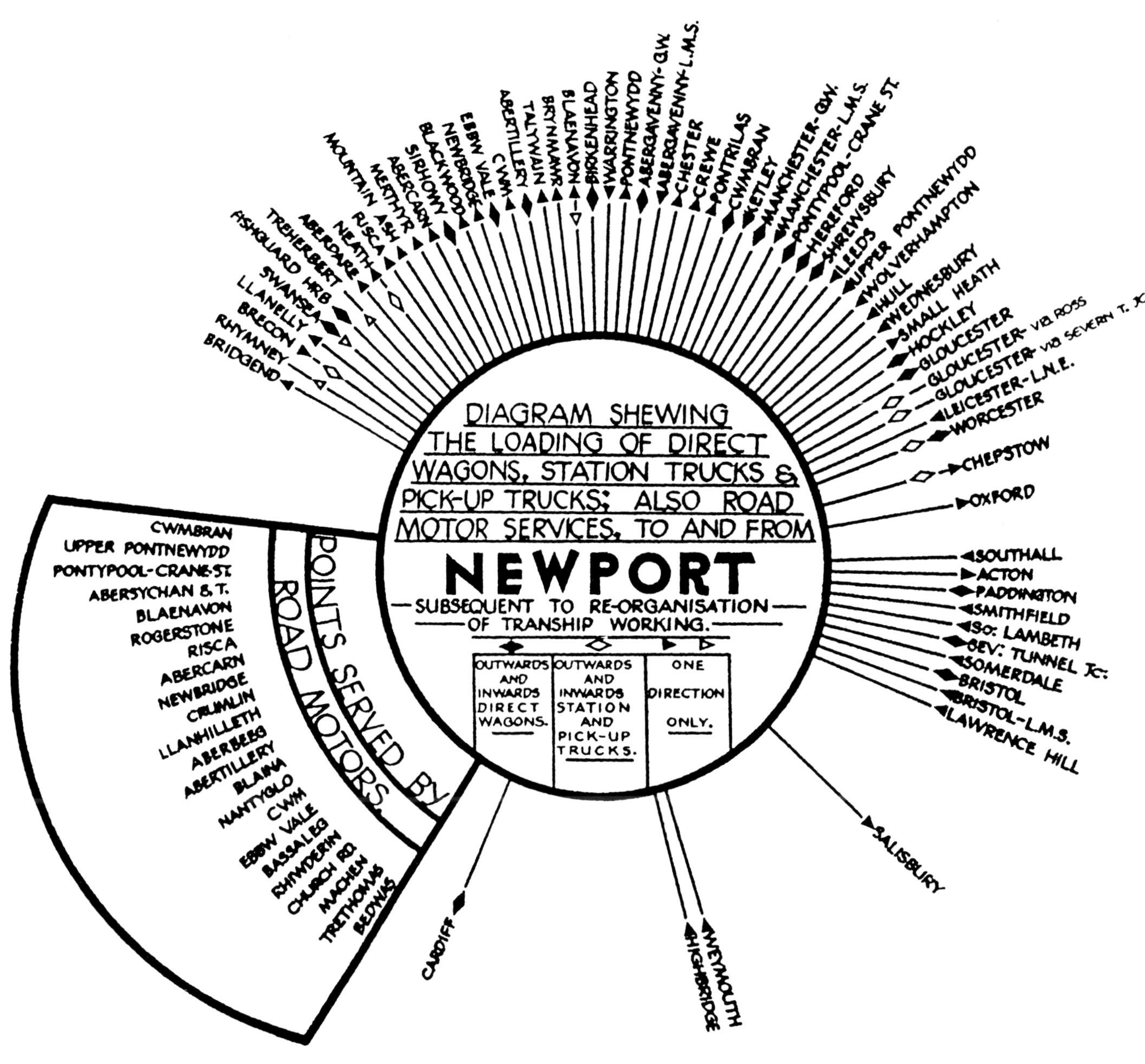

Moreover, the fast vacuum-fitted trunk goods trains between large centres gave a next-morning arrival, even with over-carrying. The freight train service was constantly under review, and re-timings, and even re-routeings, were put into place to speed up transits and delivery times. Station trucks were increasingly seen as not the fastest way of conveying goods, even in remote areas.

The original 67 rail tranship points on the GWR had been reduced to 52 by 1932, but in that year a major reorganisation took place, leaving only nine major tranship points on the system. They were Bristol, Cardiff, Chester, Hockley (Birmingham), Llanelly, Newport (High Street), Paddington, Plymouth and Wolverhampton. A revised book of instructions was issued for correct loading routes using only the new centres. As a result, not only were transit times improved in 85% of all transhipment traffic, but appreciable economies arose in wagon usage, maintenance and renewals, engine power and so on. After the goods offices at Plymouth were bombed out in 1944, the number of tranship points was reduced to eight. The station truck did not disappear with the 1932 reorganisation, but hey were now mainly employed on subidiary services with traffic local to a given egion.

After 1932, certain places (which were *ıot* general tranship centres) operated lorry ervices which distributed local tranship raffic. The places functioned as railheads or a limited number of stations within a specified area, whenever a direct load to the local destination was not possible. The eight places providing such road services, and the stations served by them, were as follows: -

Gloucester: Blaisdon Siding, Grange Court, Longhope, Mitcheldean Road, Oakle Street. *Newton Abbot*: Brixham, Churston, Dartmouth, Kingskerswell, Kingswear, Paignton, Torre. *Oxford*: Aston Rowant, Aylesbury, Bledlow, Chinnor, High Wycombe, Littlemore, Morris Cowley, Princes Risborough, Saunderton, Thame, Tiddington, Watlington, West Wycombe, Wheatley. *Reading*: Bourne End, Cookham, Henley-on-Thames, High Wycombe, Loudwater, Marlow, Shiplake, Twyford, Wargrave, Wooburn Green.

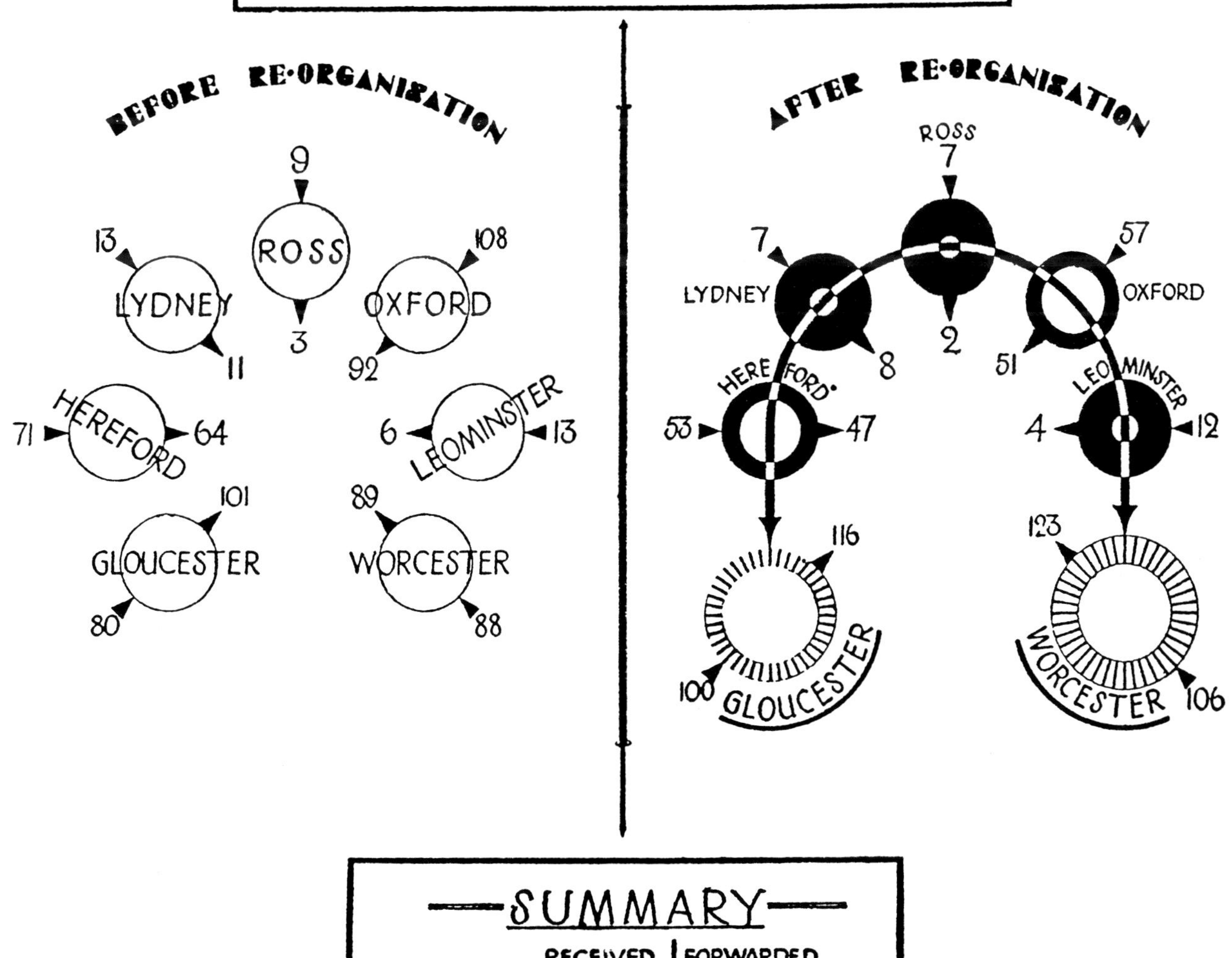

G.W.R. Tranship Arrangements.

GENERAL INSTRUCTIONS.

The tranship centres of the Great Western Railway Company are :—

BRISTOL,
CARDIFF,
CHESTER,
HOCKLEY (Birmingham),
LLANELLY,
NEWPORT (HIGH ST.),
PADDINGTON,
PLYMOUTH,
WOLVERHAMPTON.

1. Tranship centres applicable to each G.W. destination (Column 1), are shewn in Column 2, pages 7 to 30 : they appear in alphabetical order and **NOT in the order of preference for loading purposes.**

Details of loadings to stations on other Companies' systems by G.W. tranship centres appear on pages 81 to 83.

The method of disposal by each tranship point, i.e., direct wagon, station truck or road vehicle, is set out on pages 31 to 80.

2. The loadings to certain tranship points established by arrangements made during the course of the re-organisation **are not to be varied.** Reference to these lists in such cases should be with the object of confirming present practice as right or adjusting it if it is wrong.

Geographical considerations have been made secondary to quick transit.

3. The variability in traffic for different destinations, arising particularly at small stations where the existing loading ability requires to be supplemented as occasion demands, makes it essential that in forwarding traffic for transhipment the tranship centre selected should be capable of loading the *greater* portion of the traffic to destination.

4. The foregoing instructions do **NOT APPLY** to traffic for destinations in respect of which it is the practice to load into a station truck for exchange into another station truck at a station en route. These stations are minor tranship points for station truck traffic exclusively.

5. These instructions do not supersede the loading instructions issued from time to time in regard to traffic for destinations included in station concentration schemes.

6. Circular No. 1173, dated October, 1929, "Instructions relating to the forwarding of Tranship Traffic for Great Western Stations," is hereby **CANCELLED.**

ALPHABETICAL LIST OF STATIONS SERVED BY REGULAR LOADINGS FROM PLYMOUTH.

N.B.—Letters in brackets against each destination indicate method of disposal, viz :— (A) By direct wagon.
(B) By station truck.
(C) By road service.

DESTINATION.	
Alphington Road—Dealt with at Exeter.	
Ashburton	(A)
Avonwick	(B)
Bampton (Devon)	(B)
Barnstaple	(B)
Bickleigh	(B)
Billacombe	(B)
Birmingham (Hockley)	(A)
Bishop's Nympton & Molland	(B)
Bodmin	(A)
Bodmin Road	(B)
Bourne End — Road service from Reading, see page 5.	
Bovey—Loaded to Newton Abbot (for Moretonhampstead & Kingswear Branches only).	
Brent	(B)
Bristol	(A)
Brixham—Road service from Newton Abbot, see page 5.	
Brixton Road—Dealt with at Billacombe.	
Buckfastleigh	(A)
Bugle	(B)
Burlescombe	(B)
Burngullow	(B)
Cadeleigh	(B)
Camborne	(A)
Carbis Bay	(B)
Cardiff	(A)
Carn Brea	(B)
Chacewater	(B)
Churston—Road service from Newton Abbot, see page 5.	
Cookham—Road service from Reading, see page 5.	
Cornwood	(B)
Coryton	(B)
Cullompton	(B)
Culmstock	(B)
Dartmouth—See Kingswear.	
Dawlish	(B)

DESTINATION.	
Dawlish Warren	(B)
Devonport	(C)
Doublebois	(B)
Dousland	(B)
Dulverton	(B)
East Anstey	(B)
Ely (Main Line)—Dealt with at Cardiff.	
Exeter	(A)
Exminster	(B)
Falmouth	(A)
Filleigh	(B)
Fowey	(A)
Gara Bridge	(B)
Glanyllyn—Dealt with at Cardiff.	
Grampound Road	(B)
Gwinear Road	(B)
Hayle	(B)
Heathfield—Loaded to Newton Abbot (for Moretonhampstead & Kingswear Branches only).	
Hele & Bradninch	(B)
Helston	(B)
Hemyock	(B)
Henley-on-Thames — Road service from Reading, see page 5.	
High Wycombe—Road service from Reading, see page 5.	
Hockley (Birmingham)	(A)
Horrabridge	(A)
Ivybridge	(B)
Keyham	(C)
Kingsbridge	(B)
Kingskerswell — Road service from Newton Abbot, see page 5.	

Paignton's new goods shed and yard in the final stages of construction, 1931. The original shed was adjacent to the passenger station, for which plans for a sorely-needed extension of facilities had been drawn up. However, some of the ground required for the new traffic arrangements was occupied by the goods sidings and as the old shed and yard were proving to be inadequate, the new depot was constructed on a new site nearer to Goodrington.
NATIONAL RAILWAY MUSEUM

Ruabon: Acrefair, Aberderfyn, Cefn, Chirk, Gobowen, Johnstown & Hafod, Legacy, Preesgweene (for Weston Rhyn), Rhos, Rhostyllen, Trevor, Whitehurst.
Shrewsbury: Adderley, Audlem, Coalbrookdale, Crudgington, Ellerdine Siding, Hodnet, Horsehay & Dawley, Madeley (Salop), Market Drayton, Nantwich, Peplow, Tern Hill.
Worcester: Bransford Road, Droitwich Spa, Fernhill Heath, Malvern Link.
Wrexham: Balderton, Brymbo, Coed Poeth, Gresford, Llanfynydd, Minera, Moss, Plas Power, Rossett, Wheatsheaf Junction.

Motor lorries were employed on inter-ompany tranship work in London etween the principal goods depots. Even), as a result of the 1932 reorganisation, it vill be found that regular traffic from Iockley to Stewart's Lane (SR) was routed) South Lambeth, from where it was arted. Perhaps more interesting was that raffic from Bristol, Cardiff and Hockley to ishopsgate (LNE) was routed to mithfield, and carted from there.

The successor to the 1932 rearrange-ments was the 'Zonal' collection and deliv-ry scheme, introduced immediately ollowing the end of WW II, to be escribed in the *Cartage* volume in this ries.

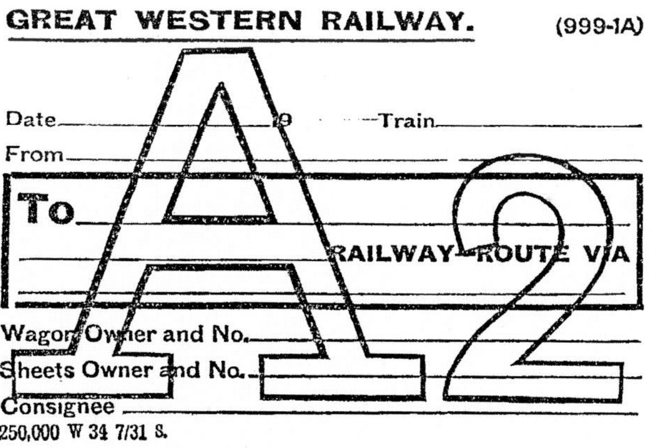

GREAT WESTERN RAILWAY. (999-1A)

A2

Date 19 Train
From
To
RAILWAY ROUTE VIA
Wagon Owner and No.
Sheets Owner and No.
Consignee
250,000 W 34 7/31 S.

(B) Label No. 999-14.—For use when traffic in Classes 1 and 2 is sent " to be weighed " en route to a foreign company.
Same as (A) only printed on back as hereunder:—

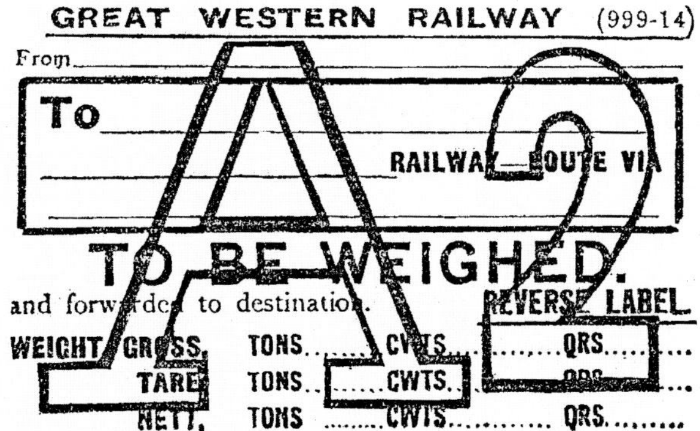

GREAT WESTERN RAILWAY (999-14)

A2

From
To
RAILWAY ROUTE VIA
TO BE WEIGHED.
and forwarded to destination. REVERSE LABEL.
WEIGHT GROSS. TONS........ CWTS........ QRS........
TARE TONS........ CWTS........ QRS........
NETT, TONS........ CWTS........ QRS........

5000—Est. 794—10,31—(17)

LIST OF REGULAR LOADINGS MADE TO R.C.H. DESTINATIONS BY GREAT WESTERN TRANSHIP CENTRES (continued).

DESTINATION.	COMPANY.	G.W. Tranship Centres Serving Stations Shewn in Col. 1.	ROUTE.
Col. 1.	Col. 2.	Col. 3.	Col. 4.
Bishopsgate ..	L.N.E.	Bristol, Cardiff, Hockley ..	Carted from Smithfield.
		Paddington	Carted.
Carlisle	L.N.E.	Hockley	Crewe & Carlisle, N.B.
Hull	L.N.E.	Hockley, Wolverhampton ..	Crewe & Leeds.
Ipswich	L.N.E.	Bristol	Acton, HackneyWick & Stratford.
King's Cross ..	L.N.E.	Bristol, Hockley, Paddington.	Carted from Smithfield.
Leeds	L.N.E.	Hockley	Crewe.
Leicester	L.N.E.	Bristol, Cardiff, Hockley, Paddington.	Banbury.
Nottingham ..	L.N.E.	Bristol	Banbury.
		Hockley	Market Drayton and Egginton.
Sheffield	L.N.E.	Bristol	Banbury.
		Hockley	Crewe & Guide Bridge
Starbeck	L.N.E.	Hockley	Crewe & Leeds.
York	L.N.E.	Bristol	Severn Tunnel Junction, Chester, Warrington, Patricroft and Normanton.
		Hockley, Wolverhampton ..	Crewe & Leeds.
Glastonbury and Street.	S. & D.	Bristol	Highbridge.
Axminster	S.R.	Bristol	Yeovil.
Barnstaple Junction.	S.R.	Bristol	Barnstaple.
Bideford	S.R.	Bristol	Barnstaple.
Bournemouth ..	S.R.	Bristol	Salisbury.
		Hockley, Wolverhampton ..	Basingstoke.
Bricklayers' Arms	S.R.	Bristol, Paddington, Wolverhampton.	Carted from South Lambeth.
Brighton	S.R.	Bristol	Salisbury & Havant.
		Hockley, Wolverhampton ..	Kensington.
Broad Clyst	S.R.	Bristol	Yeovil.

No. 2.

(A) Specimen of " EMPTY HOME " Label No. 3005 to be used for all Empty " Non-Common User " stock returning Home :

GREAT WESTERN RAILWAY. (3005)

NON-COMMON USER WAGON

EMPTY HOME

ROUTE VIA

____

Owner________________Number________________

________________________Forwarding Station.

________________________Date Returned.

IMPORTANT.—When Foreign Wagons, which have to pass over Intermediate Companies' Lines to reach home, are returned empty they must be labelled by exactly the same route (naming all junctions) as received.

(B) Specimen of " FOR CLEANSING AT...................................THENCE EMPTY HOME " Label No. 3005/1 to be used for all Empty Foreign Cattle Wagons sent to an intermediate station for cleansing before being returned Home :

(3005-1)

GREAT WESTERN RAILWAY.

NON-COMMON USER.

From________________________ Date________

TO____________________STATION TO BE CLEANSED.

THENCE TO________________________COMPANY,

Via________________________________

DATE CLEANSED____________

IMPORTANT.—When Foreign Cattle Wagons, which have to pass over Intermediate Companies' Lines to reach the LOADING COMPANY are returned empty, they must be labelled by exactly the same route (naming all Junctions) as received.

No. 3.

Labels (No. 999-1) to be used on wagons conveying packing, sheets or ropes :

GREAT WESTERN RAILWAY. (999-1)

DATE______________193 TRAIN______________

FROM______________________________

EMPTY

To ________________________

____________________RAILWAY-ROUTE VIA

____

WAGON NO.________ Sheets only

1,000,000 W 34 5/31. S.

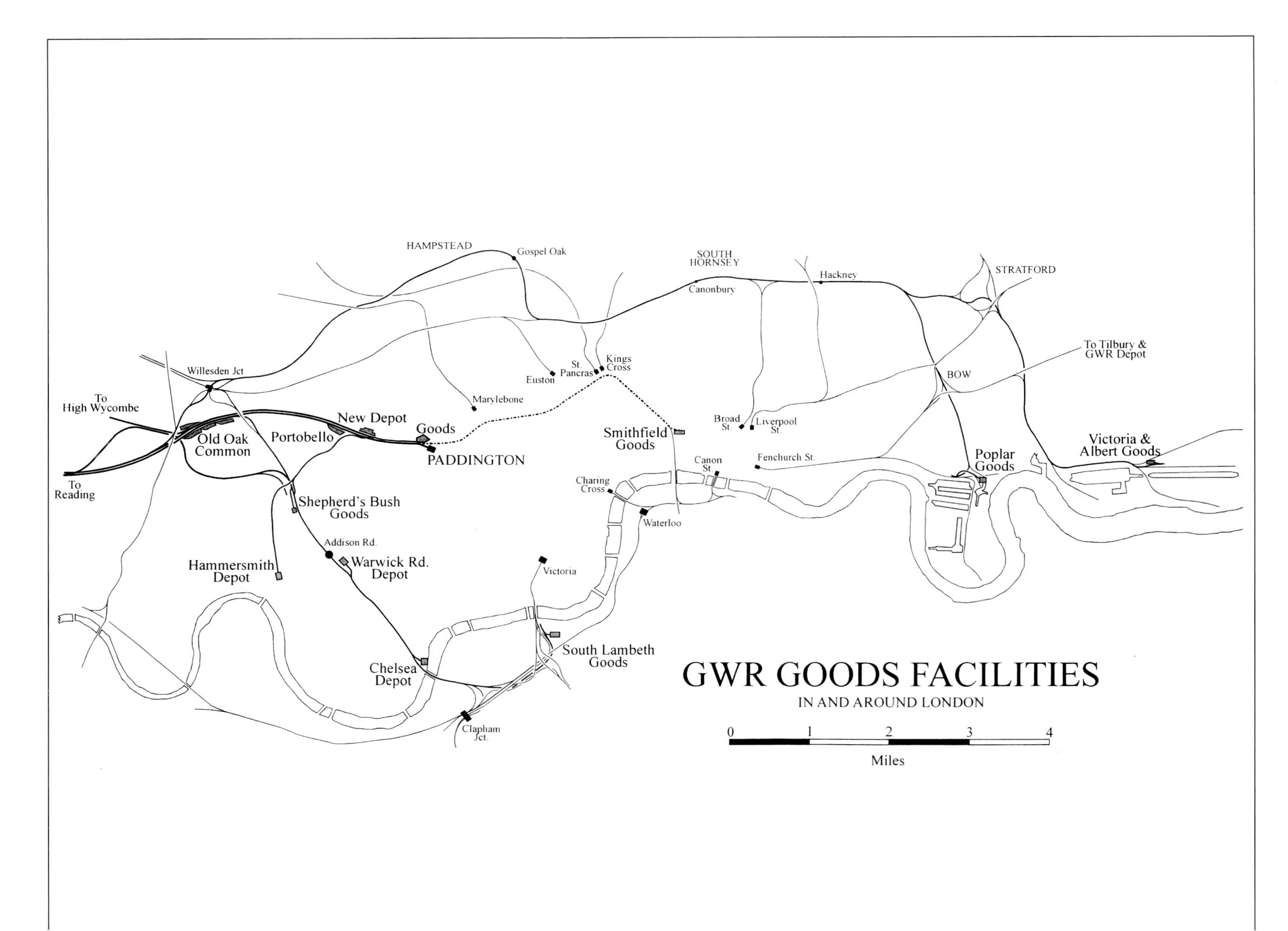
GWR GOODS FACILITIES
IN AND AROUND LONDON
HAMPSTEAD
Gospel Oak
SOUTH HORNSEY
Canonbury
Hackney
STRATFORD
To Tilbury & GWR Depot
BOW
Willesden Jct
To High Wycombe
To Reading
Old Oak Common
Portobello
New Depot
Goods
PADDINGTON
Marylebone
Euston
St. Pancras
Kings Cross
Smithfield Goods
Broad St.
Liverpool St.
Fenchurch St.
Canon St.
Charing Cross
Waterloo
Poplar Goods
Victoria & Albert Goods
Shepherd's Bush Goods
Addison Rd.
Warwick Rd. Depot
Hammersmith Depot
Victoria
South Lambeth Goods
Chelsea Depot
Clapham Jct.
0
1
2
3
4
Miles

CHAPTER THREE

THE LONDON AREA DEPOTS

THE depots at Paddington and those in the surrounding districts formed the most important group of goods facilities at one place on the Great Western system. They served not only the adjacent West London areas, but also the other main districts within and surrounding the capital, from Paddington and the outlying depots in central, east and south London. Evolution of this comprehensive system of depots effectively started with the opening of Paddington Goods in 1839, and continued for some ninety years.

A gateway to the south was opened in May 1844 in the form of the West London Railway line (joint GW and L & NW from 1854) to Kensington, followed by the West London Extension onwards to Clapham in 1863. Hammersmith was reached by the Hammersmith & City line in 1864, the concern being transferred jointly to the Great Western and Metropolitan companies in 1867. All these offered the prospect of modest goods facilities, which increased considerably in importance as time progressed.

Further to the west, the Brentford branch (with its access to the Thames and the Grand Junction Canal) was opened to goods traffic in April 1859. The various transfer facilities will be discussed in the *Docks* volume.

The GWR's association with Smithfield Market began in earnest in May 1869, when the company opened its goods depot there, with access provided by the Metropolitan company's metals. In the docks, Poplar depot was opened in May 1877, following the completion of the link to Acton Wells Junction and the North & South Western Jct. Railway near Willesden in the previous year.

In later years, the Victoria & Albert depot was opened in April 1902, and the complex at Park Royal was established from around 1905. As with Brentford, the Poplar and Victoria & Albert sites will be studied further in the *Docks* volume. Finally, the huge and important depot at South Lambeth was opened in 1911, with access by the WL and WLE lines via Kensington and Clapham.

Collectively, these facilities provided a considerable income for the company. In 1913, the goods receipts for Paddington alone amounted to some £726,000, South Lambeth £547,000, Smithfield £231,000, and Poplar £144,000. These figures do not include the income from goods in transit passing through these locations from the Great Western system and elsewhere.

THE DEPOTS – An Overview

The main Great Western depot for the London area was, of course, that at Paddington, with very extensive facilities to handle virtually every type of material and commodity. Mileage yards were at Paddington (New Yard, on the main line, which also dealt with full truck loads of returned empties as did the later Ladbroke Grove Empties Shed), Westbourne Park and Old Oak Common.

'Satellite' Great Western depots around Paddington were at Chelsea Basin (on the West London Extension Railway, reached via Old Oak Common, which mainly dealt with barge traffic on the Thames); Kensington (Warwick Road, also on the WLER via Old Oak Common); Brentford (local and docks goods traffic); Poplar and Victoria & Albert Docks (via the North London line); and Smithfield (via the Metropolitan).

There were additional yards at Hammersmith (GW & Metropolitan

London Goods Stations

This folder, which is published by the Great Western Railway as A GUIDE FOR THE USE OF TRADERS who have goods for despatch to the Metropolitan area, sets out in simple reference form the principal districts and thoroughfares of the inner Metropolis which are served by the various goods stations and depots of the Company, also the handling facilities which are available.

Goods for transport, incorrectly labelled, incur the risk of delay and additional handling, etc., and DESPATCH DEPARTMENTS making full use of the information in this folder, will do much towards obviating these undesirable features.

PLEASE CO-OPERATE BY USING THIS INFORMATION.

The principal G.W.R. goods stations in the inner metropolis are :—

PADDINGTON

Which serves West and North London, the West Central area, and the markets at Spitalfields, Covent Garden, Billingsgate, Leadenhall and Borough.

SMITHFIELD

In the heart of the City, which serves the Central Meat Market, under which it is situated, and Central and East London and the City generally.

SOUTH LAMBETH

On the south side of the river, serving the Southern, South-Western, and South-Eastern Districts of London.

All these stations are equipped with modern appliances for handling merchandise safely and speedily.

Other G.W.R. goods stations include :—

BRENTFORD DOCK

Owned by the Great Western Railway Company (adjoining the River Thames), with dock and wharf facilities for dealing with all descriptions of traffic for import and export, and for waterside premises. Large and well appointed warehouses are available for storage of grain and other traffics.

VICTORIA & ALBERT

Situated in the East side of London, and between the Royal Albert, Royal Victoria, and King George V Docks, with which it has direct rail communication serving vessels berthed in these docks. This depot also deals with general traffic for Barking, East Ham, Woolwich, Ilford and neighbouring suburbs.

ACTON & WEST EALING

The Goods Depot at Acton serves the districts of Acton, Ealing, Hanwell, and West Ealing, with regular cartage collections and deliveries daily throughout the area. The depot at West Ealing provides accommodation for coal and other traffics not usually requiring cartage by the Company.

PARK ROYAL

Which serves the wide industrial area in North-West London, including Cricklewood, Neasden, and Wembley, and many new factory estates in the vicinity. Regular daily collections and deliveries are made throughout the district.

GREENFORD

Which serves the districts of Greenford, Perivale, Northolt, South Harrow, and Sudbury Hill, including many housing and industrial estates in the vicinity.

BRENTFORD TOWN

Which is situated on the Great West Road and deals with traffic for the factories established alongside this road and in the neighbourhood.

The Company's London District Goods Manager, whose Office is at 14, Bishop's Bridge Road, Paddington, W.2 (Tel. Padd 7000 Ext. 2697), will be pleased to give information regarding G.W.R. facilities in London.

Issued by the Great Western Railway.

David Blee, Chief Goods Manager, Paddington Station. Telephone PAD. 7000. Extn. 2465.

GOODS TRAFFIC

FOR THE

LONDON DISTRICT.

A perusal of the following short account of the Company's arrangements for dealing with Goods Traffic in the London District, and of the accompanying map, will enable the Staff to understand better the instructions given herein.

The Company's London **Goods** Stations are at **PADDINGTON,** adjoining the Passenger Station; at **SMITHFIELD,** in the heart of the City; at **SOUTH LAMBETH,** in the South of London; at **BRENTFORD,** on the River Thames; at **POPLAR** and **VICTORIA AND ALBERT,** in the East of London, and in the midst of the Docks. To each of these Stations a **CARTAGE STAFF** is attached. The Districts served by them are indicated on the list, pages 46 to 62, and on the accompanying map. **Goods Depots** are also situated at **PADDINGTON** (New Yard), **WESTBOURNE PARK** (Mileage Yard), **HAMMERSMITH, SHEPHERD'S BUSH, KENSINGTON** (Warwick Road), **CHELSEA BASIN,** and **OLD OAK COMMON.** They are subsidiary to Paddington, and are convenient places for dealing with Coal, Building Materials, Hay, Straw, and other traffic, in truck loads, not requiring cartage by the Company.

Receiving Offices are established in the most important business centres, and from these the Company make frequent daily collections of Merchandise traffic.

A list of these Offices is given on page 88.

The Company, through their agents, the Thames Steam Tug and Lighterage Co., Ltd., collect and deliver **by Barge** to and from the Docks, Riverside or Canalside premises, and ships in the River Thames; arrangements are also in operation for dealing with traffic, by truck or cart, to and from all the Docks in the London District.

The Stations to and from which the Company have arrangements for collection and delivery **by Barge** are **BRENTFORD, POPLAR,** and **VICTORIA AND ALBERT.** At Chelsea Basin traffic is barged in and out of the Company's Dock, which communicates direct with the River Thames, but Freighters have to make their own arrangements.

The Special functions and characteristics of the various Goods Stations are set out below:—

PADDINGTON. This station adjoins the Paddington Passenger Station, and is approached from Praed Street (via South Wharf Road or London Street), Bishop's Road and Harrow Road. There is extensive warehouse accommodation and every facility for dealing with all descriptions of traffic; hydraulic cranes are also provided, and there is a high level yard for Coal. Traffic to or from barges on the Grand Junction Canal can be transferred from or to Railway Wagons, but, before accepting any such traffic for conveyance to Paddington Station, the Agent there must be communicated with, in order that arrangements may be made for delivery to barge.

For the purpose of serving the West, North-West, and South-West Districts of London, accommodation is also provided for traffic, not requiring cartage by the Company's teams, at the undermentioned Depots, which are subsidiary to Paddington, viz.:—

PADDINGTON (New Yard).	**SHEPHERD'S BUSH.**
WESTBOURNE PARK (Mileage Yard).	**KENSINGTON (Warwick Road).**
	CHELSEA BASIN.
HAMMERSMITH.	**OLD OAK COMMON.**

These Depots are situate in or near some of the most important business centres in the Districts named, and they afford valuable facilities for dealing with Coal, Building Materials, Hay, Straw, Minerals, and Station to Station traffic.

SOUTH LAMBETH. This Station is situate in the Battersea Park Road, and affords easy access to the South, South-West, and South-East Districts of London. The principal districts served are:—

Battersea.	Deptford.	Peckham.
Bermondsey.	Kennington.	Putney.
Blackheath.	Lambeth.	Rotherhithe.
Brixton.	Lewisham.	Southwark.
Camberwell.	New Cross.	Wandsworth.
Clapham.	Norwood.	

It has ample facilities for dealing with all descriptions of Mineral and Merchandise traffic, except Live Stock. There is extensive Warehouse accommodation, and the appliances are of the most up-to-date kind, including electric power cranes, lifts, and a gantry crane capable of dealing with weights up to 35 tons.

CITY STATION.

SMITHFIELD. This Station is situate in the heart of the City, underneath the Central Meat Market, and is the only Goods Station connected with the Market by hydraulic lifts, by means of which Meat, Poultry, etc., is delivered direct from the railway trucks to the salesmen's shops without cartage, perishable goods being thus delivered promptly in the best possible condition. The Station is also convenient for general traffic to or from the City warehouses and Central London. It has warehouse accommodation and hydraulic crane power.

RIVER AND DOCK STATIONS.

The conveniences and accommodation at the River and Dock Stations, named below, enable the Company to collect and deliver all descriptions of traffic from and to waterside premises and vessels in the docks and River Thames, at the lowest possible rates, and with the greatest possible despatch. Extensive warehouses and powerful cranes are provided.

BRENTFORD. This Station, which is on a Branch Line connected with the Great Western Main Line at Southall, is situate on the River Thames, and has ample Dock accommodation for barged traffic of all descriptions, which is transferred direct to or from the Railway Wagons, and lightered **from or to premises anywhere on the River Thames, or on the Canals connected therewith, in the London District, including the various Docks.** There is extensive warehouse accommodation at this Station for Grain and similar traffic; ample sidings for dealing with local Coal and Mileage traffic, Hay, Straw, etc.; appliances for tipping Coal from Truck to Barge and for transferring from Barge to Truck; hydraulic cranes for lifting weights up to 40 tons; also provision for articles on wheels and Live Stock for the neighbourhood. General Goods for Brentford Town, Kew, Gunnersbury, and other places in the vicinity are dealt with here, the Company's vehicles collecting and delivering in the district.

The instructions on pages 20 and 22 respecting traffic for the Docks must be rigidly adhered to.

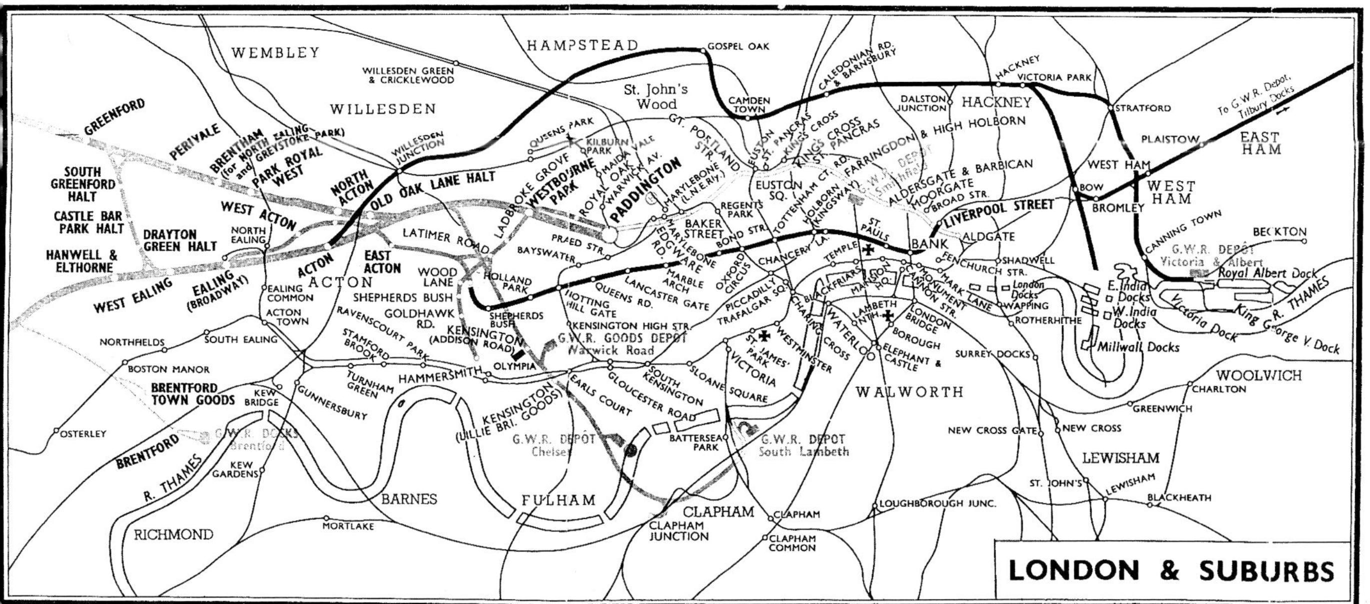

oint) and Shepherd's Bush (Uxbridge Road depot, on the West London Jt. Rly, eached from Old Oak Common). Coal vas also handled at Kensington (Warwick Road).

Outlying London area depots on the nain line were at Acton, West Ealing and outhall (serving Acton, Ealing, Hanwell nd West Ealing) and Hayes & Harlington. The depots at Greenford serving Greenford, Perivale, Northolt, outh Harrow and Sudbury Hill) and Park Royal (serving Cricklewood, Neasden and Wembley) were both on the Acton & High Wycombe line. All dealt vith general traffic for cartage delivery as vell as general mileage traffic. The GWR rading estate was located at Park Royal; lthough some elements were in place by 909, the main construction took place in he early 1920s.

During the years before the Great War, he large new depot at South Lambeth wiftly became second only to Paddington n importance. This depot was further xpanded during later periods.

In addition to all the places in London vhere goods were loaded and unloaded, here was the huge marshalling yard at Acton, where goods trains arrived from, r departed to, all parts of the railway sys- em. Acton was also an exchange point or wagons from other companies, with laily connections with the L & NWR, Midland, GNR and GER via the North London line.

Receiving Office at 26 Charing Cross Road, photographed in 1922. For a list of all London offices, see page 87 of Volume One. NATIONAL RAILWAY MUSEUM

GREAT WESTERN RAILWAY.

PADDINGTON GOODS STATION.

DIAGRAM SHEWING POSITIONS OF TRUCKS STANDING IN SHED FOR DOWN LOADING.

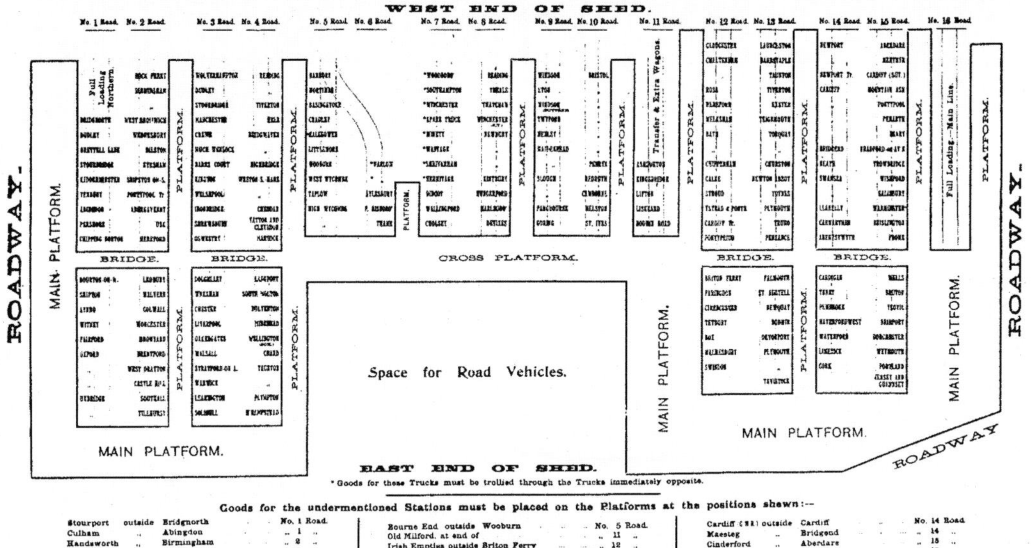

* Goods for these Trucks must be trollied through the Trucks immediately opposite.

Goods for the undermentioned Stations must be placed on the Platforms at the positions shewn:—

Stourport	outside	Bridgnorth	No. 1 Road.
Culham	..	Abingdon	.. 1 ..
Handsworth	..	Birmingham	.. 2 ..
Alcester	..	Wednesbury	.. 2 ..
Hook Norton	..	Shipston-on-Stour	.. 2 ..
Oldbury	..	Usk	.. 2 ..
Woodstock	..	Southall	.. 2 ..
Staines	..	Brentford	.. 2 ..
Cookham	..	Littlemore	.. 5 ..
Bourne End	outside	Wooburn	No. 5 Road.
Old Milford, at end of			.. 11 ..
Irish Empties	outside	Briton Ferry	.. 12 ..
Stonehouse	..	Cardiff Tr.	.. 12 ..
Corsham	..	Box	.. 12 ..
Dawlish	..	Teignmouth	.. 13 ..
Brixham	..	Torquay	.. 13 ..
Paignton	..	Churston	.. 13 ..
Cardiff (??)	outside	Cardiff	No. 14 Road.
Maesteg	..	Bridgend	.. 14 ..
Cinderford	..	Aberdare	.. 15 ..
Lydney	..	Merthyr	.. 15 ..
Chepstow	..	Mountain Ash	.. 15 ..
Monmouth	..	Pontypool	.. 15 ..
Llantrisant	..	Penarth	.. 15 ..
Penygraig	..	Barry	.. 15 ..

PADDINGTON (LONDON).

Goods Agent	1	Counter	4	~~Senior Checkers~~	3
Assistant Goods Agent	1	~~Depots~~		Checkers	126
Chief Clerk	1	~~Hay Bank~~	2	Repairer	1
Clerks—		~~Shepherds Bush~~	1	Timekeepers	5
General	9	Warehouse	4	Weighbridgemen	12
Staff	18	Spare	17	Callers Off	65
Cash	3	Cartage	11	Capstanmen	22
Accounts—	1	Shed	6	Loaders	174
General	12	District Inspectors	2	Number Takers	5
Inwards	19	Cartage Inspector	1	Officemen	11
Outwards	28	Market Inspectors	3	Rope Splicers	2
Abstracts	7	Yard Inspectors	9	Porters	311
Rebates	4	Chief Foreman	1	Motor Drivers	33
Ledger Deductions	18	Capstan Foremen	7		
Station Accounts	23	Cartage Foremen	7	Carters	303
Correspondence—		Cattle Foremen	3	~~Shunt Horse Driver~~	1
Inwards	27	Foremen	5	Chain Horse Drivers	33
Outwards	23	~~General Foremen~~	4	Vanguards	336
Rates	2	~~Goods Foremen~~	2	Leading Fireman	1
Copy of Entry	7	Shed Foremen	32	Firemen	5
Townsmen	3	Working Foremen	14	Messengers	35
Invoicing	41	Shunters	38	Charwomen	9
Inwards	33	Tracers	8		

The staff employed at Paddington Goods between 1913 and 1926.

PADDINGTON & ENVIRONS

Some of the staff at Paddington goods depot in 1912.

By 1845, the Paddington terminus in London was well established, with the engine shed and passenger station situated between the new Westbourne and Bishop's Road bridges, aligned east-west. A goods shed was also provided at this 'temporary' terminus, just to the east of Bishop's Road bridge, alongside Eastbourne Terrace, around the end of what is now No.1 platform at Paddington. It measured 330ft in length by 120ft wide (excluding the verandah), with platforms 11ft in width. Three roads ran through, with a centrally-placed traverser connecting them.

It was decided in the early 1850s to reconstruct the passenger terminus to the south-east of the Bishop's Road bridge, with the new station in that area then occupied by the goods depot and the station approach road.

Paddington Goods was relocated to the site of the original broad-gauge passenger terminus during the 1850s, and by the 1860s occupied some 13 acres, made up of about 6 acres of shed under cover, 6 acres of open yard and cart road east of Westbourne Bridge, and the remainder a high level coal yard by the side of the Grand Junction Canal, and adjoining the passenger terminus (with tracks almost at right-angles to the yard lines), all served by wagon turntables. The high level was reached by a wagon lift (Brunel's original hydraulic 'coal truck hoist') and wagons were then hauled by hydraulic capstans via a rail viaduct within the main yard.

In later years, the depot served West and North London, the West Central area, and the markets at Spitalfields, Covent Garden, Billingsgate, Leadenhall and Borough, but originally it was the *only* GW goods depot in London. In addition, there were GWR Receiving Offices scattered throughout London, (and listed in our *Introductory* volume to this series), which fed goods into Paddington.

Apart from minor alterations (platforms lengthened by removal of wagon turntables; and narrowing of the gauge in 1892, which gave widened platforms), the original depot did not change much for 60 years. Had not additional depots been opened in the London area at Smithfield (1869), Poplar (1878), Victoria & Albert Docks (1902) and South Lambeth (1913), it would have been impossible for the GWR to have kept pace with the demands of a rapidly-increasing volume of merchandise up to WWI. The growth of GWR London goods traffic is shown by comparing the figures for 1867 (the last year that Paddington Goods was the only GW depot in London) and 1899, when it was sharing its business with some half-dozen other depots:

1867: 821,000 tons of merchandise and goods carried, bringing in £621,000 earnings
1899: 1,057,000 tons, producing £810,000 earnings

Despite being all under one roof, those lines and platforms to the right of the central cart road were called the 'old shed', and those to the left the 'new' shed. There were 11 platforms in total, goods for the North (Oxford, Birmingham, Birkenhead, Manchester, etc.) being handled in the new shed, and traffic for Bristol, Wales and the West in the old. The platforms were connected by a series of Brunel-designed cross bridges which would disappear out of sight when wagons were moved in and out of the depot. On the east side of the depot was the hydraulic power house and the returned empties shed (formerly the cattle bank), a separate shed being a boon for this sort of 'nuisance' traffic. Fish trains used to be berthed beyond the empties shed until a fire in 1896 damaged the

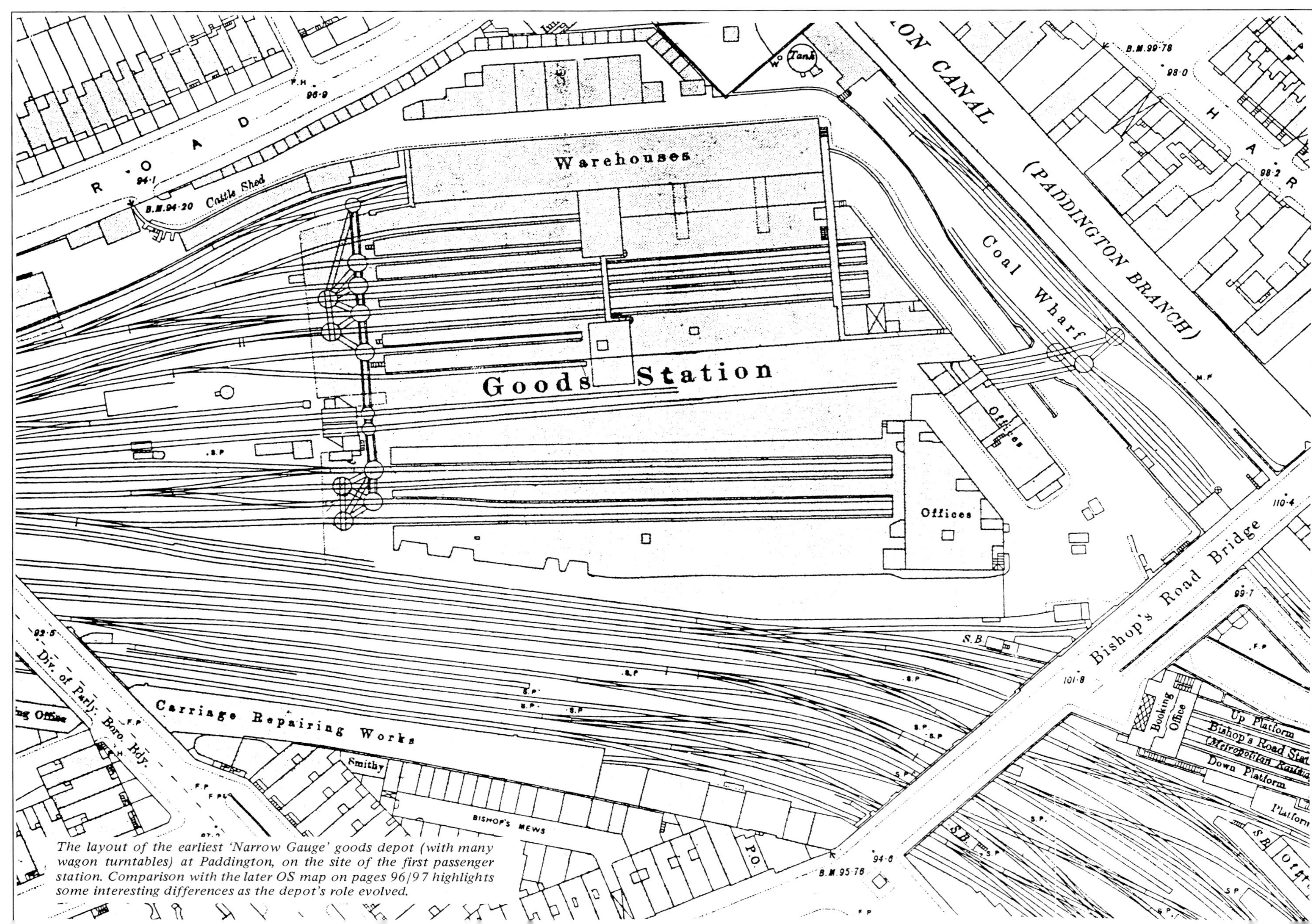

The layout of the earliest 'Narrow Gauge' goods depot (with many wagon turntables) at Paddington, on the site of the first passenger station. Comparison with the later OS map on pages 96/97 highlights some interesting differences as the depot's role evolved.

Part of the goods yard throat where the tracks divided and entered the original Paddington goods depot, looking east. The warehouse on the left backed on to the Harrow Road, whilst the main line was out of the picture to the right of the wagon lift. The date is unknown, but van No. 79581 with original louvred ventilators at the foot of the lamp post dates from 1912. There are many details on view in the yard, including hydraulic capstan and reels; stone setts in the road; and planks between tracks. The curved awning extension in the centre is not present in the 1900 picture, shown on page 84. NATIONAL RAILWAY MUSEUM

nearby (and very large) warehouse. After that, the fish tracks were covered over with old longitudinal sleepers, and the platform so made used for storing flour, grain and Irish bacon. Goods could also be stored on No. 1 (North Staffs and Birmingham) goods platform because it was so wide and sheltered.

By the end of the 19th century, the total capacity for berthing rail vehicles was 215 vans or 280 open wagons, plus 17 under the flour store. Thirty-six inwards and thirty-eight outwards goods trains were handled at the depot daily; in addition, there were numerous 'specials' and 'returned empties'. All this meant some 600 inwards loaded wagons and 700 outwards loaded wagons.

Paddington in late Victorian times, after the opening of other GW London goods yards, was essentially a station for mixed general traffic. According to season, over

The wagon hoists at Paddington lifted vehicles up to an overhead rail bridge that ran through the depot to the high-level coal yard at the back of the depot site. Water-driven at 1500 psi, the pressure for the hoists was supplied by the London Hydraulic Co. of Deptford. Photographed in 1900.

Paddington goods depot in 1900, looking east, with the wagon hoists in the centre of the view and the south wall of the depot on the extreme right. In addition to the usual consignments, Paddington Goods also handled road vehicles by rail; a horse-drawn furniture removals van belonging to Avant & Co. of Dawlish is seen at centre right on a 'Hydra' or 'Loriot'.
NATIONAL RAILWAY MUSEUM

1,000 tons of fruit and vegetables (including 69,000 packages of asparagus) arrived annually from Worcester, Evesham, and from other agricultural areas; 7,000 tons of potatoes and 13,000 packets of hops, from Herefordshire and Worcestershire; train-loads of beans and potatoes from the Channel Islands; broccoli from Cornwall, and so on.

Perhaps the next most important full truck loads were sides of bacon from Ireland and Wiltshire. In 1899, regularly three days a week, the Irish boats brought over some 650 bales of bacon which required 14 wagons for their conveyance to London (1,700 bales could be stored in the 'arches' at Paddington Goods). Meat from Birkenhead went to Smithfield, but freshly-slaughtered meat from Deptford was a regular outwards traffic from Paddington at that time; nineteen road waggons arrived each evening, whence the carcases were shouldered by porter into railway refrigerator vans ('Micas'). All meat and fish traffic was handled at the 'full load' banks; 300 tons of fish were unloaded daily.

Over 100 tons of Huntley & Palmer biscuits from Reading came to Paddington every day in Victorian times, but much was for export, so after the opening of the Poplar depot in 1878 the quantity dwindled to 40 tons/day for London consumption. Thirty tons of Cadbury's chocolate and 30 tons of Fry's cocoa also were received daily. There was a great deal of hardware from the Midlands. It seems that wicker chairs were so popular at that time that 5 or 6 van loads a day were received from the Bridgwater area. Paper from the Ely Paper Mills on the western outskirts of Cardiff was a significant traffic, on which the bulk of London's newspapers and magazines were printed, over 600 reels (6ft long by 3ft in diameter) being received daily.

Outwards traffic was extremely varied: in addition to manufactured goods, leather from the Borough market, spring mattresses and bedsteads seemed to feature prominently, as well as many tons of 'smalls'.

Most of the major through goods trains carrying smalls traffic travelled overnight, so work at a depot was very busy in the morning for 'Inwards' traffic, and busiest in the afternoon and throughout the evening for the 'Outwards' traffic. Just before WWI, during the afternoon, the early loads of goods collected by the company's road vehicles – fruit, vegetable and fish empties – and traffic from the London termini of other railways arrived along with goods that traders carted themselves (and for which they claimed a cartage rebate). That continued until 6.30 p.m. when the goods station was closed to the public for receipt of goods, by which time some 150–200 lorry loads would have been dealt with (recall that 'lorry' in those days meant a horse-drawn vehicle).

The Receiving Offices scattered about the metropolis also closed at 6.30 p.m., though some of these did not deal with goods traffic; for example: 7 & 8 Charing Cross Road; King William Street; Leadenhall Street; 11–15 Monument Buildings (staffed by the SR after the grouping) and Smithfield (Long Lane), during the early 1920s. Others, such as Battersea (York Road), in 1912, dealt only with goods.

Since the GWR motor vehicles also ceased collecting from traders' premises at 6.0 p.m., the bulk of outwards traffic came into Paddington between 7.0 and 9.0 p.m. A line of vans and carts, extending from the north side of Bishops Road to beyond Praed Street underground station, each awaiting its turn to pass over the weighbridge, was a common sight in late Victorian times (vans carrying fruit, vegetables, meat and other perishables were given a special pass to go through). In Edwardian days, about 160 road vehicles on average passed over the weighbridge into the depot between 7.0 and 8.0 p.m., to reach a total of about 600 vehicles by the end of a day. The last of the day's road vehicles to turn up – from Poplar, and Victoria and Albert Docks – arrived as late as midnight. The reason that goods were carted from these outlying depots rather than being brought around via the North London Railway to Paddington was that GWR locomotives were not permitted on the NLR, and the GW did not wish to pay for the movement by rail. Of course, this applied to 'cartable' goods; wagon loads or goods too large or awkward to handle had to come round by rail.

By midnight, most outwards railway wagons had been loaded and put out into the yard where the marshalling foreman had put them into proper order for their trains, before being handed over to the running department. The time of peak loading activity at Paddington Goods occurred at 8.0 p.m., and by midnight only trucks for the later, short-distance goods trains remained to be finished off, together with some clearing-up into the 'late stores' of goods which may have missed their trains. It was then that the men went to supper, although some inwards trains would already have started to arrive in the yard, and were held in reserve for berthing.

The task of unloading wagons from those inwards trains began in earnest at

.o a.m. The first arrivals at Paddington vould have been the short-distance trains om Slough, Reading and Wycombe and, ccording to the season, broccoli, fish or otato trains that had come up as special ains the previous day. Most perishable affic was intended for early market sales nd had, therefore, to be out of the depot y 6.0 a.m. In fact, the goods depot at 'addington was also responsible for the elivery of all fish, poultry, meat, flowers and so on) received by train at the *passen-er* station. In 1908, for example, 72 horse ams and one 5-ton motor lorry (68 men nd boys) came on at 2.0 a.m. for this vork, and drew a special market pay-llowance. Sometimes, 'callers-up' were ent out to bring in up to 100 regular day nen to augment the staff at busy night eriods. After the passenger department ad been dealt with, the market and per-shable goods from the goods depot itself vere got out, then the regular smalls traffic vas dealt with.

In 1908, the authorised number of armen and van guards was 910 men and

The Chief Goods manager's Office, Paddington, against the Bishop's Road Bridge in 1907, looking west from the roof of Bishop's Road suburban station. This building would later bear the lettering 'Great Western Railway Goods Depot'. NATIONAL RAILWAY MUSEUM

ORGANIZATION OF OFFICE STAFF AT PADDINGTON GOODS STATION, 1908.

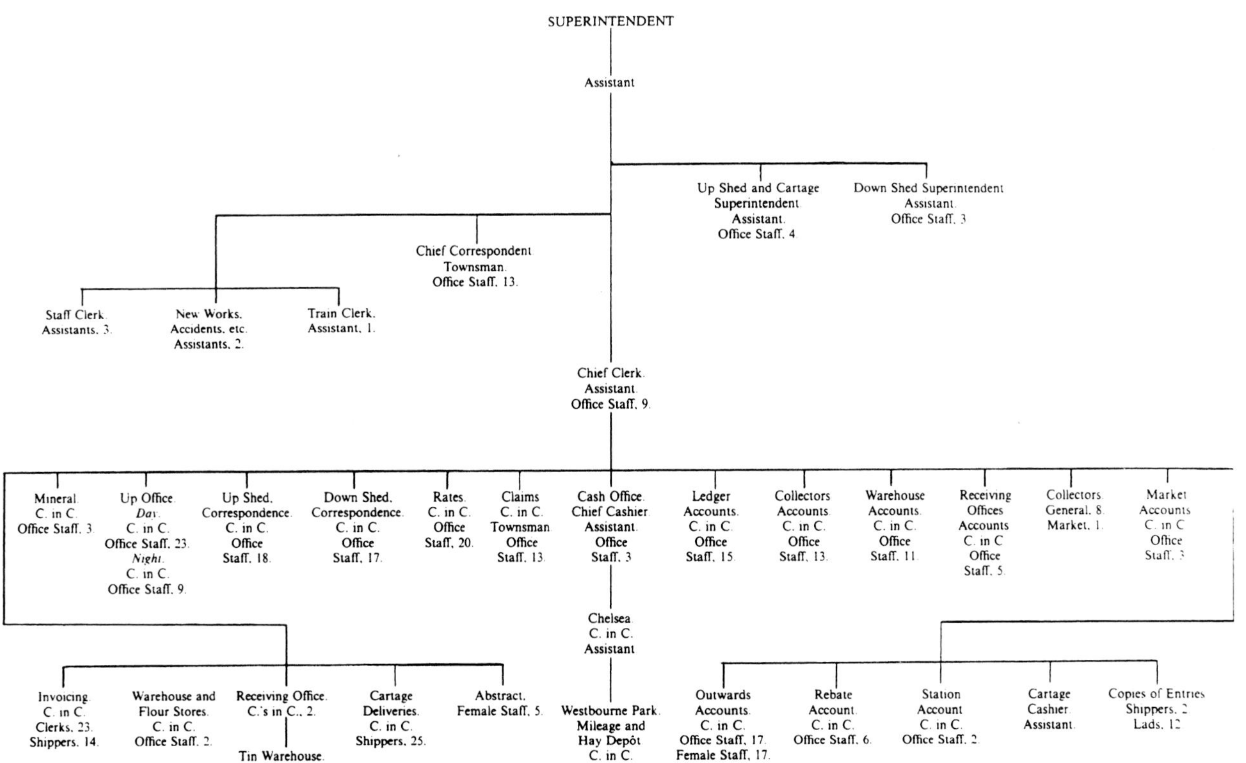

TOTAL OFFICE STAFF: 364.

The high-level coal yard at the rear (east end) of Paddington Goods, with its tracks running parallel to the Paddington branch of the Grand Union Canal that ran behind the depot. As the width was limited, wagon turntables were necessary to swing trucks onto the various coal sidings from the two approach tracks through the depot; the high-level access bridge can be seen on the left, bringing the two tracks from the wagon hoists. The picture was probably posed (as so many were) as Dia O11 open No. 86459 was a goods, not coal, vehicle, and was newly-painted in post-Grouping 16in lettering. The shunting horse was attached by chain to the drawbar hook. Coal sacks had been draped over the steelwork of the far rail bridge member to dry. Just beyond, on the upper floor of the old depot, the 'Down Booking And Receiving Office' notice can be seen. A wooden hut had been tipped on its side, and was surrounded with rubbish, whilst the yard itself was empty, so it may have been preparing for closure. Returned empties traffic, dealt with in part of the warehouse in the distance, was removed to Ladbroke Grove in 1924 prior to reconstruction of the depot. The derrick crane at the far end of the coal yard could be used 'by prior arrangement' to interchange traffic

Looking south-eastwards from Paddington Goods Offices during the First World War, with a view along the eastern side of Paddington station. The two sidings in the foreground (corresponding to the two on the left in the adjacent high-level yard photo) originally extended back about halfway along the passenger station, but by this time the high-level yard had been cut back to make room for new platforms (the new fourth arch to the passenger station was almost complete). Coal merchants' pitches and offices can be seen against the boundary wall with the canal, with bagged house fuel on road wagons to the left of the chimney. The entrance to the goods depot was down the road on the right and under the Bishops Road bridge, whilst the road in the centre turned through a right-angle below the photographer and climbed up to join Bishops Road bridge near to that station. This photo was taken about two years later than that on page 32 of Volume One. NATIONAL RAILWAY MUSEUM

›oys, with some 600 cartage vehicles and a ›tud of 1,000 horses. Including this cartage ›taff, there were over 2,000 people ›mployed at Paddington Goods. In the ›ffices, some 250 clerks made some 7,000 ›ook entries each night and issued 1,100 ›nvoices, whilst about 700 porters were ›mployed in the sheds and yard. In addi›ion to these, there were 30 policemen. ›ften, the shed and cartage staff at large ›epots worked on bonus schemes, which ›vere introduced by the GWR on 1st ›anuary 1900; for example, in 1908 at ›addington Goods, a gang of five (checker, ›aller-off and three trolleyers) were each ›aid 6d for every ton loaded or unloaded ›bove what was considered as a fair average ›oad for a day's work (a working day then ›eing 10½ hours). For outwards (or 'down ›oading') goods, the average load was set at ›5 tons per gang i.e. about 2½ tons per ›our. For inwards traffic, it was 40 tons for ›eneral smalls traffic, but 50 tons for heavy ›raffic. More inwards traffic could be dealt ›vith than outwards because the gangs merely moved the goods from the rail wagons to one of the 36 pitches representing the districts into which the London delivery area was divided.

An important programme of extensions for Paddington passenger station was drawn up in 1906, and work was in progress between 1909 and 1916. One of the chief works was the replacement of the series of old brick arches across the line from Bishops Road out to Old Oak Common by long-span steel girder structures (which are still there today), intended to give future flexibility with permanent way alterations.

Improvements continued during the 1920s, and the Victorian goods depot itself at Paddington was rebuilt in the mid/late 1920s to help improve on what was really a very restricted area in which to move so large a volume of traffic; the old platforms were narrow and irregular, and trolleying was impeded by the large number of fixed cranes. Work began in 1925 on the reconstruction of that half of Paddington goods shed lying nearer to the main line, and this was completed in 1929.

In late Victorian times, Paddington Goods despatched 32 long-distance goods trains each weekday, and 38 were received at short intervals, the marshalling of which was covered by a staff of 67, including inspectors, foremen, shunters, capstan men and others. The GWR's fast vacuum-fitted goods trains were introduced in the early 1900s; nine 'C' (vacuum) and five 'E' (Express Goods, class 'A') services departed from Paddington Goods daily in 1913 between 8.0 p.m. and 2.0 a.m., with nine 'C', three 'Accelerated E' and one 'E' in 1927. There were, in addition, other slower trains and transfer services that departed (and arrived) daily at Paddington depot.

The subsequent alterations to the passenger stations at Paddington and Bishops Road in the early 1930s meant further modifications. The goods invoicing and cartage offices facing the main line had to be demolished, and this, in turn, entailed the removal of most of the surviving old

The north-east corner of Paddington Goods (i.e. at the road exit), looking east, showing the north-western corner of the cartage vehicle bay and park, as indicated by the legend 'Space for Road Vehicles' on the diagram of the old depot at Paddington for Down Loading on page 80. This 1909 photograph shows a great variety of road wagons, and diverse goods and methods of packing, including a crate going to 'W & G, 8 Rue Gluck, Paris'. Shed cranes and a platform weighing machine (protected by metal barriers) are in evidence. A number of slightly different styles of painting of road vehicles may be seen, but only some had shafts for horses (including wide shafts for a horse pair), others being attached by chains to

igh-level goods yard, and providing, on art of that site, a new block of offices and n alternative road approach; the latter ook the form of a viaduct, with mess ooms and kitchens below. A new parking rea for storage of motor and horse vehicles on the old high level was reached from the new approach road. The fire station also had to be resited. The remainder of the hydraulic appliances at the station were electrified, amongst other improvements.

All new cart roads were paved with 5in-deep granite setts on a 6in bed of concrete, asphalt being used elsewhere and in the shed and warehouses. Where track was laid in or crossed roadways, the edging for the

Continued on page 101

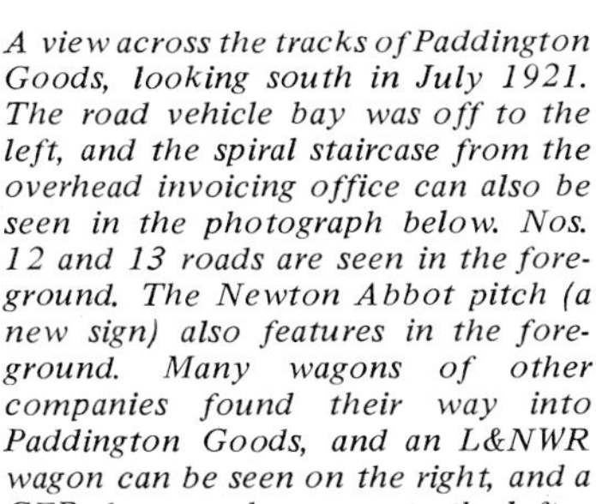

A view across the tracks of Paddington Goods, looking south in July 1921. The road vehicle bay was off to the left, and the spiral staircase from the overhead invoicing office can also be seen in the photograph below. Nos. 12 and 13 roads are seen in the foreground. The Newton Abbot pitch (a new sign) also features in the foreground. Many wagons of other companies found their way into Paddington Goods, and an L&NWR wagon can be seen on the right, and a GER sheet on the wagon to the left.

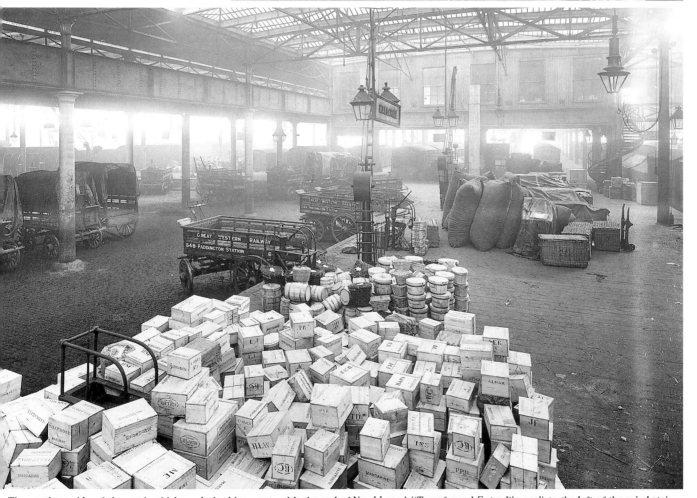

The northern side of the road vehicle park, looking west, with the end of No. 11 road ('Transfer and Extra Wagons') to the left of the spiral staircase from Invoicing. This picture was taken on the same occasion as the earlier one portraying the vehicle yard, but with the photographer's back to the platform office. A large number of margarine boxes and casks are seen under the suspended 'Margarine' sign and along the platform in the foreground. Barriers had been positioned around the platform scales equipment. NATIONAL RAILWAY MUSEUM

A view from the other (south-western) corner of the road vehicle bay, looking towards the cartage exit in the east wall. This is the third picture taken on the same occasion in 1909, giving a remarkable record of that venue. Four similar cranes can be seen down No. 4 platform on the right, with guard rails around their control levers. McVitie & Price biscuit boxes are seen scattered along the bottom of the picture, including returned empties and rope sheave. A pile of skins and fleeces may be seen at the foot of the pillar on the left, tied up

The entry into Paddington depot at the east end of the site in July 1921. A large variety of horse lorries belonging to the Great Western, private firms and hauliers look as if they were milling about in some confusion, and on the left, Great Western wagon No. 2429 seems to have been moving against the flow of traffic – but everything was probably going to plan, this being Paddington. A few private motor vehicles including 'Wyman & Sons, Fetter Lane' are seen on the extreme right, at the foot of the incline that led up and behind the old warehouse in the far distance.
NATIONAL RAILWAY MUSEUM

The entry to Paddington Goods, looking towards the rail overbridge and the high-level coal yard, but a little less crowded. This view shows Paddington four-horse teams, with additional horses possibly attached just for the incline out of the yard, as was the practice at certain places. The horses attached to the wagons were in extra-wide shafts, whilst the collars of the front pairs were attached by chains to the wagon shafts. The boxed loads must have been heavy to justify the four-horse teams, though the pairs may have been able to handle the weight on more level ground. Paddington's two-storey 'Mint' stables are shown in the top left of the photo on page 32 of Volume One (now part of St. Mary's Hospital).
NATIONAL RAILWAY MUSEUM

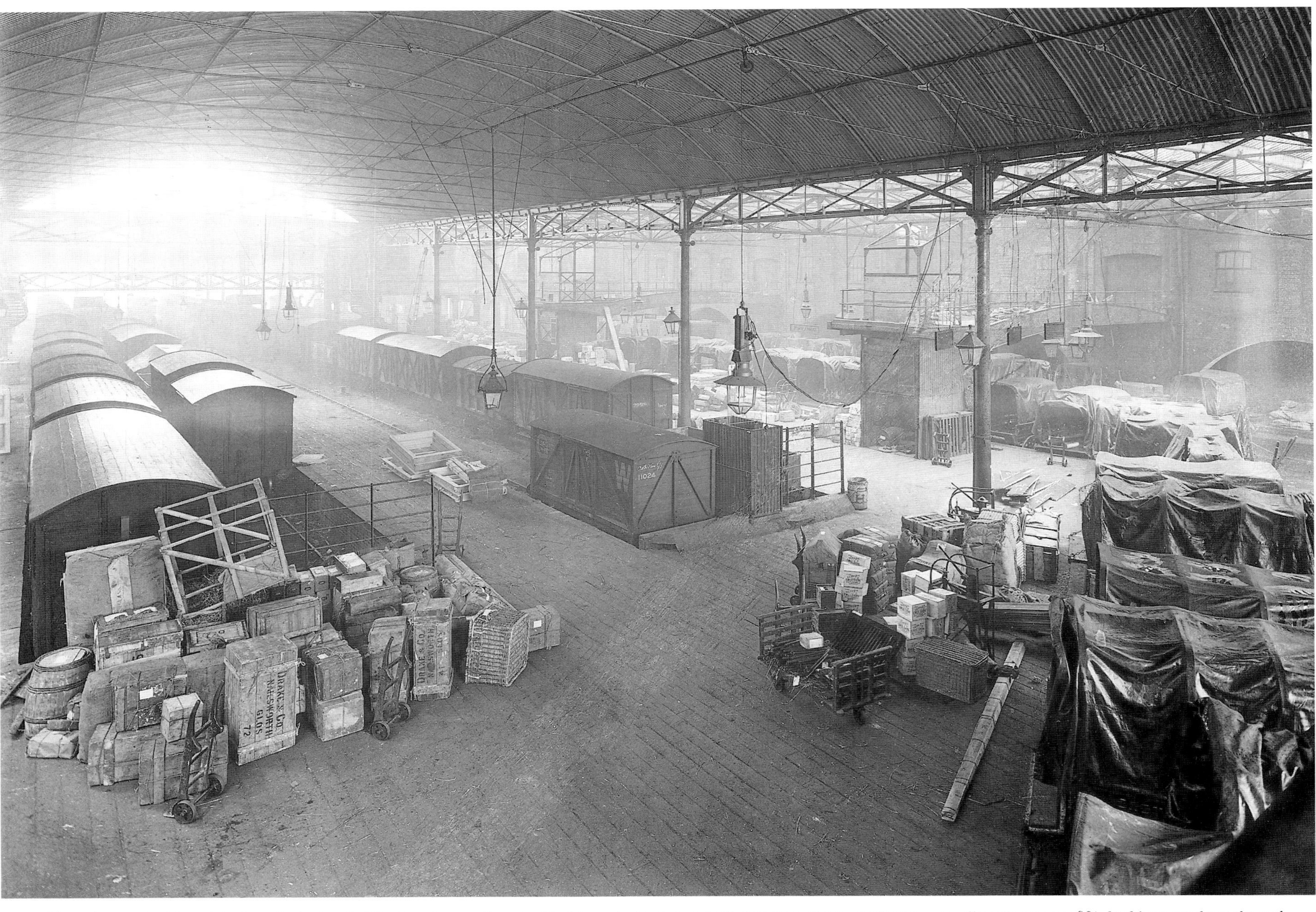

The other part of the original goods shed at Paddington, for northern traffic (closer to the bacon bank and four-storey warehouse – see diagram on page 99), looking west from the end of the cartage bay, with the goods platforms to the left and the continuation of the cartage bays on the right. This part had a curved roof, whilst the other part shown in earlier pictures had a pitched glass roof. Covered carts are seen in the end of the cartage bay on the right, and others along the internal roadway along the back of the picture. Plate girder bridges from the warehouse spanned the cart road on their way to the lift shafts on the platform, near to the columns. Outside-framed wooden goods van No. 11024 at the stop blocks had 'Cloth Van 813' chalked on its end, whilst Dia V7 'Mink C' No. 79519 dated from 1906. Cases of Scotts emulsion are seen at the platform scales near the carts on the right, whilst, on the left,

Two views of the Paddington goods, showing reconstruction under way. The first, from 27th July 1926, was looking eastwards into the shed (Bishop's Road bridge is just visible over the boundary wall on the right). New tracks and platforms are seen in place, with the new shed framework being clad with corrugated sheeting. Dia N6 Loco Coal wagons on the left were being used for building spoil. The second view, taken in March 1927, was from inside the remains of the old goods shed, looking east towards the cartage area and former high-level yard. The two cranes were shown in earlier photographs, on the edge of the former cartage bay. The far end of the deep girder (formerly carrying overhead tracks from hoist to high-level coal yard) had already been removed, leaving the columns standing outside the new shed. Building processes predominated in this area, with a steam-driven cement mixer in use on the right, whilst a ballast wagon filled with broken bricks is seen on the far line, framed by the cranes. Nevertheless, goods work had to continue, as a line of wagons in the foreground shows. NATIONAL RAILWAY MUSEUM

An aerial view of Paddington taken in April 1931, looking south, with the new goods depot prominent in the centre of the picture, and the passenger station to its left. Between the passenger and goods structures, the depot's entrance road still descended under the Bihop's Road bridge and the CGM's office to feed the enlarged cartage yard at the east end. The truncated high-level coal yard remained on the station side of the road, but had been removed on the depot side, replaced partly by a roadway that curved round behind the warehouse to join Harrow Road. Westbourne bridge spanned the yard throat. Ranelagh bridge, with its turntable and loco sidings, can be seen further to the right. The Paddington branch of the

Reconstruction of the new depot was nearly complete in April 1931. The high-level coal yard had been removed on the west side of Bishop's Road, and the new base and retaining wall (on the right) against the canal towpath passed behind the warehouse which, with the cartage wiehgbridges at the entrance, were the only parts of the original depot to survive. Temporary track carrying loaded spoil wagons connected to a shed line extended into the cartage area. NATIONAL RAILWAY MUSEUM

A similar view a little later, looking west over the roof of the new structure, with a guard wall built on the road vehicle park in the bottom right-hand corner (the lowered site of the former coal yard). The old cart weighbridge survived at the bottom left corner, and there was still a great deal of building debris on site. NATIONAL RAILWAY MUSEUM

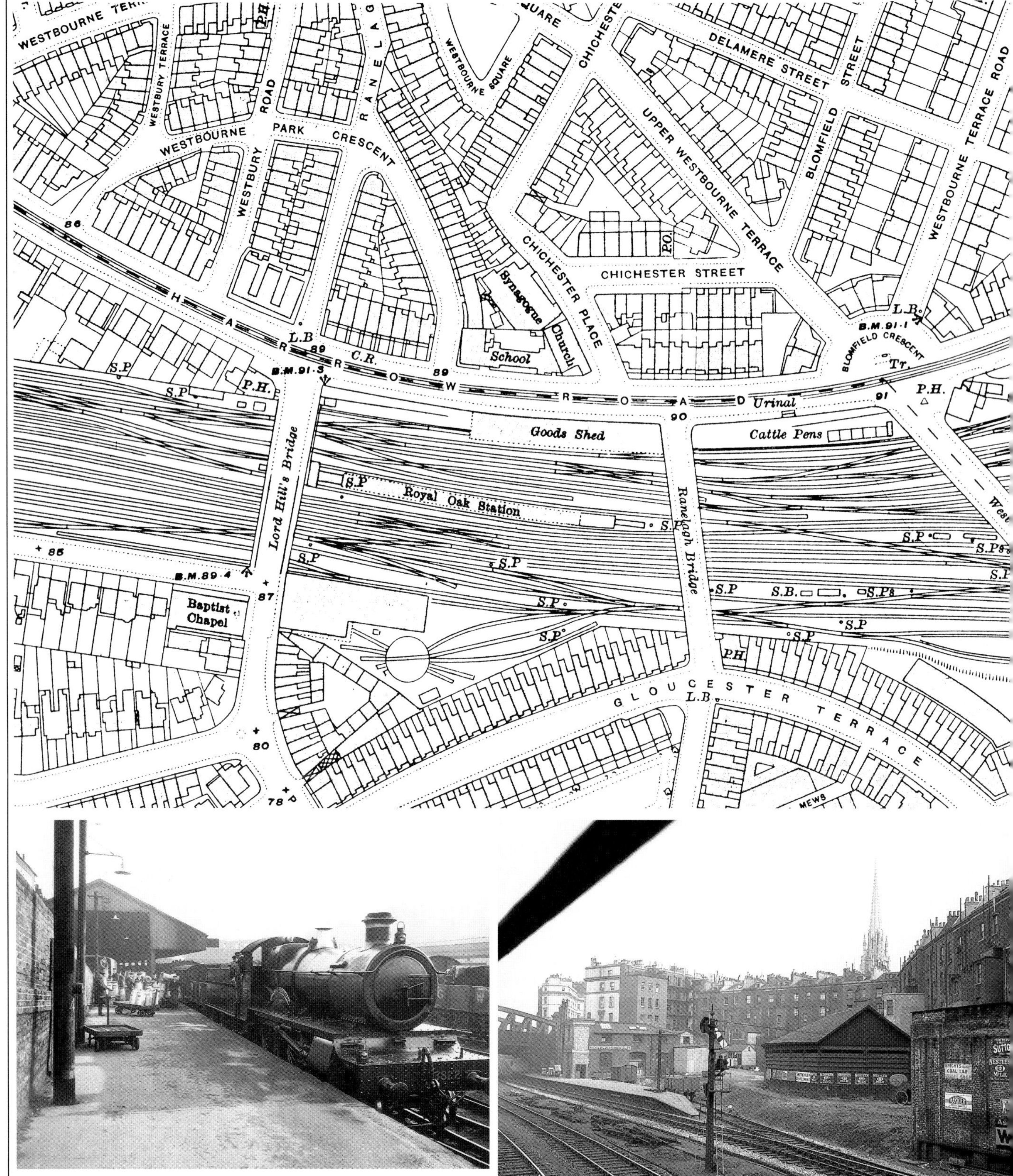

Milk empties traffic in 1928 at the goods shed backing on to Harrow Road near royal Oak station. Ranelagh bridge appears in the background between the awning and 3822 County of Brecon. *Road access to the platform was from Lord Hill's bridge, down the ramp on the left; see the view on page 107.*

NATIONAL RAILWAY MUSEUM

The end of passenger platform 1A beyond Westbourne bridge, built i 1908 on the site of the old broad gauge carriage shops which stood t against Bishop's Mews. Westbourne bridge is seen on the left, and the spi of Holy Trinity right centre. New parcels facilities were to be built here.

NATIONAL RAILWAY MUSEU

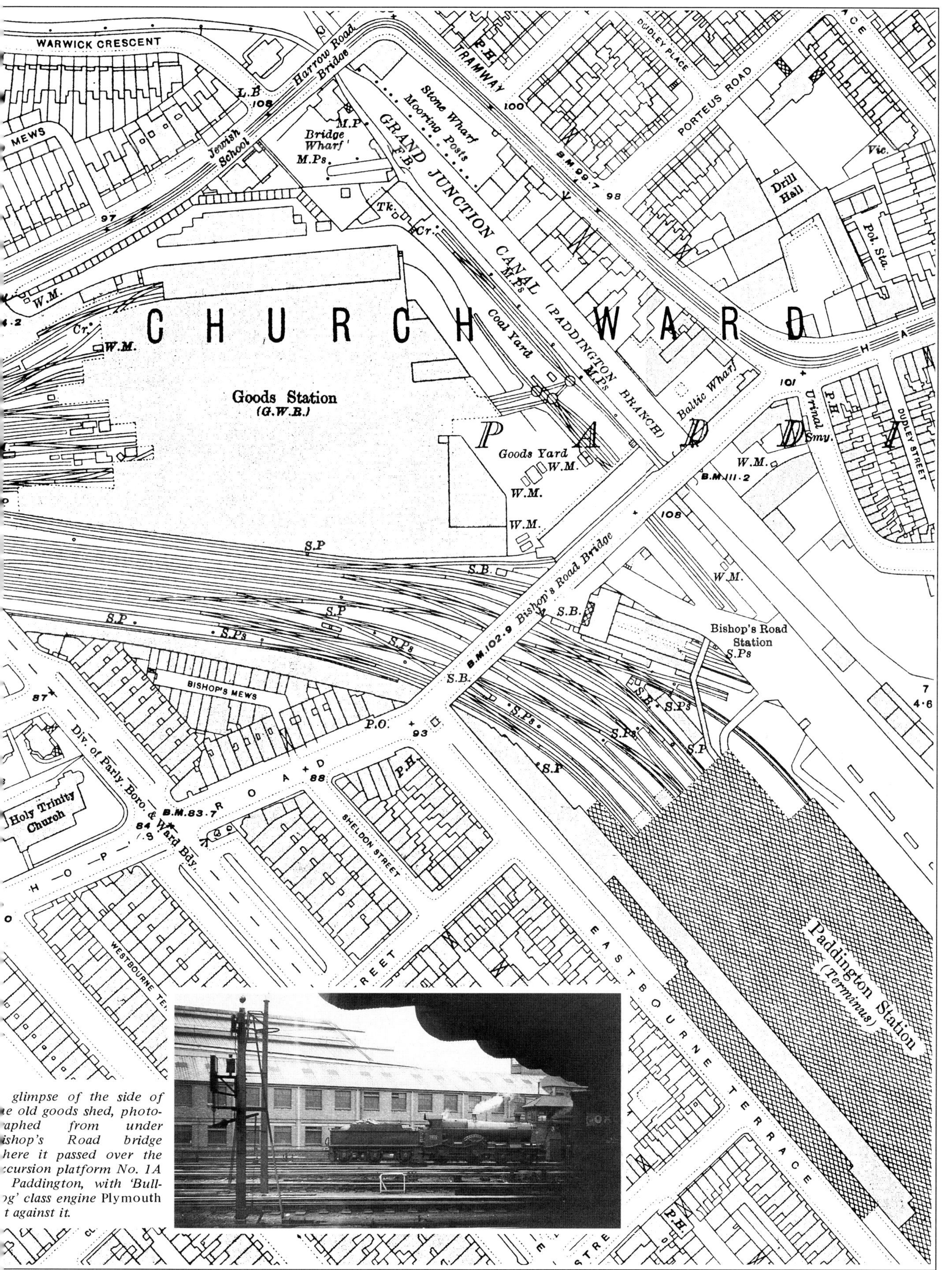

glimpse of the side of
e old goods shed, photo-
aphed from under
ishop's Road bridge
here it passed over the
ccursion platform No. 1A
Paddington, with 'Bull-
og' class engine *Plymouth*
t against it.

Taken from 25-inch Ordnance Survey for 1916. Crown copyright reserved.

The rebuilding of Bishop's Road station in September 1933, after which it was incorporated as platform Nos. 13 to 16 of Paddington station. This view was looking east (the end of the GWR goods offices on the left). The old Bishop's Road station comprised two platform faces with three tracks between. The new Arrival signal box and equipment building at the end of platforms 10/11 are seen in the centre, whilst new water columns (behind signals) had been located at the west ends of the new platforms for the suburban service and Smithfield goods train locos.

A view looking north-west from platform 10/11, with the dominant Goods Offices forming the backdrop. 'Great Western Railway Goods Station' lettering was now hung on the building; this was not attached when the structure opened in 1908, nor in later times, as can be seen on other views. The building also had a deeper coping above its third storey than when opened. On the extreme right, at high level, the Geo. J. Cockerell & Co. Coal Office building (with sign) was just about all that remained of the old high-level yard. New platforms (13-16) for suburban and Hammersmith trains were nearing completion to the right, with the realigned road access to Bishop's Road from the cab rank road alongside the main station beyond. (See also view on page 92.)

NATIONAL RAILWAY MUSEUM

The roads between the north-eastern side of Paddington station and the goods depot were also much modified in the reconstruction. This view, taken from the goods offices in 1936, shows (in the foreground) a mechanical horse parked on the new, descending road access to the goods depot, now on the left *side (and roughly along the same alignment as the old road that climbed towards Bishop's Road bridge), whilst the new high-level road to join Bishop's Road is seen on the right. The end of the new Bishop's Road booking office entrance is visible at the extreme right. Virtually all that remained of the high-level yard can be seen on the left, with the canal boundary wall beyond. Cartage vehicles were now stored on the site of the old coal yard, which was retained at its original height only to the east of Bishop's Road bridge. The new footbridge and parcel lifts connecting the main-line station with the rebuilt H & C platforms can be seen in front of the train sheds, with taxis lined up against the left-hand arch of the station, awaiting their move onto platforms. (See also view on page 85.)* All photos: NATIONAL RAILWAY MUSEUM

Left: *Bomb-damaged 'GWR Paddington Suburban Station' signs on the roof of a rather grubby Bishop's Road station entrance in 1946.* Right: *The road entrance (realigned in 1933) to Paddington goods depot, running down under Bishop's Road bridge and the goods offices, probably again in 1946. The large 'goods Station' lettering on the CGM's offices had been removed, probably as security during the war. The police office is seen on the right, and on the left the road climbing to Bishop's Road bridge, with the remains of the old high-level yard to the right.*

Left: *The south-easternmost corner of the cartage yard at the depot, between the old high-level coal yard on the left and the descending entrance road to the depot on the right. This 1933 view shows the new mess for Paddington Goods, built beneath the new access road on the right, with benches outside.* Right: *The interior of the new mess, looking east, with the GWR clock just coming up to noon on 15th September 1933.*

Left: *The demolition of Bishop's Mews to make way for the construction of the new parcels depot to the west of the station, on the down side.* Right: *Construction of the new Parcels Receiving Office (rear view) is under way in this view, with the Departure signal box to the front, in March 1932. Bishop's Road bridge features on the left, with the awnings on the right built on the cleared site in the picture alongside.* NRM

Looking west from the end of platforms 10/11, Paddington, with the completed parcels depot on the far side of the trackwork, and Paddington Goods to the right. Diesel parcels railcar No. 17 (introduced in 1936) was a frequent visitor to the parcels platform, and is seen alongside in this view. The exit from the parcels depot came up from platform level to Orsett Terrace under the GWR office building on the near side of Westbourne bridge, seen beyond. L. E. COPELAND

Left: *A view along the parcels platform in 1935. Various signs identify the pitches of outwards parcels, including South Wales, Northern, and Main Line (behind the clock).* Right: *The front facade of the completed Parcels Receiving Office in Bishop's Road, with the bridge to the right, seen during 1933 as originally built; later, two extra storeys were added. The ground floor of the GWR building was also let out to tobacconists and the Marnic Motor Co. The entrance to the new parcels depot was through the gates on the left, from which the road descended to platform level. The exit was into Orsett Terrace, off the end of Westbourne bridge, a couple of hundred yards away.* NATIONAL RAILWAY MUSEUM

ad within the track was formed by 5in x ½ in bulb angle coach-screwed into the eepers, 2in off the rail on the inside.

The old tunnel to the Metropolitan ailway had to be demolished for part of s length in the Bishop's Road reconstruc- on, being replaced by a covered way. The rder work involved use of the heaviest ate girder then available, with a 133ft an weighing 126 tons carrying the goods id taxi approaches.

Arrangements for parcels traffic were ompletely changed at the same time. ormerly dealt with on the 'Lawn' (the area etween the end of the passenger tracks id the GWR Royal Hotel), a new depot or parcels was provided, having a road ntrance from Bishops Road and exit to)rsett Terrace. The old down excursion nd milk platform (Platform 1A built as an xtension to Platform 1 in 1908) was set ack, and a separate line provided to it for arcels traffic. A new subway was built to onnect the parcels depot with Platforms 1) 8, the rest being reached by means of ie new footbridge connecting the main ation with the rebuilt Bishops Road. The riginal station there had been built in 863, when trains on the mixed-gauge line) Farringdon Street commenced; the road gauge remained until 1869. The ame Bishop's Road was dropped from eptember 1933, when the four platforms ecame Paddington platforms 13–16.

In the 1920–1940 period, some 600,000 ons of goods were handled annually at 'addington. There were roughly 330 loaded rucks inwards and 400 outwards daily, car- ying some 70,000 separate packages in all bulked into some 3,700 inwards consign- ients and 7,000 outwards). In addition, ome 160 tons of transfer traffic, en route to ther depots and to other railway compa- ies, was dealt with daily. Over 900 road ehicles used the depot each day, the 3WR's own cartage fleet at Paddington onsisting of 300 horse teams and 40 motor ehicles at the end of the 1920s.

The principal operational changes to goods handling after the 1920s/early 1930s ebuild of Paddington Goods was the mployment of quick-acting, self-pro- elled platform trucks and trailers to eplace hand trolleying. A feature of the iew shed was the absence of fixed cranes on the platforms, the only obstructions eing the roof supports, but these were laced 10ft away from the platform edges, eaving a 11ft-wide gangway in the centre of each of the seven 600ft-long platforms for unobstructed trolleying purposes. Counter-balanced lifting platform bridges were provided about halfway down all the platforms to enable movement between platforms without having to go round the end. During shunting, the leaves were swung up at right-angles to the platform surface and locked in place.

The edges of the platforms next to the tracks were coped for a depth of 3ft 9in with Australian brush boxwood and other hardwoods to prevent damage to wagon drop doors.

On the north side of the shed, where there was a 50ft roadway between the plat- forms and the old bacon bank and four- floor warehouse, similar bridges connected the outer platform of the new shed to the old buildings.

The new layout was simpler than the old, with wide, clear and straight platforms between the fourteen tracks enabling the platform trucks and trailers to be operated very quickly. Different makes of power truck were tried out, including a fleet of 12 petrol trucks made by Low Loaders Ltd.

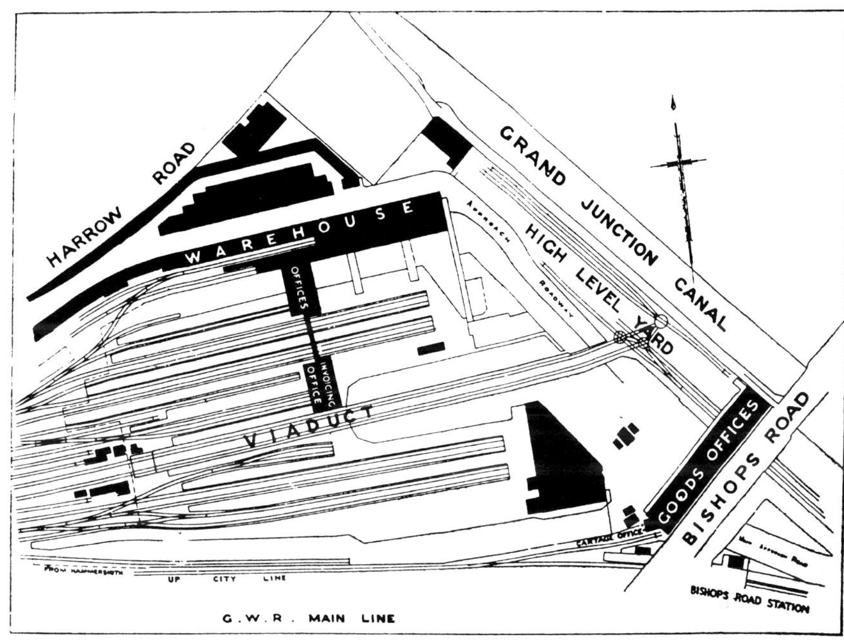

Paddington goods shed, before rebuilding.

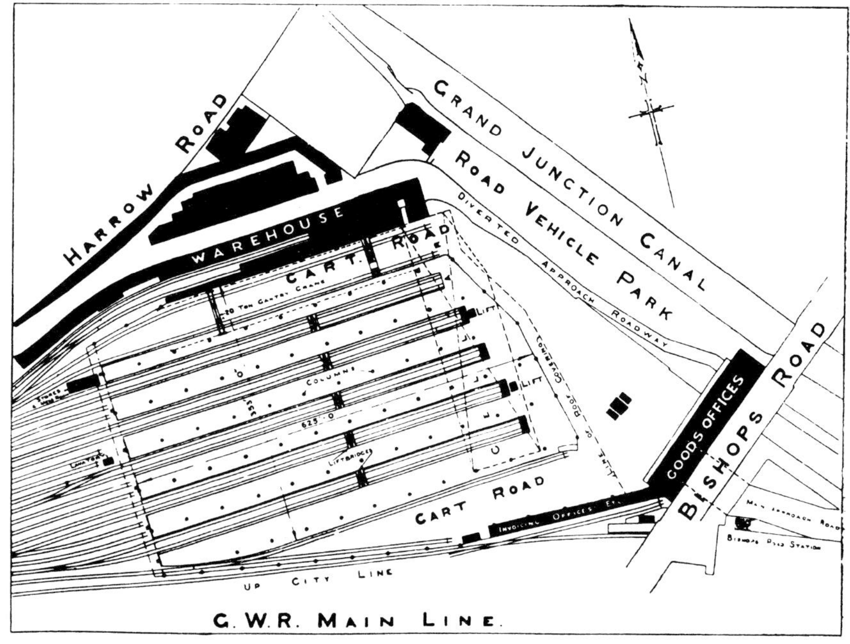

Paddington goods shed, after rebuilding.

The rebuilt, spacious new Paddington goods shed came into use between July and October 1926, and this photograph dates from May 1927. Ransomes & Rapier 2-ton mobile cranes and 'petrol barrows/tractors' (Douglas, LowLoader and Lister Auto Truck types) were some of the mechanical handling innovations introduced to speed up transit. This was a posed picture of loading among what were surely unloading operations (the sheet on the 'Open' is seen partly off, not on), whilst little work appears to have been going on beyond the five staff in the foreground! The 'British Grown Pure Indian Tea' chests were a very common sight at the depot. Destination signs were again evident

Ransome & Rapier mobile petrol-lectric cranes also speeded up goods andling, and had the freedom of move-ıent allowed by the wide central gang-/ays. Consignments too heavy to be ıan-handled into or out of wagons could e easily dealt with by the cranes, and voided the shunting required when fixed ranes had been used. Really heavy loads vere dealt with by a 20-ton overhead elec-ric travelling gantry crane within the shed n the north side.

Another improvement was the provision f illuminated indicators, giving the desti-ations of wagons at the various loading erths.

Faster operation in and out of the depot vas also ensured with twin machine cart veighbridges located in the main cart oadway in front of the shed. The new veighbridges were of greater capacity than he old types intended for horse lorries, nd were supplied to handle the increasing umber of motor lorries being used for C&D work after WWI.

A photograph taken on goods platform No. 2 after nationalisation of Paddington goods shed, showing a petrol-electric mobile crane with a crate containing a 'Ford Exchange Reconstructed Engine'. This platform handled outbound traffic for the West Country, as evidenced by the sign above. A 'Down Stores – Private' shed is seen to the right of the crane.
NATIONAL RAILWAY MUSEUM

All railway companies used women employees to replace the men called into the forces during the Second World War, and in this posed view on one of the platform bridges at Paddington goods in July 1941, some of the women porters are shown at work. A 'Mink A' van is seen on the left, with rail-mounted scotches to prevent wagons from accidentally colliding with the trolleying bridges; it was chalked for Camborne, Grampound Rd. and Burngullow. Boards above the shed foreman and inspector indicated the stations served from that platform. The second board indicated Morris Cowley, Thame, Witney, Fairford S(tation) T(ruck), Campden ST, Pershore ST, Evesham, Oxford (Fruit and News), Oxford (twice); and the nearer board indicated High Wycombe, Bicester & Hockley ST, Watlington ST, Princes Risboro', Beaconsfield, Gerrards Cross, Ruislip, Denham ST, Windsor & Eton, Slough. Destinations on these boards were painted on slats that could be slid in and out as required. Compare with chalked destinations for platform 2, in the photograph above of the crane.
NATIONAL RAILWAY MUSEUM

An aerial view of the approaches to Paddington, seen on 2nd June 1947, with the goods depot in the centre, the CGM's office at the top right-hand corner of the site, and the warehouse to the left of the main building. The four bridges on the approach are seen here: Bishop's Road, Westbourne, Ranelagh and Lord Hill's respectively, from top to bottom. The view also shows how the rebuilt parcels platform to the right of the tracks extended almost all the way down to the Ranelagh bridge, with the extensive awning in the 'vee' of the buildings (old carriage shops site) between Westbourne and Ranelagh bridges. The Parcels Receiving Office at the near end of Bishop's Road bridge, originally with three storeys, now had five (see page 98). On the opposite side, against the Harrow Road retaining wall, a loading platform stretched almost all the way round from Lord Hill's bridge to the north-western part of the depot.
SIMMONS AEROFILMS

The western end of Paddington Goods in early nationalisation days, with Westbourne bridge across the middle of the picture. The approach roads to the depot are seen in the background, with the western face of the structure on the right. Beyond the roads, at the rear of the Barclay's pub at the northern end of Westbourne bridge, can be seen the extended loading platform, with the old broad gauge cattle shed to the right of the pub, by now employed for beer and general goods. Whilst there was much activity on the approaches to Paddington station, little is seen on the goods side, as nearly all work at this hour was probably indoors. NATIONAL RAILWAY MUSEUM

A capstan being used for shunting at Paddington Goods just after nationalisation. The control pedal can be seen under the right foot of the operator, whilst the rope was hooked to the axleguard of the third van (Dia V3/7 'Mink C'), and there were four turns around the capstan to provide adhesion for the pull. The location was at the north-west corner of the site, alongside the former broad gauge cattle shed. The end of the original four-storey warehouse can just be seen to the left of the corrugated facing to the main depot. NATIONAL RAILWAY MUSEUM

A view to the west from the roof of the offices at the end of Westbourne bridge, in 1955. Royal Oak station can be seen off Lord Hill's bridge in the middle distance, with the goods roads beyond the two electrified tracks running along the centre of the track bed at this point. Cattle pens and the milk shed can be seen on the extended loading platforms below Harrow Road, to either side of Ranelagh bridge. These are also visible in the 1947 aerial picture, though all have now been swept away in the elevated road construction works of recent years. J. R. BATTS

Shunting on the goods sidings under Lord Hill's bridge, looking west, with the shunter on the shunting truck calling the driver of the '57XX' pannier tank back. Royal Oak station was just out of the picture, to the left of the photographer.
NATIONAL RAILWAY MUSEUM

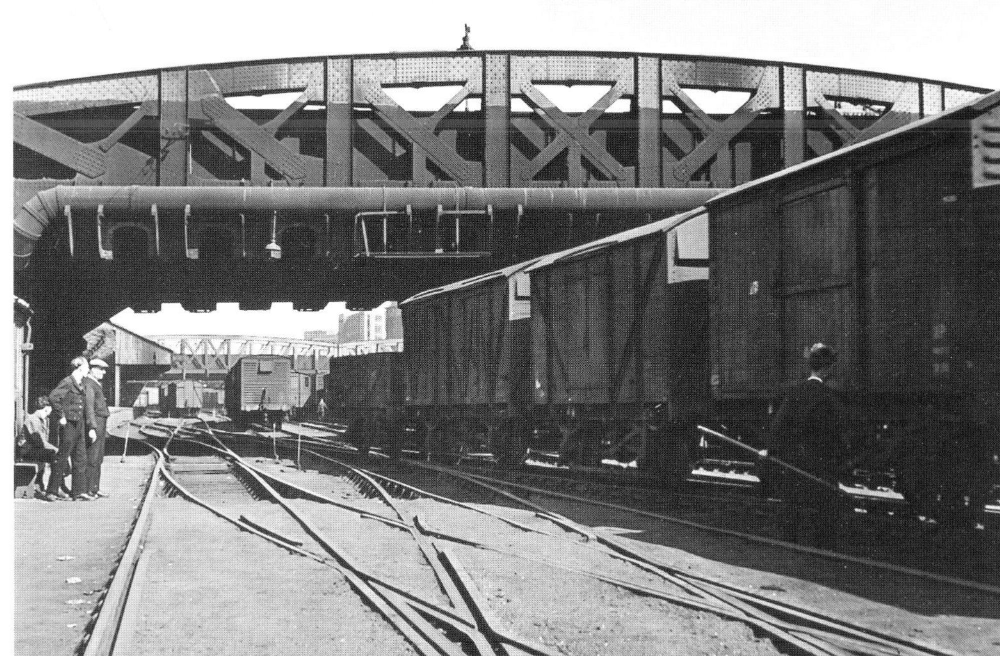

Looking eastwards under Lord Hill's bridge towards Ranelagh bridge, after nationalisation, with shunting operations under way. The shunters' cabin and office are seen behind the men on the left.
NATIONAL RAILWAY MUSEUM

The sidings outside Royal Oak station, between Lord Hill's and Ranelagh bridges, looking east, with the latter bridge in the middle distance. Various horse lorries are seen parked under the old milk shed, road access to which was down the ramp on the left from Lord Hill's bridge. '57XX' class Pannier No. 8763 is seen against the loading platform with a shunting truck branded 'Paddington'. The tracks ahead contained wagons for or from Paddington Goods depot, whilst the lion on the roof of the Barclay's pub at Westbourne bridge is visible beyond the shed.
NATIONAL RAILWAY MUSEUM

To be Substituted for Pages 25 and 26 in the Book of Instructions relating to London Goods Traffic, dated 1924.

RETURNED EMPTIES

It is most important that these instructions be understood by all concerned and strictly complied with.

All Returned Empties for, or via, London, must be invoiced and loaded as under:—

Paddington.—A separate Depot, called the "**Ladbroke Empties Shed,**" is provided for dealing with returned empties, and all empties for addresses served by the Paddington and Smithfield Stations, as appearing in list of Districts and Streets on pages 46 to 62 (with the following exceptions) must be forwarded in full truck loads, wherever practicable, and (except as hereinafter provided) labelled to "**Ladbroke Empties Shed,**" with the special label (as under) that has been adopted for the purpose. A supply of these labels can be obtained from the Stationery Department in the usual way.

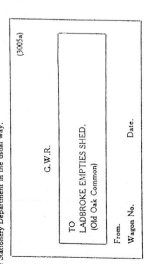

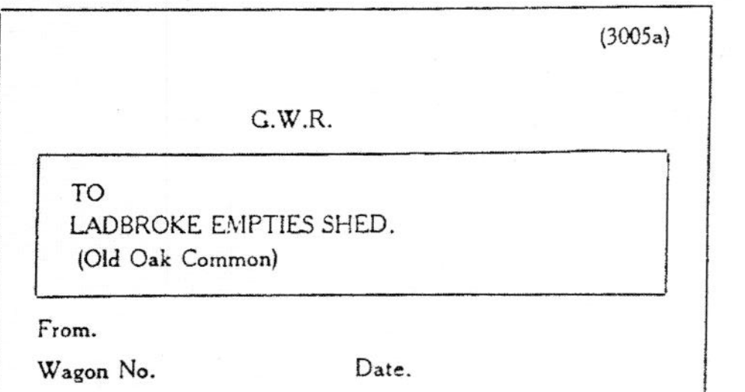
(3005a)

G.W.R.

TO
LADBROKE EMPTIES SHED.
(Old Oak Common)

From.

Wagon No. Date.

At Stations where there are not enough empties for a truck load daily, but at which sufficient can be accumulated in, say, two or three days, the empties must be held back for that time, but not for a longer period than three days unless specific instructions to the contrary are held.

Small Stations, not able to make truck loads of empties, must forward them as received daily to the most convenient Transfer Station.

All empties (with the following exceptions) must be invoiced separately to Paddington and not with General Goods, and they must not be loaded with General Goods.

Full Loads for South Lambeth (with the following exceptions) must be invoiced, labelled and forwarded direct to that Station, the labels to be endorsed "Empties." **Small lots for South Lambeth** must also be invoiced thereto, but loaded with General Goods when separate wagons are forwarded to that Station; otherwise, they must be loaded to the most convenient transfer point (accompanied by the invoices), in accordance with the instructions respecting Ordinary Returned Empties.

Returned Market and Fruit Empties.—Full truck loads of returned Market and Fruit Empties are dealt with in the Paddington New Yard, and the Wagons must be labelled to Paddington New Yard. Small lots of these empties are dealt with in the Paddington Goods Shed and they must be loaded as General Goods.

They must be securely tied in bundles and each bundle labelled with sender's and consignee's name and address.

These empties must be invoiced separately and not with General Goods.

Full loads of empties for the **Brentford Market** must be labelled and invoiced to Brentford, but small lots must be invoiced to Brentford and sent with the invoices to Paddington for transfer.

Pickfords, Limited, Returned Empties.—Messrs. Gilbey & Co.'s and other Firms' returned empties, carted by Pickfords, Limited, will be dealt with in the Paddington Goods Shed, and, when in sufficient quantity for a truck load, must be loaded separately from other empties and labelled to "Paddington, for Pickfords, Ltd." If not sufficient for a truck load, the empties must be loaded with General Goods, and in either case they must be labelled to "Paddington" and may be included on the same invoices with General Goods.

Oxygen Gas Cylinders for all consignees must be loaded and invoiced to Paddington and not to Ladbroke Empties Shed.

CHELSEA BASIN.—The following firms require their Returned Empties sent to Chelsea Basin:—

Shell Mex and B.P., Ltd.	Fulham.
Gartons, Sons & Co.	Battersea.

The empties for these firms must be invoiced to **Paddington for Chelsea Basin**, truck loads being labelled direct to Chelsea Basin and small lots sent to Ladbroke Empties Shed for transfer.

WARWICK ROAD, KENSINGTON.—The following firms require their Returned Empties sent to Warwick Road, Kensington:—

Manbre, Garton, Ltd., Winslow Rd., Fulham Palace Rd.
Hammersmith Distillery, Winslow Rd., Fulham Palace Rd.

The empties for these firms must be invoiced to Paddington for Warwick Rd., Kensington, truck loads being labelled direct to Warwick Rd., Kensington, and small lots sent to Ladbroke Empties Shed for transfer.

SMITHFIELD.—No Returned Empties are to be invoiced or loaded Smithfield, except those for the following firms:—

Booths Distillery, Ltd., 55, Cowcross St., London.
Nicholson, J. & W. Co., Ltd., 195, St. John St., Clerkenwell, London.
Walker, John & Sons, Ltd., St. George's Bond, Commercial Rd., London.
Whitbread & Co., Ltd., Britannia St., King's Cross, London.

POPLAR AND VICTORIA & ALBERT.—Returned Empties for addresses served by these Stations must be invoiced to these stations and forwarded in full truck loads whenever practicable, and may be held for not more than three days to enable this to be done. If direct loading cannot be effected, the empties should be loaded to the most convenient transfer station.

Returned Empties, for Foreign Lines, for which the route is via London
Full loads for any one Station must be loaded and invoiced through to destination.

Consignments, in less than full loads, must be dealt with in the following manner:—

If a full load can be made up for a number of Stations, on a particular Company's Railway, they must be invoiced through to the respective destinations, loaded together, and sent to that Company's London Station for transfer. For instance, a full load of transfer traffic for Stations on the L. & N.E. Railway (Great Northern Section) must be labelled to King's Cross.

If, however, a through load cannot be made up, they must be invoiced to the respective destinations, and forwarded to Ladbroke Empties Shed with other London Empties. The invoices must be sent to Paddington Goods.

Through wagons are made daily from Ladbroke Grove Empties Shed to the following Stations:—

Camden, L.M. & S.R.	King's Cross, L. & N.E.R.
Somers Town, L.M. & S.R.	Bishopsgate, L. & N.E.R.
Commercial Rd., L.M. & S.R., for Tilbury Section.	Nine Elms, Southern Rly.
Thames Haven, L.M. & S.R.	Bricklayers Arms, Southern Rly.

In future all Empties for **London District Stations** must be loaded to Ladbroke Empties Shed and ***not*** to Paddington Goods Shed. Through wagons or Station Trucks are made daily with empties from Ladbroke Empties Shed to the following destinations:—

Acton	High Wycombe	Small Heath
Beaconsfield	Langley (Bucks)	Southall
Birmingham (Hockley)	Maidenhead	Southall (Ticklers)
Brentford	Oxford	South Lambeth
Bristol	Park Royal	Staines
Colnbrook	Poplar	Taplow
Denham	Princes Risborough	Twyford
Gerrards Cross	Reading	Uxbridge
Greenford	Ruislip	Victoria & Albert
Hayes & Harlington	Slough	West Drayton
Henley-on-Thames	Slough (St. Martins Preserving Co.)	West Wycombe

When there are sufficient Empties for any one Firm to fill a truck they should be loaded together in one wagon; and in mixed loads each Firm's Empties should be loaded together in the same part of the wagon.

It is necessary that all Returned Empties be properly addressed with Sender's and Consignee's names and addresses—and they should not be accepted for forwarding under mark.

Returned Empties for Messrs. McVitie & Price, Ltd., Edinburgh Biscuit Works, Willesden, must be invoiced to Park Royal and the names of senders and branded numbers of cases shown upon the invoices when received from that station full.

Many Returned Packages of Light Goods, such as Drapery, Furs, etc., are mistaken for Empties and are loaded to "Empties Shed." This subjects them to considerable risk of damage or entire loss, and great care must be taken to see that such packages are properly invoiced in accordance with the nature of the goods upon the general invoice and loaded with the general goods.

7099—4-35

LADBROKE EMPTIES SHED

Kensal Green in later years, looking north-eastwards with the Ladbroke Grove 'returned empties' shed to the south of the main line. Paddington empties traffic moved here in 1924 in anticipation of the rebuilding of the Paddington goods depot. The gas works were a prominent landmark on the route into Paddington, and the Paddington branch of the Grand Union Canal can also be seen passing behind, on the left of the picture.

SIMMONS AEROFILMS

PLEASE EXHIBIT THIS IN YOUR DESPATCH DEPARTMENT

LIST OF METROPOLITAN DISTRICTS AND THOROUGHFARES SERVED BY THE MAIN G.W.R GOODS STATIONS

THE UNDERMENTIONED BRIEF LIST OF PRINCIPAL DISTRICTS AND THOROUGHFARES WILL BE OF ASSISTANCE IN THE FORWARDING OR RECEPTION OF MERCHANDISE, THE STATIONS COVERING THE PARTICULAR AREA BEING INDICATED IN CODE AS FOLLOWS :—**A=ACTON. B=BRENTFORD. P=PADDINGTON. PR=PARK ROYAL. S=SMITHFIELD. SL=SOUTH LAMBETH. V & A=VICTORIA & ALBERT.**

Abbey Wood	V & A
Acton	A
Acton Lane, Chiswick	A
Addison Road (North and South)	P
Adelaide Road, Hampstead	P
Agricultural Hall, Islington	P
Albany Road, Camberwell	S L
Albany Street, Regent's Park	P
Albert Embankment	S L
Albert Gate, Hyde Park	P
Aldermanbury	S
Aldersgate Street	S
Aldgate	S
Aldwych	P
Alexandra Park, Wood Green	P
Alperton	P R
Anerley	S L
Arlington Road, Camden Town	P
Asylum Road, Peckham	S L
Australian Avenue	S
Back Church Lane	S
Baker Street	P
Balham	S L
Ball's Pond Road	S
Bank of England	S
Bankside, Southwark	S L
Barbican	S
Barking	V & A
Barking Road	V & A
Barnes	P
Barnsbury	P
Bartholomew Close	S
Basinghall Avenue	S
Basinghall Street	S
Battersea	S L
Bayswater	P
Bear Lane, Southwark	S L
Beckton	V & A
Becontree	V & A
Bedford Park, Chiswick	A
Bedford Square	P
Belgrave Square	P
Belsize Park and Road	P
Belvedere Road, Lambeth	S L
Berkeley Square	P
Bermondsey	S L
Berners Street	P
Berwick Street	P
Bethnal Green	S
Bevis Marks, City	S
Billingsgate Market	P
Billiter Street and Square	S
Bishopsgate	S
Blackfriars Road	S L
Blackheath	S L
Blackhorse Road	S L
Blackwall	V & A
Bloomsbury	P
Bond Street (Old and New)	P
Borough	S L
Borough High Street	S L
Borough Market	P
Botolph Lane	S
Bouverie Street, City	S
Bow	S or V & A
Bow Common Lane, Poplar	S
Bow Lane, City	S
Bowes Park	P
Bread Street, City	S
Brentford	B
Brick Lane, Spitalfields	S
Brixton	S L
Broad Street (Bloomsbury)	P
Broad Street (Old and New)	S
Broadway (Deptford)	S L
Brockley	S L
Bromley-by-Bow	V & A
Brompton	P
Brondesbury	P
Brook Green	P
Brunswick Road, Poplar	V & A
Brushfield Street	S
Bryanston Square	P
Buckingham Palace and Gate	P
Budge Row, City	S
Bunhill Row, Chiswell Street	S
Burdett Road, Stepney	S
Cable Street, St. George's	S
Cadogan Square	P
Caledonian Road	P
Camberwell	S L
Cambridge Road, Chiswick	B
Cambridge Heath	S
Camden Road	P
Camden Town	P
Camomile Street, City	S
Campden Hill, Kensington	P
Canning Town	V & A
Cannon Street	S
Canonbury	P
Canterbury Road, Kilburn	P
Carmelite Street	S
Carpenter's Road	V & A
Carter Lane, City	S
Catford	S L
Cattle Market, Islington	P
Cavendish Square	P
Central Market, City	S
Chadwell Heath	V & A
Chalk Farm	P
Chancery Lane	S
Charing Cross	P
Charlton (Old and New)	V & A
Charterhouse St. and Square	S
Cheapside	S
Chelsea	P
Child's Hill	P R
Chiswell Street	S
Chiswick	A, B or P
City	S
City Road	S
Clapham and Clapham Park	S L
Clapton (Upper and Lower)	S
Clare Market, Strand	P
Clerkenwell	S
Clerkenwell Road	S
Cloth Fair, City	S
Coleman Street, City	S
College Park	P
Colliers Wood	S L
Commercial Road, Lambeth	S L
Commercial Road, East Stepney	S
Commercial Street	S
Cornhill	S
Covent Garden Market	P
Cowcross Street	S
Cranbourn St., Leicester Sq.	P
Craven Park	P R
Cricklewood	P R
Cromwell Road, S, Kensington	P
Crouch End	P
Crutched Friars	S
Crystal Palace	S L
Crystal Palace Road	S L
Cubitt Town	S
Cumberland Market	P
Curtain Road	S
Customs House, City	S
Dalston	S
Dawes Road, Fulham	P
Denmark Hill	S L
Deptford	S L
Deptford Market	S L
Devons Road	S or V & A
Dock Head, Bermondsey	S L
Dollis Hill	P R
Dowgate Hill, City	S
Drury Lane	P
Dudden Hill	P R
Dulwich	S L
Ealing	A
Earl's Court	P
Earlsfield	S L
Eastcheap	S
East Ham	V & A
East India Dock and Road	S or V & A
East Smithfield	S
Eaton Square, Pimlico	P
Edgware Road	P
Edmonton, Upper	P
Eltham and New Eltham	V & A
Essex Road, Islington	S
Euston Square and Road	P
Evelyn Street, Deptford	S L
Falcon Square, City	S
Farringdon Market	S
Farringdon Road and Street	S
Fenchurch Street	S
Fetter Lane, City	S
Finchley (Church End)	P
Finchley (East)	P
Finchley (North)	P
Finchley Road	P
Finsbury (City)	S
Finsbury Park	P
Fitzroy Square	P
Fleet Street	S
Fore Street, City	S
Forest Gate	V & A
Forest Hill	S L
Friday Street, City	S
Frognal	P
Fulham	P
Fulham Palace Road	P
Fulham Road	P
Garrett Lane	S L
General Post Office	S
George Lane, Woodford	V & A
Gipsy Hill	S L
Glasshouse Street, W.1	P
Globe Road, Mile End	S
Golden Lane, Barbican	S
Golden Square	P
Golders Green	P
Goldhawk Road	P
Goodge Street	P
Goodman's Yard, Minories	S
Goodmayes	V & A
Gospel Oak	P
Goswell Road and Street	S
Gower Street	P
Gracechurch Street	S
Graham Road, Dalston	S
Gray's Inn Road	S
Great Dover Street	S L
Great Eastern Street	S
Great Marlborough Street	P
Great Portland Street	P
Great Queen Street	P
Great Russell Street	P
Great Tower Street	S
Greenwich	S L
Gresham Street	S
Grosvenor Road, Pimlico	P
Grosvenor Square, Westminster	P
Grove Lane, Camberwell	S L
Grove Park	S L
Gunnersbury	B
Gutter Lane	S
Hackney	S
Hackney Downs	S
Hackney Road	S
Hackney Wick	S
Haggerston	S
Hammersmith	P
Hampstead	P
Hampstead Garden City	P
Hampstead Road	P
Hanover Square	P
Hanwell	A
Harlesden	P R
Harringay	P
Harrow Road	P
Hatcham	S L
Hatton Garden	S
Haverstock Hill	P
Haymarket	P
Herne Hill	S L
Higham Hill, Walthamstow	P
Highbury	P
Highgate	P
High Holborn	P
Hither Green	S L
Holborn	S
Holborn Viaduct	S
Holland Park and Road	P
Holloway	P
Holloway Road	P
Homerton	S
Honey Lane Market	S
Honor Oak	S L
Hornsey	P
Horseferry Road	P
Horselydown	S L
Houndsditch	S
Hoxton	S
Hyde Park	P
Ilford	V & A
Isle of Dogs	S
Islington	P or S
Jamaica Road, Bermondsey	S L
Jermyn Street	P
Jewin Street and Crescent	S
Jewry Street	S
Junction Rd. (Upper Holloway)	P
Kennington	S L
Kensal Green	P
Kensal Rise	P
Kensal Road	P
Kensington	P
Kensington (North)	P
Kensington (South)	P
Kentish Town	P
Kew	B
Kidbrooke	V & A
Kilburn	P
Kingsbury	P R
King's Cross	S
King's Cross Road	S
Kingsland	S
King's Road, Chelsea	P
Kingsway	P
King William Street, E.C.	S
King William Street, Strand	P
Knightrider Street	S
Knightsbridge	P
Ladbroke Grove	P
Ladywell	S L
Lambeth	S L
Lambeth (South)	S L
Lamb's Conduit Street	P
Lancaster Gate	P
Latimer Road	P
Laurence Pountney Hill	S
Laurence Pountney Lane	S
Lavender Hill	S L
Lawrence Lane	S
Lea Bridge	S
Leadenhall Market	P
Leadenhall Street	S
Leather Market Bermondsey	S L
Leather Lane, Holborn	S
Lee (Kent)	S L
Leicester Square	P
Leman Street	S
Leonard Street, Finsbury	S
Lewisham	S L
Leyton	V & A
Leytonstone	V & A
Lillie Road, Fulham	P
Limehouse	S
Lime Street	S
Lincoln's Inn Fields	P
Little Britain	S
Lisson Grove	P
Liverpool Road	P
Liverpool Street	S
Lombard Street	S
London Bridge	S L
London Docks	P
London Wall	S
Long Acre	P
Long Lane, Bermondsey	S L
Long Lane, E.C.	S
Lothbury	S
Lower Thames Street	S
Ludgate Hill	S
Maida Vale and Hill	P
Manchester Road, Poplar	S
Manor Park	V & A
Mansell Street, Aldgate	S
Mansion House	S
Mare Street (Hackney)	S
Mark Lane	S
Marylebone	P
Mayfair	P
Maze Pond	S L
Merton	S L
Middlesex Street	S
Mildmay Park	S
Mile End	S
Mile End Road	S
Milk Street, City	S
Millwall	S
Milton Street	S
Mincing Lane	S
Minories	S
Mint (Royal)	S
Mitcham	S L
Monkwell Street	S
Montagu Square	P
Moorfields	S
Moorgate	S
Morden	S L
Mortimer Street	P
Muswell Hill	P
Narrow Street, Limehouse	S
Neasden	P R
New Bridge Street	S
New Cross	S L
Newgate Street	S
Newington., S.E.	S L
New Kent Road	S L
Newman Street, Oxford Street	P
New North Road, Hoxton	S
New Oxford Street	P
New Southgate	P
Nine Elms	S L
Norbury	S L
Norfolk Street, Strand	P
North Audley Street	P
North End Road, Earl's Court	P
North End Road, Hampstead	P
Northumberland Avenue	P
Norwood	S L
Notting Hill	P
Nunhead	S L
Old Bailey	S
Old Change	S
Old Ford	S or V & A
Old Kent Road	S L
Old Oak Rd., Shepherd's Bush	A
Old Street	S
Olympia	P
Oxford Street	P
Paddington	P
Palace Gates	P
Pall Mall	P
Palmer's Green	P
Park Lane	P
Park Royal	P R
Parliament Street	P
Paternoster Row	S
Paul Street	S
Peckham	S L
Penge	S L
Pentonville	S
Philpot Lane	S
Piccadilly	P
Pimlico	P
Plaistow	V & A
Plumstead	V & A
Poplar	S or V & A
Portland Place, Marylebone	P
Portland Road, Notting Hill	P
Portman Square	P
Portobello Road	P
Poultry	S
Praed Street	P
Pudding Lane	S
Putney	S L
Putney Heath	S L
Queen's Park	P
Queen Street, E.C.	S
Queensway, Bayswater	P
Queen Victoria Street	S
Rathbone Place	P
Raynes Park	S L
Redcross Street, E.C.	S
Red Lion Street and Square	P
Regent's Park	P
Regent Street	P
Roehampton	S L
Roman Road, Old Ford	S
Rood Lane, City	S
Rosebery Avenue	S
Rosoman Street, Clerkenwell	S
Rosslyn Hill and Park	P
Rotherhithe	S L
Royal Mint	S
Rushey Green	S L
Russell Square	P
Rutland Gate	P
Sackville Street	P
St. Giles'	P
St. George's, East	S
St. James's Park	P
St. James's Square	P
St. John Street, Finsbury	S
St. John's Wood	P
St. Luke's	S
St. Martin's Lane	P
St. Martins-le-Grand	S
St. Mary Axe	S
St. Pancras	P
St. Paul's Churchyard	S
Salusbury Road, West Kilburn	P
Savile Row	P
Scrubbs Lane, Willesden	A
Seething Lane	S
Seven Kings	V & A
Seven Sisters Road	P
Shacklewell	S
Shad Thames	S L
Shadwell	S
Shaftesbury Avenue	P
Shepherd's Bush	A or P
Shoe Lane	S
Shooter's Hill	S L
Shoreditch	S
Silver Street, City	S
Silvertown	V & A
Sloane Square and Street	P
Smithfield	S
Smithfield, East	S
Smithfield Market	S
Snaresbrook	V & A
Snow Hill	S
Soho	P
Somers Town	P
Southampton Row	P
South Audley Street	P
South Ealing	A
Southfields	S L
Southgate Road, Islington	S
Southwark	S L
Spitalfields	S
Spitalfields Market	P
Stamford Hill	S
Stamford Street	S L
Stepney	S
Stockwell	S L
Stoke Newington	S
Stonebridge Park	P R
Strand	P
Stratford	V & A
Stratford Market	P
Streatham	S L
Stroud Green	P
Sudbury	P R
Sumner Road, Peckham	S L
Sussex Square, W.2	P
Sydenham	S L
Temple	S
Thames St. (Upper and Lower)	S
Theobald's Road	P
Throgmorton Avenue and Street	S
Tooley Street, Bermondsey	S L
Tooting	S L
Tothill Street, Westminster	P
Tottenham	P
Tottenham Court Road	P
Tower Bridge Road	S L
Tower Street and Hill	S
Trafalgar Square, Charing Cross	P
Tufnell Park	P
Tulse Hill	S L
Turnham Green	P
Twyford Abbey	P R
Union Street (Borough)	S L
Upper East Smithfield	S
Upper Ground St. (Blackfriars)	S L
Upper Holloway	P
Upper Street, Islington	P
Upper Thames Street	S
Upton Park	V & A
Uxbridge Road :—	
1 to 3 and 2 to 168	P
11 to 289 and 192 to 432	A
Vauxhall	S L
Victoria Embankment	P
Victoria Park	S
Victoria Street, Westminster	P
Walbrook	S
Walham Green	P
Walworth	S L
Walworth Road	S L
Wandsworth	S L
Wandsworth Common	S L
Wanstead	V & A
Wanstead Park	V & A
Wapping	S
Warwick Road, Kensington	P
Watling Street	S
Waterloo Road	S L
Wembley	P R
Westbourne Grove and Park	P
West Brompton	P
West Ealing	A
West End (Hampstead)	P
West End Lane	P
West Ferry Road, Millwall	S
West Green	P
West Ham	V & A
West India Dock Road	S
West Kensington	P
Westminster	P
Westminster Bridge Road	S L
West Smithfield	S
Whitechapel	S
Whitechapel Road	S
Whitecross Street	S
Whitefriars Street, City	S
Whitehall	P
White Hart Lane	P
Willesden	A or P R
Willesden Green	P R
Wilton Road, Pimlico	P
Wimbledon	S L
Wood Lane, Shepherd's Bush	P
Wood Green	P
Woodford	V & A
Wood Street, E.C.	S
Woolwich	V & A
Wormwood Scrubs	A
Worship Street	S
York Road (Battersea)	S L
,, ,, (King's Cross)	P
,, ,, (Lambeth)	S L
Zoological Gardens	P

FACILITIES AVAILABLE AT G.W.R LONDON AREA GOODS STATIONS AND DEPOTS

Tele. No.	Station or Depot.	Facilities.						Crane Power
Acorn 0161.	ACTON	G	M	L			C	6 0
Ealing 1891.	BRENTFORD	G	M				C	6 0
,, ,,	BRENTFORD DOCKS	G*			W	B		40 0
Flaxman 1467.	CHELSEA BASIN	G				B		10 0
Riverside 2438.	HAMMERSMITH	G†						

Tele. No.	Station or Depot.	Facilities.						Crane Power
Western 7098.	KENSINGTON (Warwick Road)	G†						
Paddington 7000	OLD OAK COMMON	G†						
Paddington 7000	PADDINGTON	G	M	L	W		C	20 0
Elgar 7031.	PARK ROYAL	G	M	L			C	6 0

Tele. No.	Station or Depot.	Facilities.						Crane Power
Shepherd's Bush 2677	SHEPHERD'S BUSH	G	M					6 0
Clerkenwell 2923.	SMITHFIELD	G			W		C	6 0
Macaulay 4321.	SOUTH LAMBETH	G	M		W		C	35 0
Albert Dock 1366.	VICTORIA & ALBERT	G	M		W		C	7 0
	WESTBOURNE PARK	G†						
Ealing 0488.	WEST EALING	G	M				C	6 0

Code Letter	Facility.
G	Goods Station.
G†	Mineral and Station to Station traffic only.
G*	Waterborne Traffic only.
M	Wheeled Traffic.
L	Livestock.
W	Warehouse accommodation.
B	Barging facilities.
C	Cartage Depot.

Printed by Jordison & Co., Ltd., London

OUTER MAIN LINE

ACTON

The goods shed and yard on the northern side of the main line at Acton, with a down express headed by 'Saint' 4–6–0 No. 2912 St. Ambrose *(as running between 1907 and 1910) passing on the main line. In 1932 the relatively modest yard beyond was renamed the Up Yard, and an extensive new arrangement to the left became the Down Yard.*

Acton goods yard, looking west in 1921. The line of 'Mica' meat vans on the left worked mostly between either Birkenhead or Fishguard and Smithfield, the London end of the operation being mounted at Acton. The goods platform with scalloped awnings on the right was originally the intercepting goods shed to remove goods from 'foreign' company wagons arriving via the North London lines (see photo on page 41 of Volume One).
NATIONAL RAILWAY MUSEUM

WEST EALING

West Ealing station, looking east, showing the goods shed on the right in the Old Yard which had three sidings. A larger yard was provided on the opposite (up) side (the New Yard), including the loading platform, possibly around the time of the building of the Greenford Loop in 1903/4. The Dia V12/14 'Mink' No. 93218 at the shed entrance appears new, and so dates the picture to around 1910-12. An unusual split arrangement of passenger platforms is to be seen, with the Up Relief to the far side of the bridge carrying the high-level station building, visible through the arch.
L&GRP

West Ealing in 1924, looking north along the station road, with the station building seen on the right of the picture at the brow of the overbridge. The entrance to the old goods yard was to the left, behind the line of nine coal order offices (though with a confectionery shop next to the station entrance). The firms holding offices here were Booth Brothers; Walter Moore & Co; the Clay Cross Company; Cameron's Coals; Garrick, Davies & Partners Ltd; Spencer Whatley Ltd; Edwin A. Cornwall; Hinchcliffes; New Wallsend Collieries Co Ltd; and Harvey Roberts.
NATIONAL RAILWAY MUSEUM

SOUTHALL

As at Acton, the goods yards at Southall were of some importance. Part of Southall East Yard (up side) and local goods sidings is seen here in 1950, looking north-west across the engine shed trackwork and the main lines. The road entrance to the Up yard and the shed itself was to the far left. NATIONAL RAILWAY MUSEUM

A freight on the Down Relief headed by Dean '2371' No. 2376 passing Southall goods depot in 1934. As with many sheds whose work expanded over the years, extensions had been added to the former structure to provide additional covered space for handling consignments. B. Y. WILLIAMS

HAYES

The newly-painted goods shed at Hayes, looking east, seen around the turn of the century, with the old carriage shed immediately beyond, bearing a Lilleshall company coal factor sign (to the left of the shed, above the roof of the lock-up on the platform). The small goods yard was beyond. Although the local goods facilities here were modest, the private companies served by the railway had more extensive sidings.

Hayes station, looking west after the Grouping. By this time, the goods shed (to the right) had been enlarged at its far end by a platform with an overall canopy, a common type of extension to the sheds. Amongst the early firms at Hayes was the Gramophone Company, which became part of the EMI empire, whose factory (served by sidings) can be seen in the background. LENS OF SUTTON

GREENFORD

An aerial view of Greenford in postwar years, looking north-eastwards across the goods yard and industrial complex, with the houses of Hill Rise to the bottom right. The BR and LPTB stations feature on the extreme right, with the goods yard in the centre of the picture, the goods shed itself located centrally at the rear of the sidings; initially Greenford was provided with a small lock-up shed on a loading platform, but this was enlarged in the interwar years. The huge Lyons factory can be seen beyond the goods yard, with rail access from just to the left of the station. In the left foreground we can see more rail-connected sites, dating mostly from the late 1920s, connected to the main lines by a branch that passed beneath the electrified lines of the LPTB. J. LYONS & CO. LTD.

Greenford station in 1920, looking west from the Down platform, with the goods yard on the Up side in the middle distance. In the near future, the Lyons factory would come to dominate the background to the right (the private siding agreement with the GWR was dated November 1920). L&GRP

A view westwards from the Torquay Street footbridge (see OS map on pages 118/9), with Subway Junction signal box in the centre left. This picture was taken after installation of the Paddington & Southall colour light signalling scheme of 1931/2. The Hammersmith & City lines descending to the left of the box crossed under the main line, with Crimea Sidings yard (and the Westbourne Park mileage and hay depot at the far end) to the left. Paddington New Depot and Yard of 1908 is seen on the right of the picture, to the north of the main line; this later became the site for the Alfred Road depot. The furthest track to the right, curling around behind the goods shed, was part of the Portobello Jct. to Paddington goods relief line, opened in 1880 to relieve congestion on the main line. G. N. SOUTHERDEN

A rare glimpse of Westbourne Park mileage yard and hay depot in 1934, looking east with a new GWR mobile crane suspending a BX2 container (of 1930) between the road and the 'Scorpion' carriage truck. Turntables shown on old maps of this depot up to the Great War period had now gone. The London depot of Hill, Evans & Co. Ltd. (Worcester vinegar producers) features behind the depot. NATIONAL RAILWAY MUSEUM

WESTBOURNE PARK YARDS

References to the goods depot/yard at Westbourne Park' in GWR documents nd photographs is, perhaps, confusing, as *hree* separate yards existed there, all of vhich developed when facilities for local raffic were moved from Paddington after he high-level yard was demolished in the 920s' rebuilding. Furthermore, to add onfusion, the name of one of the three ards (Paddington New Yard) changed its ame in 1939 to Alfred Road yard.

The original Westbourne Park Mileage nd Hay Depot (the 'Crimea' sidings) was n the *south* side of the main line, opposite ubway Junction signal box, and its head-hunt sidings curled south-westwards longside the Hammersmith & City lines owards Ladbroke Grove station. Rail access could be either from the east, or from the west in a tortuous route via Portobello yard and Junction signal box, which crossed the Hammersmith & City lines at an acute angle just south of the passenger platforms. This depot dealt with 24,000 wagon-loads of hay and straw annually before the First World War.

The high-level coal yard at Paddington, before its removal in the 1920s reconstruction, had dealt with about 6,000 tons per month, the wagon lift hoisting some 850 wagons each month, up and down. Most of these wagons were for private firms, to whom space in the Paddington coal yard was leased. The bulk of GW domestic coal traffic was even then carried on at the Crimea sidings, where there was room for 280 wagons. Westbourne Park took on the Paddington private owner coal traffic after the high-level yard was demolished. The volume of traffic passing in and out of the yard is reflected in its having eight road weighbridges at the street entrances and one wagon weighbridge on the northern side of the yard, next to the H & C lines.

On the *north* side of the main line, and just south of the Grand Junction Canal, was Paddington New Yard, opened in April 1908 on the site of the old (broad gauge) loco sheds, which had been moved to Old Oak Common in 1906. The site of the New Yard was redeveloped to include a new two-storey warehouse just before WWII for the heavy, seasonal perishable goods traffic coming into London (for

A view looking west from behind the H&C Westbourne Park station in 1937, with the backs of houses on Tavistock Crescent to the left. The track from Westbourne Park (Crimea) mileage and hay yard (behind the camera) crossed the H&C on the level to enter the Portobello/St. Ervans yard, but also provided a connection onto some sidings alongside the H&C route to Hammersmith. The H&C signal box is seen behind the GWR siding signal.
NATIONAL RAILWAY MUSEUM

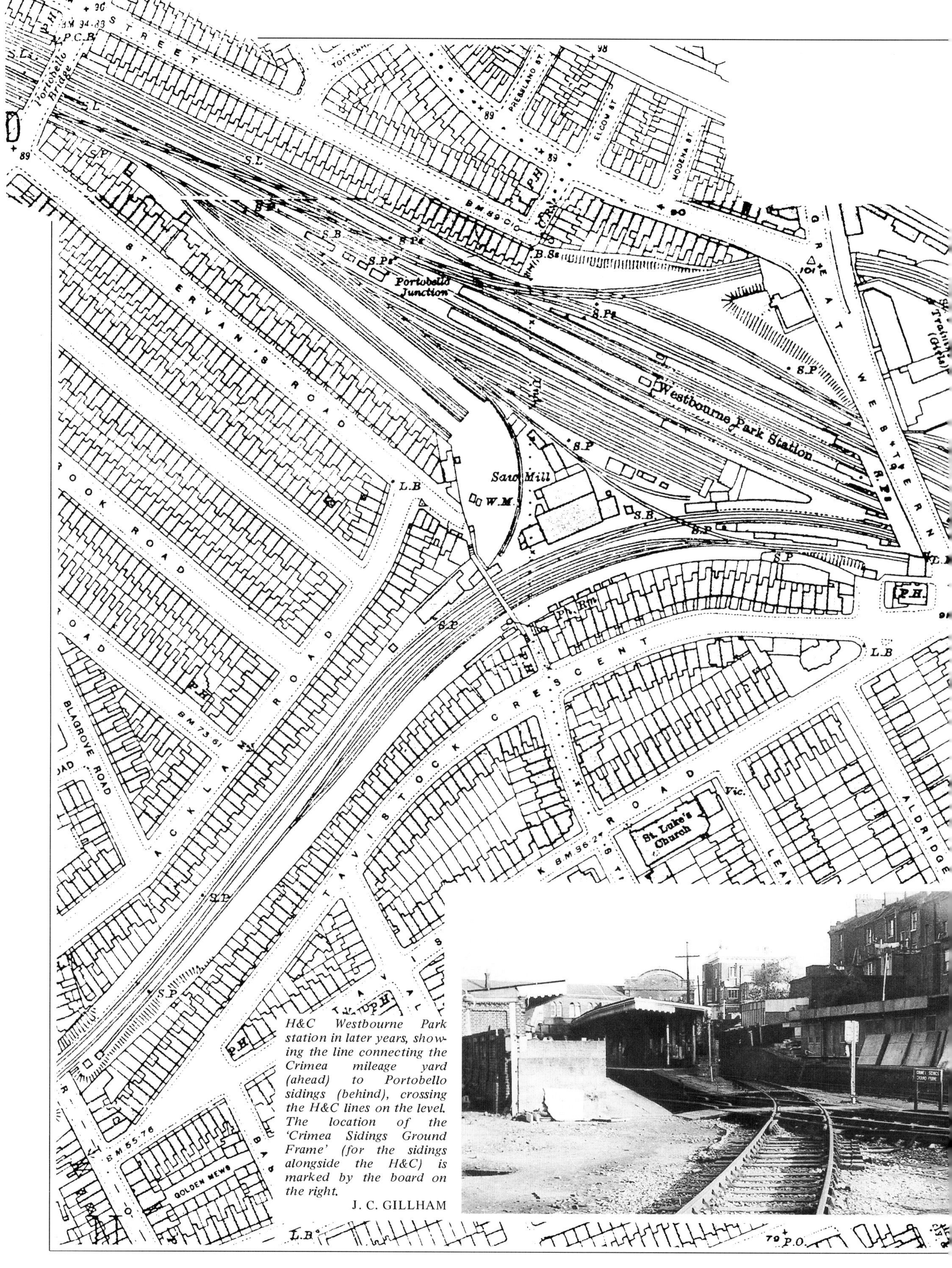

H&C Westbourne Park station in later years, showing the line connecting the Crimea mileage yard (ahead) to Portobello sidings (behind), crossing the H&C lines on the level. The location of the 'Crimea Sidings Ground Frame' (for the sidings alongside the H&C) is marked by the board on the right.

J. C. GILLHAM

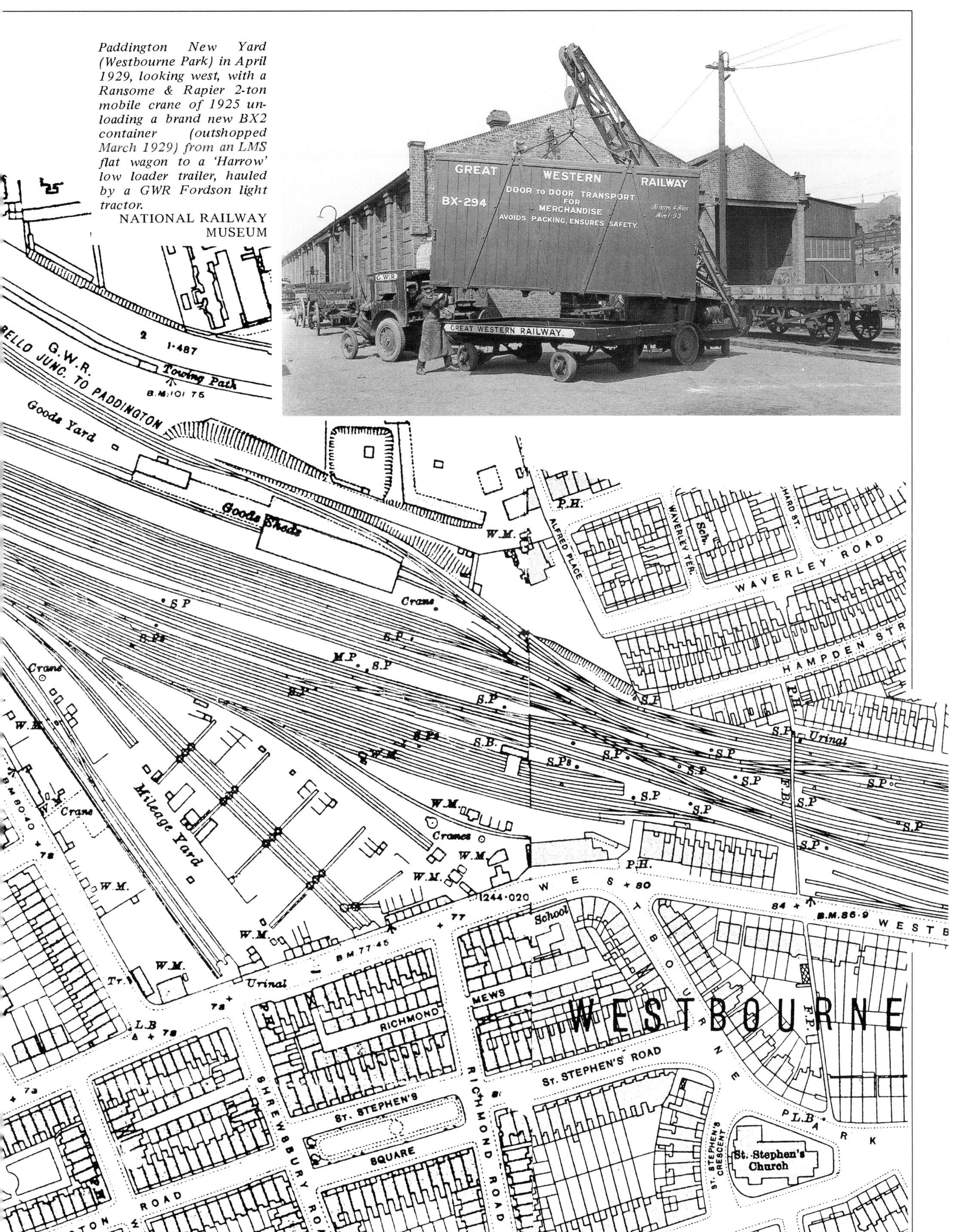

Paddington New Yard (Westbourne Park) in April 1929, looking west, with a Ransome & Rapier 2-ton mobile crane of 1925 unloading a brand new BX2 container (outshopped March 1929) from an LMS flat wagon to a 'Harrow' low loader trailer, hauled by a GWR Fordson light tractor.
NATIONAL RAILWAY MUSEUM

Taken from 25-inch Ordnance Survey for 1914. Crown copyright reserved.

The demolition of Paddington New Yard goods shed in preparation for the building of the Alfred Road depot on the same site, looking south in April 1938. The elusive Crimea Sidings can be seen on the far side of the main line, occupied by numerous private owner wagons. The Westbourne Park station building (GWR and H&C) on Great Western Road is seen on the skyline to the right. The Portobello to Paddington goods relief line features in the foreground.
NATIONAL RAILWAY MUSEUM

Preparation work for the footings of supporting columns at the east end of the new Alfred Road warehouse had been completed in this view of 3rd June 1938. The Charrington's advert on the far side of the tracks, above the sheeted wagon, was on the Westbourne Tavern, whilst the footbridge from which the previous photograph of Subway Jct. (etc) was taken features on the far left, with Subway Jct. signal box in the centre, below St. Stephen's church spire.
NATIONAL RAILWAY MUSEUM

Left: *The framework at the west end of the new Alfred Road warehouse under construction, seen on 3rd June 1938. The usual traffic was still using the yard.* Right: *This new concrete retaining wall and guard rail were constructed behind the Alfred Road building to replace a brick wall and grass embankment. Access to the yard was down the ramp beside the GWR Alfred Road motor repair depot (to the right). The additional goods shed of the Paddington New Yard is seen at the bottom of the ramp, with the new warehouse off to the left.*
NATIONAL RAILWAY MUSEUM

An almost-completed Alfred Road warehouse for seasonal traffic in November 1938. The upper storeys were supported on columns, with the tracks and platforms passing underneath. The rear of the building came right up against the access road with the guard rail, which may be seen through the columns. A notice 'Drivers and others are warned against projecting scaffolding' indicates that construction was still in hand.
NATIONAL RAILWAY MUSEUM

Unloading cardboard boxes from Minsterley Creameries at Alfred Road soon after nationalisation; this shows the postwar practice of unloading directly from wagon to road vehicle (see Cartage volume*) whenever possible. The versatility of the mechanical horse and trailer, and its manoeuvrability, made it a welcome addition to the road fleet.*
NATIONAL RAILWAY MUSEUM

A view westwards from the upper storey of Alfred Road warehouse, with Westbourne Park GWR (right) and H&C (left) station buildings on Great Western Road bridge across the centre of the picture. Crimea mileage yard is again apparent in the top left-hand corner of the photograph, beyond the GWR main lines and the electrified H&C tracks. The line to

example, 1,200 tons/week of broccoli from Cornwall and 600 tons/week from the Worcester district). After these alterations, it became known as the Alfred Road Goods Depot, and shared an entrance with the GWR Motor Repair Garage which had been built on the site of 'Alfred Villa' (formerly the company house for the London Divisional Locomotive Superintendent, located in an elevated position overlooking the area where the BG sheds had been). On this northern boundary of the New Yard was the double-track dedicated goods line, opened in 1880, from Portobello Junction to Paddington Goods, to relieve congestion on the main line approaches. The line passed through the short Cape Horn Tunnel below Great Western Road – a well-known landmark called 'The Mousehole' by enginemen – and remained a through route until the widening of the main lines in 1906 when girder bridges replaced the old arches towards

The southern edge of New Depot yard, looking east towards Paddington, probably in the 1920s, with Subway Jct. box in the centre right of the view. To the right of the cabin, a wide walkway over the depression carrying the H&C tracks afforded access to Crimea yard; this bridge is shown on the OS map (on page 118/9), but was later removed. The end-loading ramp of Paddington New Yard can be seen on the extreme left, whilst Torquay Street footbridge, seen beyond the box, joined that road with Westbourne Park Villas. NATIONAL RAILWAY MUSEUM

The main line at Subway Jct. in 1950, with Alfred Road yard and crane on the left, and Crimea sidings on the right. Torquay Street footbridge still spanned the tracks in the distance, as one does to this day. NATIONAL RAILWAY MUSEUM

A view of St. Ervans siding, looking west towards the Portobello (Golborne Rd.) bridge in 1950. This was the throat of the yard, with Portobello sidings to the right. The engineer in the picture was using the 'Shapman Mains & Service Finder'.
NATIONAL RAILWAY MUSEUM

St. Ervans Road in June 1947, showing the rear and east elevations of Portobello Jct. signal box, on the right. The occasion was a demonstration of modern goods handling equipment to traders and the press, including a Coventry Climax forklift truck with oil drums, and a Foden low-loader on the left, in contrast to a 'high-loaded' horse lorry. Loudspeakers to

The St. Ervans Rd. mileage yard was being used for more 'conventional' tasks in this 1939 picture of a Ransomes & Rapier mobile crane unloading corrugated steel components of Anderson air-raid shelters onto a 'Dyak F' trailer, attached to a 3-ton Scammel.
NATIONAL RAILWAY MUSEUM

Right: *Anderson air-raid shelter components leaving St. Ervans Road mileage sidings on horse-drawn vehicles in April 1939. The rear of houses in St. Ervans Road overlooked the yard.*
NATIONAL RAILWAY MUSEUM

Below: *The entrance to the Portobello/St. Ervans Road yard was located at the south-eastern end of St. Ervans Road, with a cart weighbridge and office just inside the yard. Here, the yard office at the end of the houses at the entrance can be seen.*
NATIONAL RAILWAY MUSEUM

addington. The sidings at the Mousehole emained – albeit truncated – until 1967, erving Alfred Road Depot.

On the *south* side of Westbourne Park ation, to the west, was the Portobello ard, situated opposite the signal box. To dd to the confusion, part of this yard was lso known as St. Ervans Road Goods. It as the location for many of the Great Vestern's official photographs showing oods operations, and may be recognised y the backs of the tall terraced houses, e.g. e view of the Ransomes & Rapier crane nloading Anderson Air Raid Shelters. The ard was equipped with a 12-ton weighridge at the entrance from St Ervans oad, near the footbridge, and a 30-cwt rane. At the south end of the footbridge as the road entrance to the Tavistock Crescent Hay Bank, which formed part of e Crimea sidings.

BRENTFORD DEPOTS

Brentford, on the branch from Southall, dated from 1865. Originally, the goods facilities at the docks on the Thames dealt with local traffic at a dedicated goods shed with a small yard, as well as transit goods and minerals to and from the East London Docks and other waterside venues. The goods shed was located to the north of the basin, near to the northern edge of the site, alongside the grain warehouse.

However, the volume of docks traffic became so great during and after WWI that new riverside and basin extension work required all the available space within the area, and the town's goods facilities were therefore rebuilt on the far (Southall) side of the passenger station. In November 1930, the separate goods shed and yard (Brentford Town Goods) was opened adjacent to the A4 for local goods.

Brentford dealt with around 400,000 tons per annum in Edwardian times, rising to 600,000 tons in the late 1930s.

The riverside facilities at Brentford will be dealt with in detail in the *Docks & Marine* volume of this series.

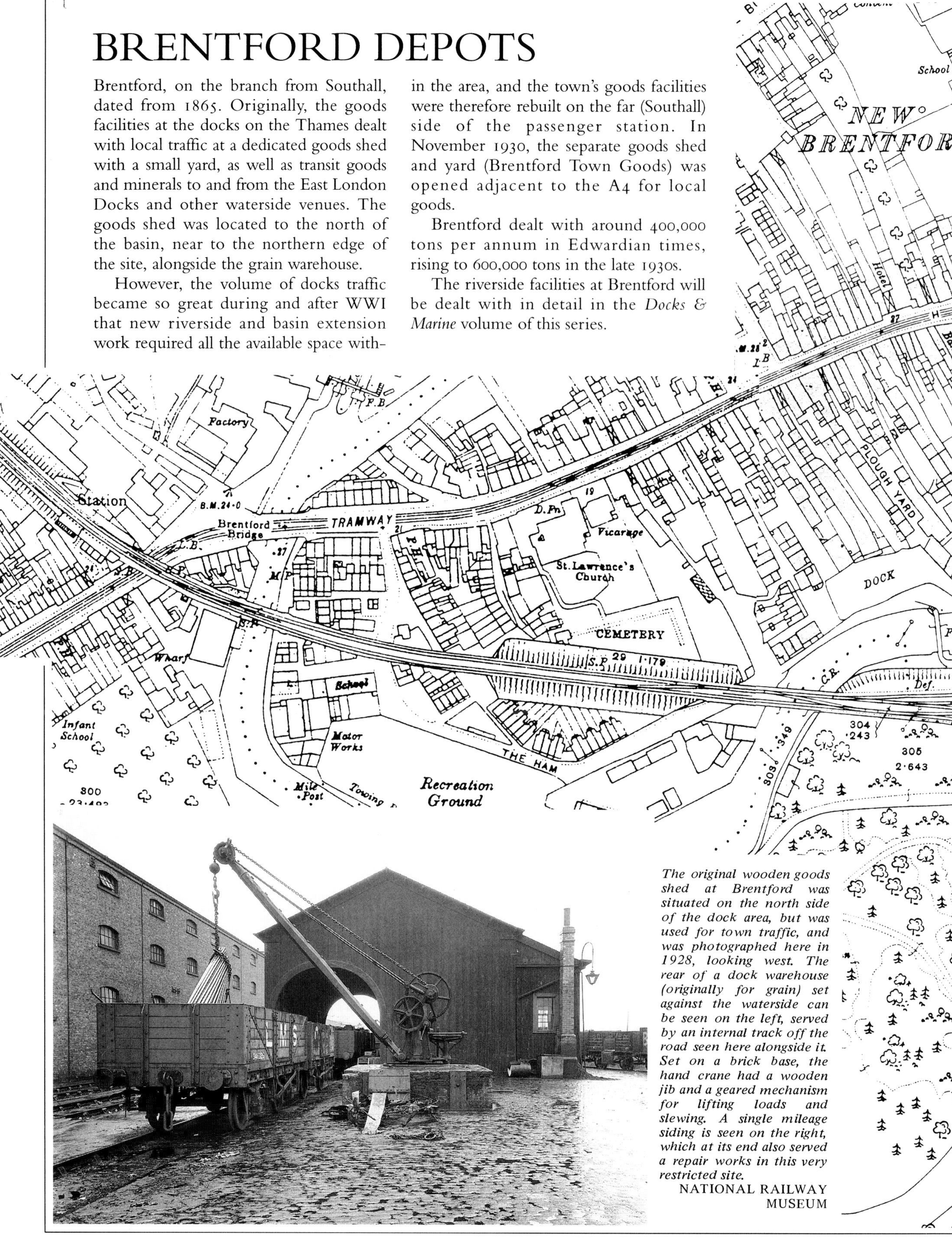

The original wooden goods shed at Brentford was situated on the north side of the dock area, but was used for town traffic, and was photographed here in 1928, looking west. The rear of a dock warehouse (originally for grain) set against the waterside can be seen on the left, served by an internal track off the road seen here alongside it. Set on a brick base, the hand crane had a wooden jib and a geared mechanism for lifting loads and slewing. A single mileage siding is seen on the right, which at its end also served a repair works in this very restricted site.
NATIONAL RAILWAY MUSEUM

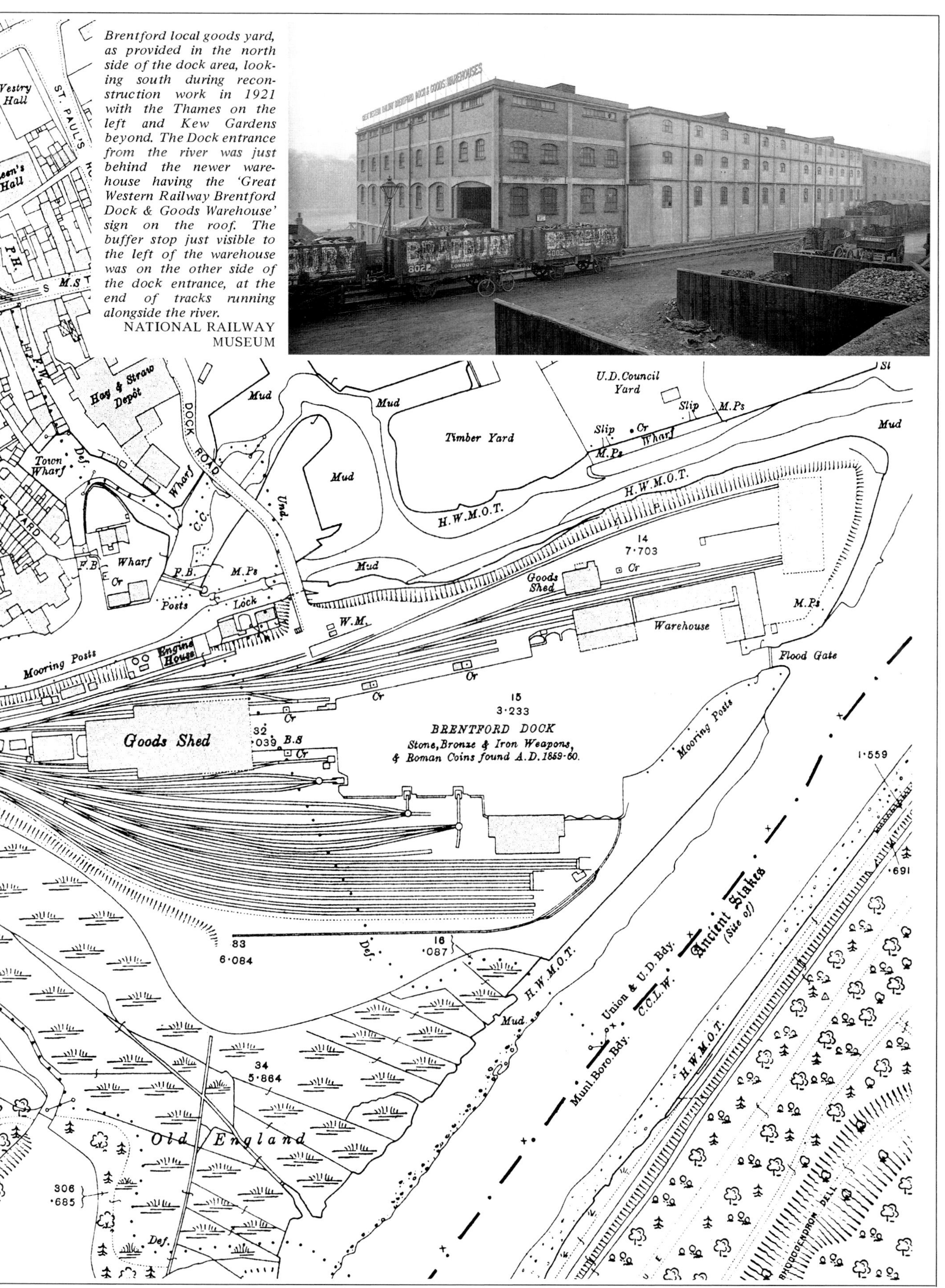

Brentford local goods yard, as provided in the north side of the dock area, looking south during reconstruction work in 1921 with the Thames on the left and Kew Gardens beyond. The Dock entrance from the river was just behind the newer warehouse having the 'Great Western Railway Brentford Dock & Goods Warehouse' sign on the roof. The buffer stop just visible to the left of the warehouse was on the other side of the dock entrance, at the end of tracks running alongside the river.
NATIONAL RAILWAY MUSEUM

Taken from 25-inch Ordnance Survey for 1915. Crown copyright reserved.

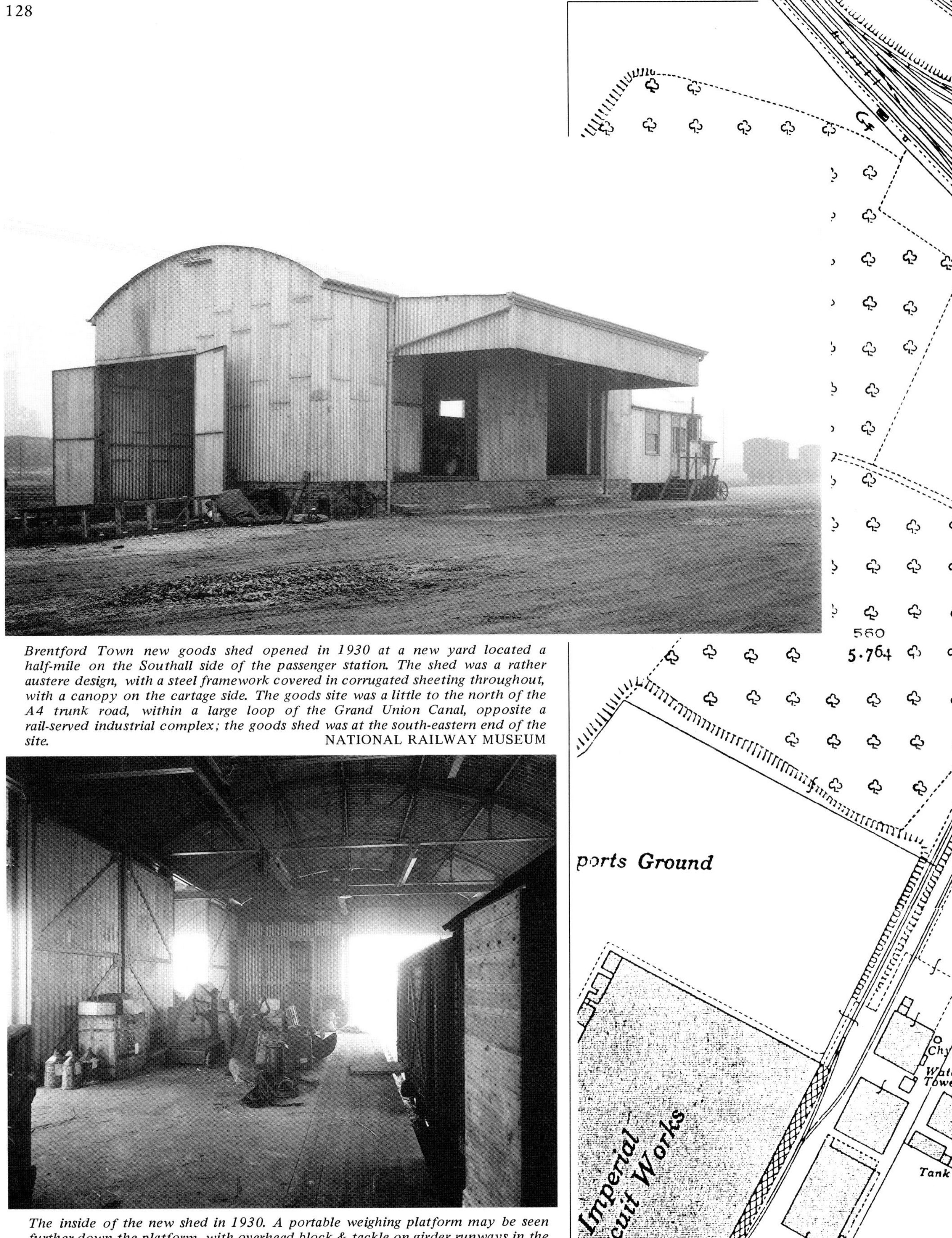

Brentford Town new goods shed opened in 1930 at a new yard located a half-mile on the Southall side of the passenger station. The shed was a rather austere design, with a steel framework covered in corrugated sheeting throughout, with a canopy on the cartage side. The goods site was a little to the north of the A4 trunk road, within a large loop of the Grand Union Canal, opposite a rail-served industrial complex; the goods shed was at the south-eastern end of the site. NATIONAL RAILWAY MUSEUM

The inside of the new shed in 1930. A portable weighing platform may be seen further down the platform, with overhead block & tackle on girder runways in the roof space for lifting, and a slatted 'lock-up' at the rear for more valuable items. Note the well-worn board in use to bridge the gap between the van and platform, for sack trucks. NATIONAL RAILWAY MUSEUM

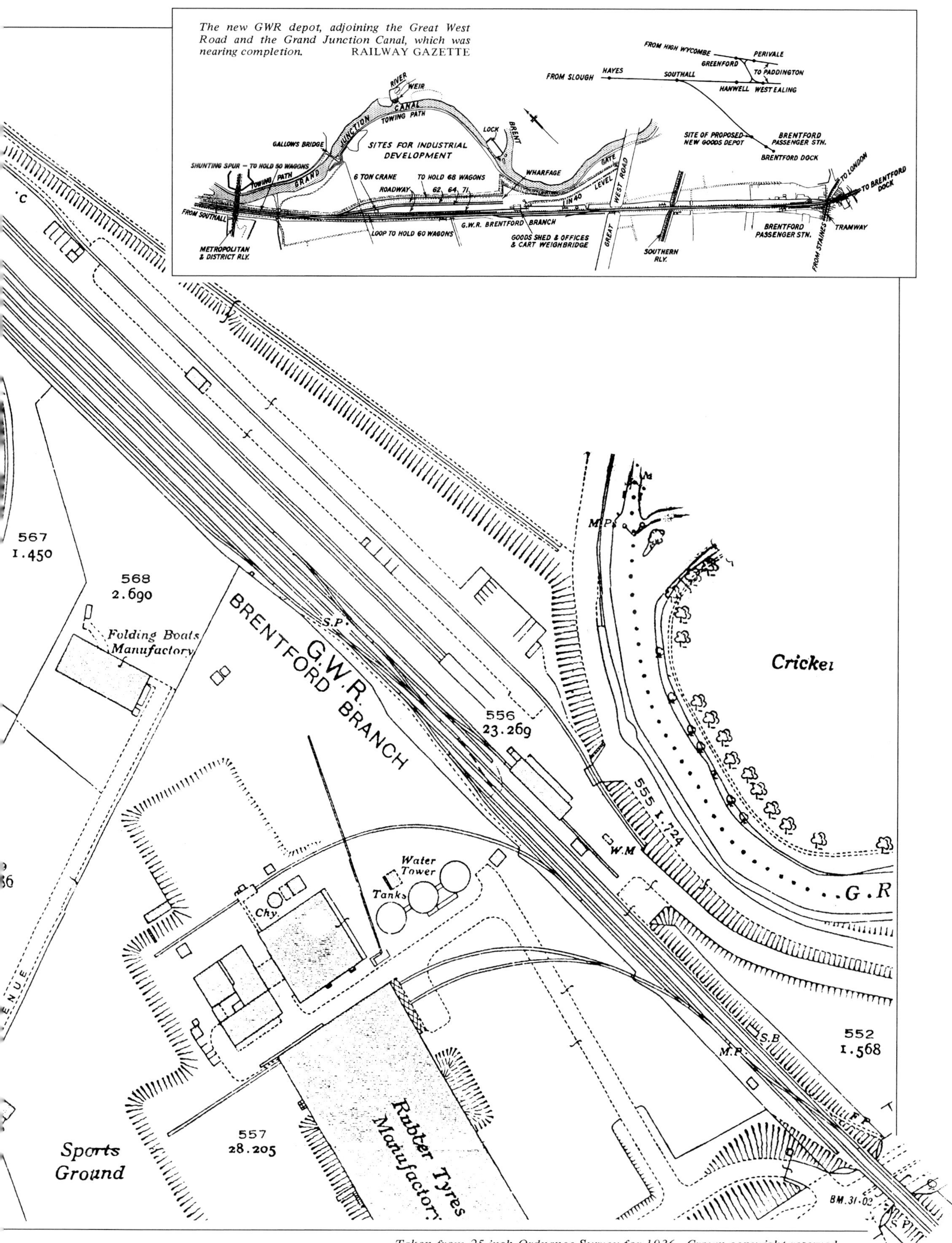
The new GWR depot, adjoining the Great West Road and the Grand Junction Canal, which was nearing completion. RAILWAY GAZETTE
FROM HIGH WYCOMBE
PERIVALE
GREENFORD
TO PADDINGTON
FROM SLOUGH
HAYES
SOUTHALL
HANWELL
WEST EALING
SITE OF PROPOSED NEW GOODS DEPOT
BRENTFORD PASSENGER STN.
BRENTFORD DOCK
RIVER
WEIR
GRAND JUNCTION CANAL
TOWING PATH
LOCK
BRENT
GALLOWS BRIDGE
SITES FOR INDUSTRIAL DEVELOPMENT
SHUNTING SPUR – TO HOLD 50 WAGONS
6 TON CRANE
TO HOLD 68 WAGONS
ROADWAY
62
64
71
WHARFAGE
GATE
LEVEL
GREAT WEST ROAD
TO LONDON
TO BRENTFORD DOCK
FROM SOUTHALL
METROPOLITAN & DISTRICT RLY.
LOOP TO HOLD 60 WAGONS
G.W.R. BRENTFORD BRANCH
GOODS SHED & OFFICES & CART WEIGHBRIDGE
SOUTHERN RLY.
BRENTFORD PASSENGER STN.
TRAMWAY
FROM STAINES
567
1.450
568
2.690
Folding Boats Manufactory
G.W.R. BRENTFORD BRANCH
S.P.
556
23.269
M.P.
Cricket
555
1.724
W.M
Water Tower
Tanks
Chy.
G.R
552
1.568
S.B
M.P.
F.P.
BM.31.02
S.P.
Rubber Tyres Manufactory
557
28.205
Sports Ground
ENUE

Taken from 25-inch Ordnance Survey for 1936. Crown copyright reserved.

A panoramic view of the new mileage yard at Brentford on 8th September 1931, with three mileage roads at the rear, and two shed/reception roads in the foreground, against the double-track branch; the signal at centre left was located just beyond the Down branch line. A considerable number of coal pitches ('wharfage' on inset map on page 129) was located between the two far sidings, but lorries behind the signal were being loaded directly from the wagons on the third line. GWR loco coal wagons were also being used for domestic coal. The end-loading ramp for two tracks is seen on the right, with the goods shed just out of picture to the right, and the Grand Junction Canal looping around in the distance.

NATIONAL RAILWAY MUSEUM

CANNOCK CHASE
COWLEY
BRYNNA
ANTHRACITE
CHARRINGTONS
LMS

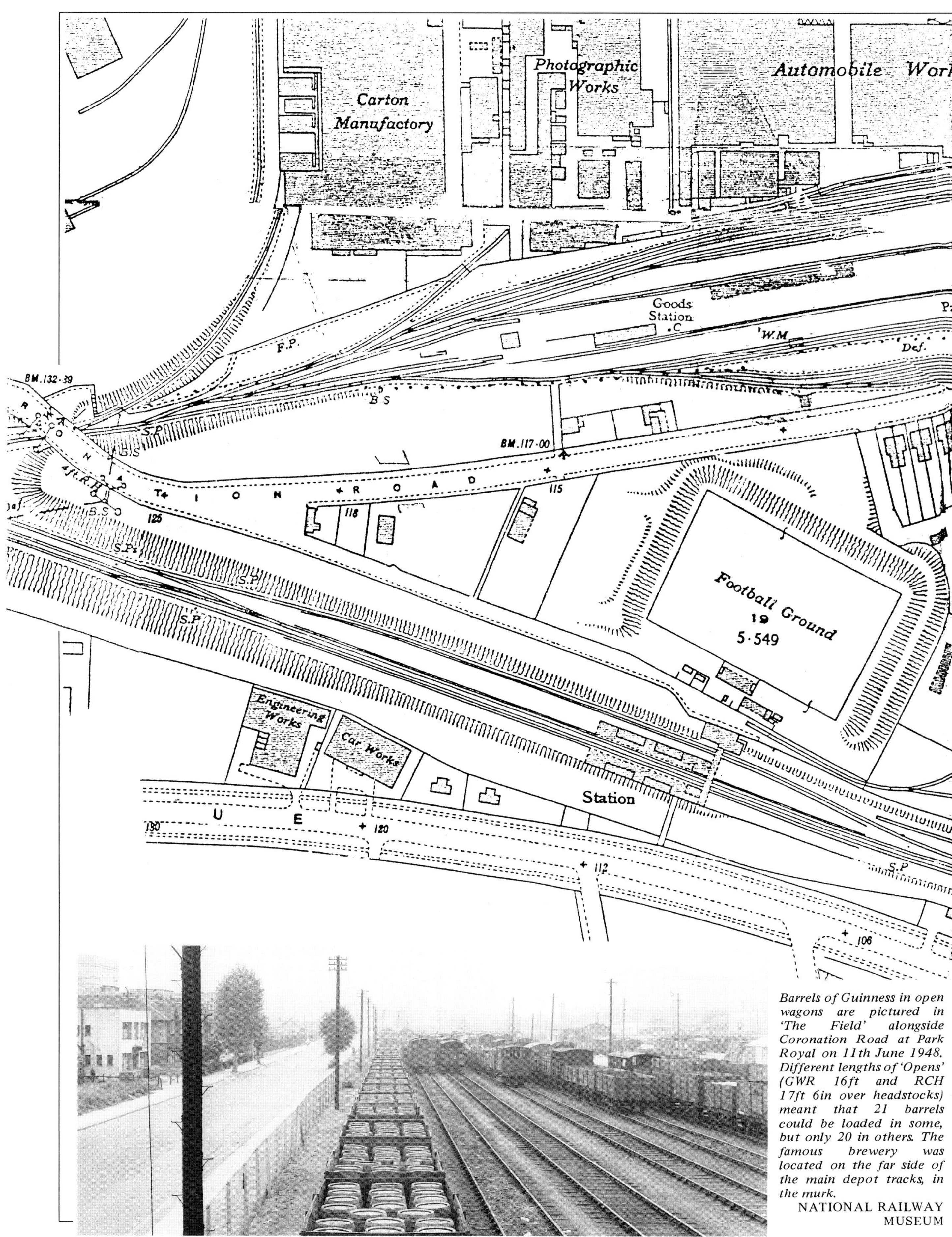

Barrels of Guinness in open wagons are pictured in 'The Field' alongside Coronation Road at Park Royal on 11th June 1948. Different lengths of 'Opens' (GWR 16ft and RCH 17ft 6in over headstocks) meant that 21 barrels could be loaded in some, but only 20 in others. The famous brewery was located on the far side of the main depot tracks, in the murk.

NATIONAL RAILWAY MUSEUM

PARK ROYAL

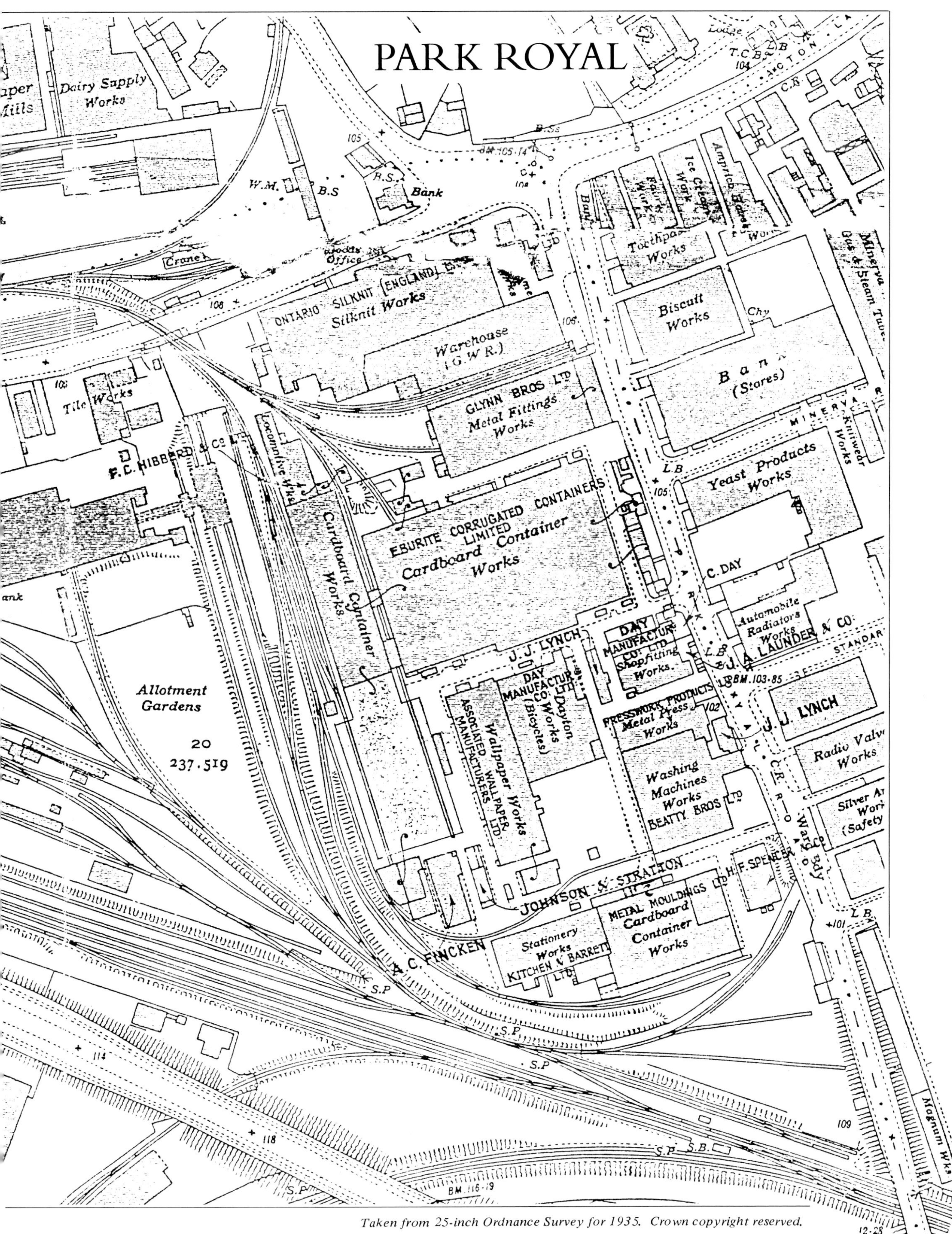

Taken from 25-inch Ordnance Survey for 1935. Crown copyright reserved.

Looking south-westwards from the goods depot area towards the Coronation Road bridge, where shunting was taking place on the throat of the estate lines. The debris scattered along the line may have been the result of a bad shunt, with perhaps an insurance claim in the offing.
NATIONAL RAILWAY MUSEUM

Park Royal goods shed and platform, 1936, looking south-west. The shed was virtually surrounded by estate buildings, and much of its business was probably concerned with those companies whose premises were not connected by rail.
NATIONAL RAILWAY MUSEUM

The 30-cwt crane at Park Royal, just outside the goods shed. It was worked from the goods platform by a long loop of chain around a large wheel, with various gearing levers involved. Slewing appears to have been by rope attached near to the top of the jib. Again, the curved jib prevented fouling against sides of taller rail vehicles.
COLLECTION J. SCOTT-MORGAN

addition to its goods connections for ie surrounding communities in ricklewood, Neasden and Wembley, ark Royal was the location for the WR Trading Estate. The line from hich the facilities were served – the cton & Wycombe Railway (GWR) – as constructed in sections, with the first, om Old Oak to Park Royal, opened in ne 1903. At first, it was more associated ith its role as the headquarters of the oyal Agricultural Society, with extensive ow facilities provided. However, upon e spectacular failure of its Royal Shows, e RAS horse ring gave way to football – particular, Queen's Park Rangers, who oved from their ancestral home in ensal Rise to the Park Royal site in 904.

The extensive showgrounds, connect- d as they were to the railway, provided an xcellent venue for light industrial use, id by the 1920s such companies as J. Lyons & Co., with their confectionery business, were established. Also on the site at that time (and after) were Mono Service Containers Ltd (containers for foodstuffs); R.H. Neal (builders materials); Walter Scott & Middleton Ltd (contractors materials); Hall, Lewis & Co. (wagon repairing materials); St. Martins Preserving Co. (jam factory); William Kayley (scrap iron), and the Guinness Brewery as well as many others.

Park Royal Goods sat centrally within the southern part of the industrial complex, reached by the spur running to the north of the main lines which also served the estate companies.

A view down one of the side roads in the GW Park Royal trading estate leading west from the main Park Royal Road, in 1951, with J. J. Lynch and the Daytona works on the left, and Eburite on the right. Park Royal Road was behind the camera. The sign 'GWR Caution Buried Electric Cables' outside the small Eburite office indicates the company's involvement.
NATIONAL RAILWAY MUSEUM

Part of the Park Royal estate system from Coronation Road level crossing gates in 1951, looking east. The small loco shed features centre right, with the bunker of an engine visible. From 1926-1946, a GWR Sentinel patent geared steam shunting engine No. 13 was employed here, and at the Lyons factory at Greenford.
NATIONAL RAILWAY MUSEUM

The road entrance to the Guinness factory at Park Royal on 29th May 1946 (off top left-hand edge of OS map). The repair of the level crossing had recently taken place.
NATIONAL RAILWAY MUSEUM

Outside the Guinness factory on 29th May 1946, with the shunter demonstrating how road traffic was stopped for the passage of trains. The notice in the centre of the road island reads 'Main gate locked while trains are passing level crossing'.
NATIONAL RAILWAY MUSEUM

Two more views of the level crossings outside the Guinness and Mono Containers factories, showing the arrangement of road and rail. In the lower picture, an L&NE high-sided sleeper wagon loaded with barrels was emerging from the factory rail access, chalked with the shortened destination 'GUIN'. NATIONAL RAILWAY MUSEUM

SMITHFIELD

Smithfield GWR goods depot, dating from 1869, was situated beneath the new Central Meat Market, and was reached via the underground lines (the mixed gauge of the Metropolitan Railway became standard gauge in 1869 when through Great Western passenger trains were withdrawn). The GW and Metropolitan Railways contributed towards the construction of the depot and paid rent thereafter (£1,000 each per annum originally), on a 100-year lease, to the Corporation of London, who had built the new market. Instead of slaughtering animals on site as previously, that market was moved to Islington, and dead meat was now brought into Smithfield having been slaughtered elsewhere (either locally as at Deptford, for example, or imported locally (V & A Docks), or from far-away places such as Birkenhead, New Milford and later Fishguard).

Goods trains to Smithfield travelled from Paddington to just west of Farringdon Street station, thence to Aldersgate Street station over the (up) 'widened lines' (which were at a lower level than what later became the Circle line) where they set back into the reception lines for the goods depot; this was situated on the south-east side of the 'Snow Hill' spur to Holborn Viaduct. Down goods trains (back to Paddington) crossed this spur on the level and rejoined the Metropolitan main line west of Farringdon Street station.

Smithfield goods served not only the meat market, but was also the depot for ordinary goods traffic for Central London and the City; other railways (Midland & Great Northern) had goods depots in this congested area. As an example of its traffic, the two special linoleum wagons (diagram O6/7 of 1905 and 1890 respectively) were marked 'To run between Staines and Smithfield only'.

All traffic for Smithfield had to be loaded in 4-wheeled vacuum-braked vehicles (maximum length 25 vehicles plus 'Toad', worked by condensing locos) and no dangerous goods were permitted. Trading in the meat market began at 4.0 a.m., so many of the trains from Acton arrived in the early hours of the morning.

The cramped goods depot was about 600ft long by 250ft wide. There were four main sidings parallel to the widened lines,

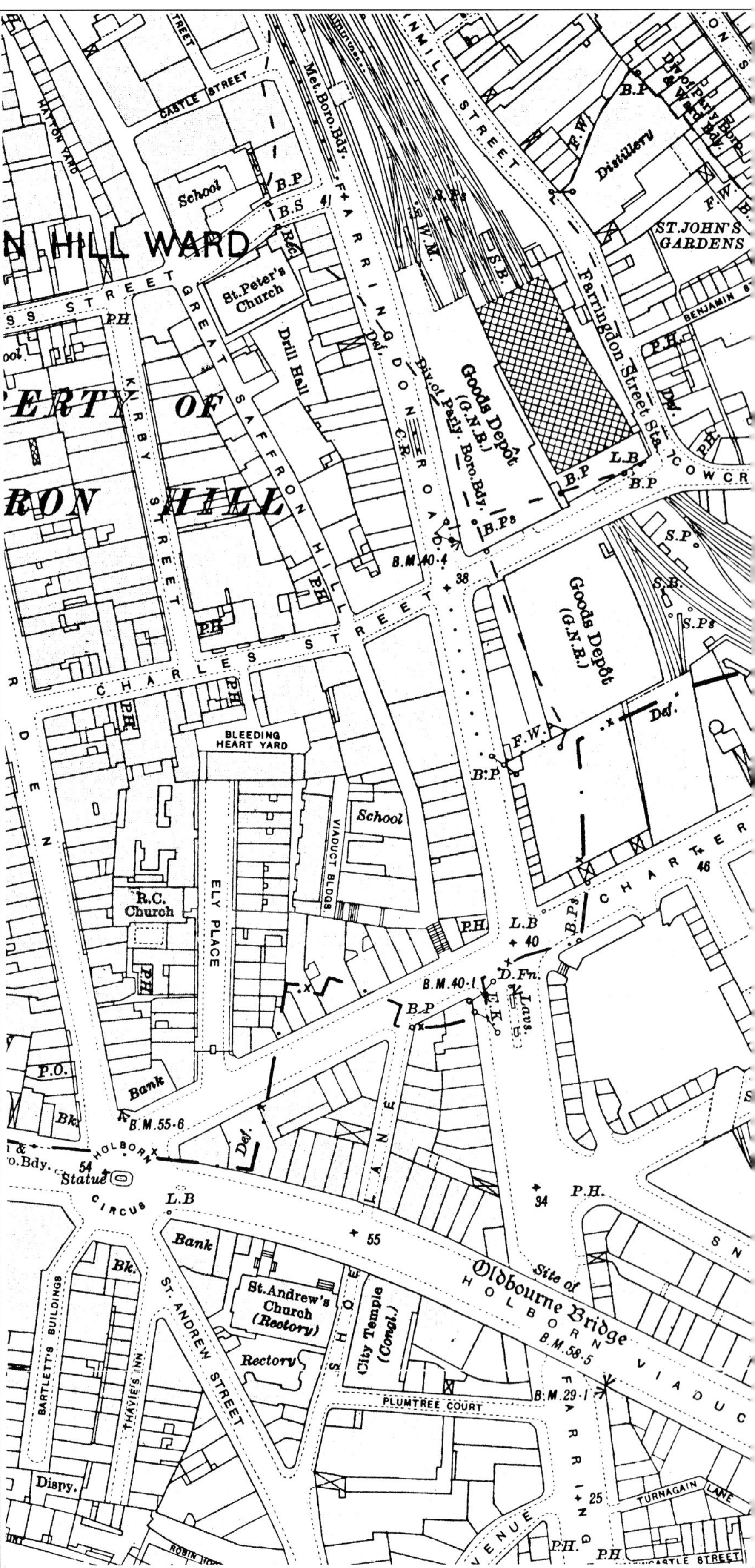

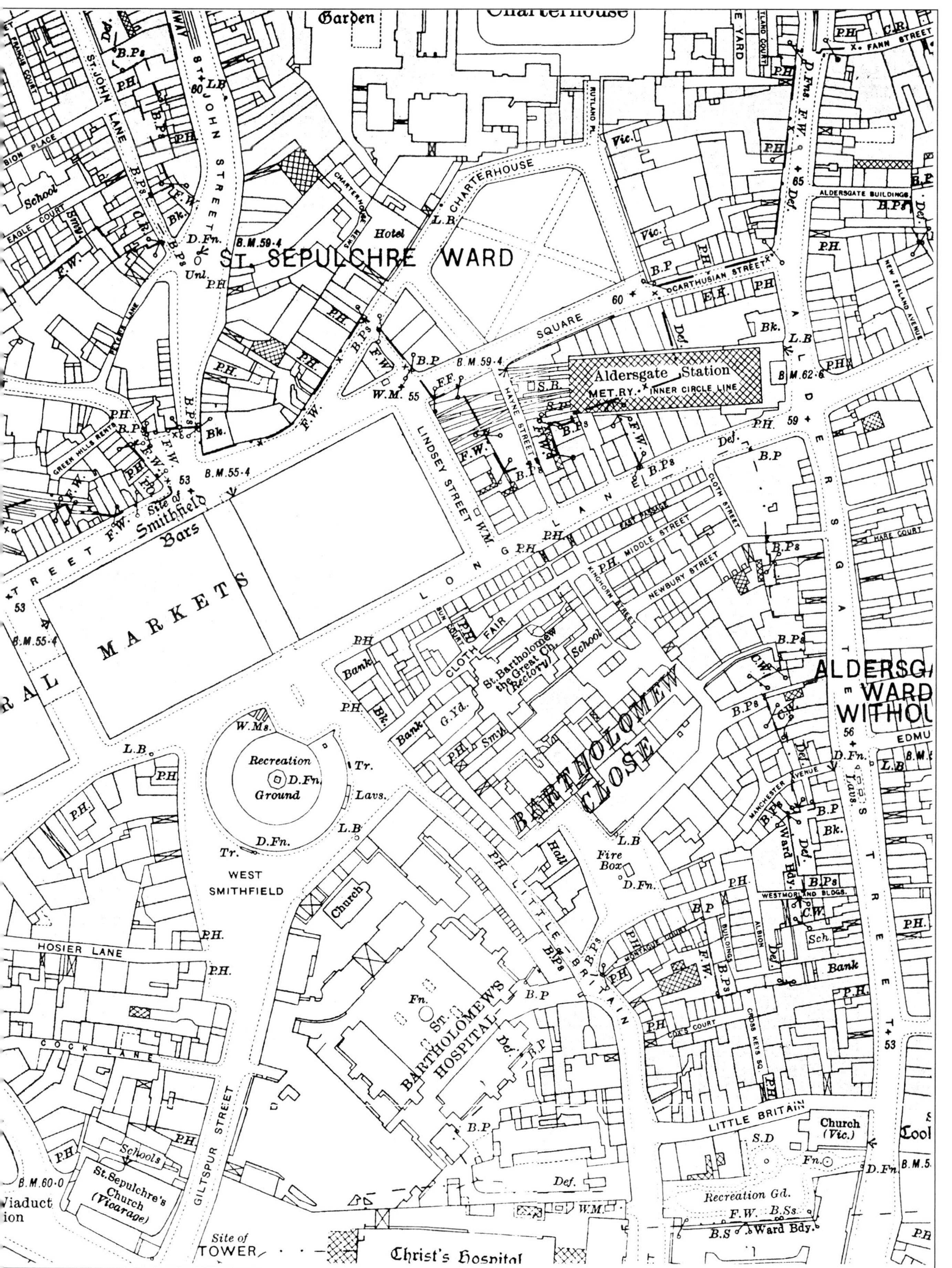

Taken from 25-inch Ordnance Survey for 1916. Crown copyright reserved.

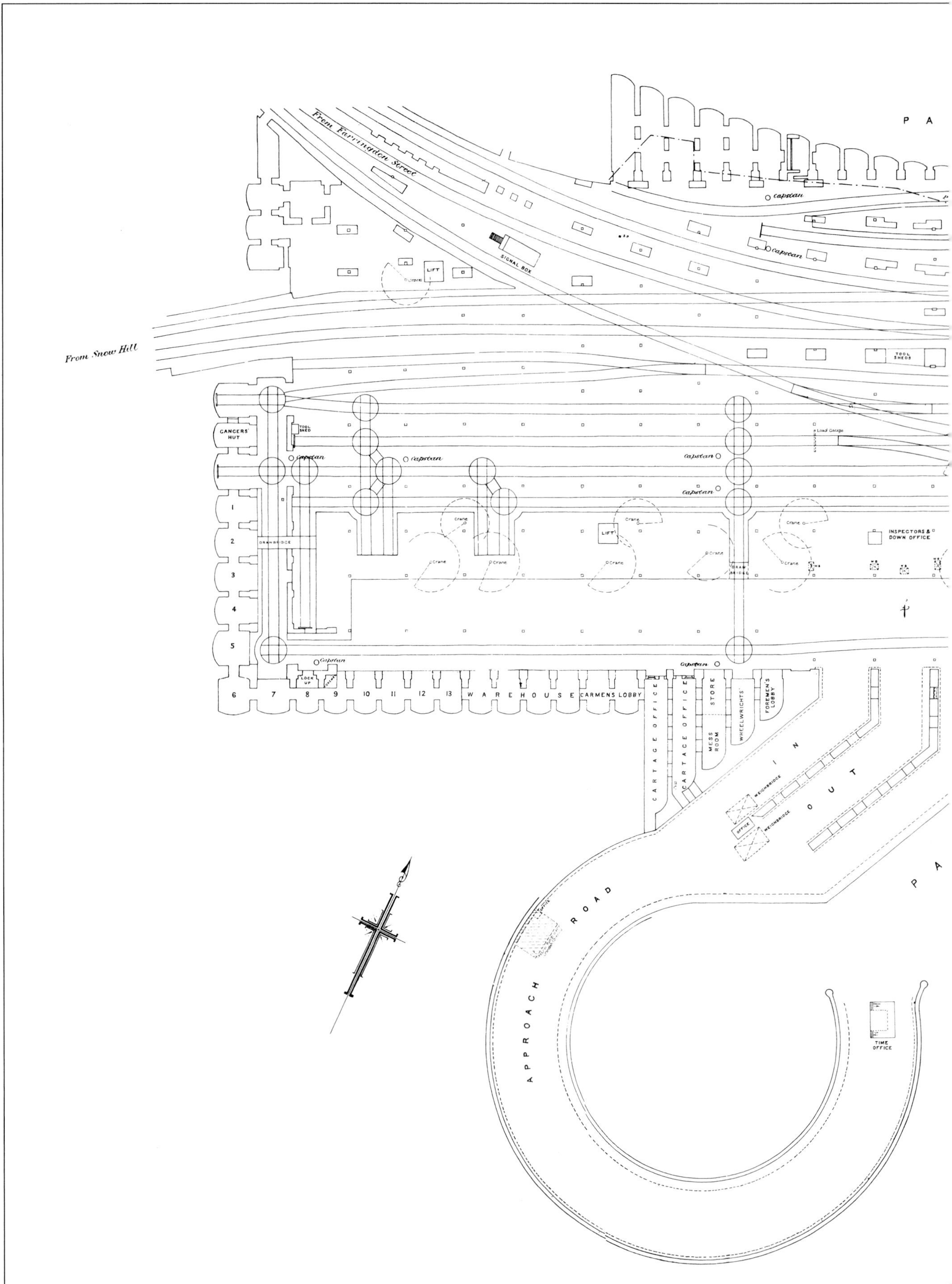
From Farringdon Street
From Snow Hill
SIGNAL BOX
LIFT
Capstan
TOOL SHEDS
GANGERS' HUT
TOOL SHED
Crane
DRAWBRIDGE
INSPECTORS & DOWN OFFICE
Load Gauge
LOCK UP
WAREHOUSE
CARMENS LOBBY
CARTAGE OFFICE
STORE
MESS ROOM
WHEELWRIGHTS
FOREMEN'S LOBBY
IN
OUT
WEIGHBRIDGE
OFFICE
APPROACH ROAD
TIME OFFICE
1
2
3
4
5
6
7
8
9
10
11
12
13

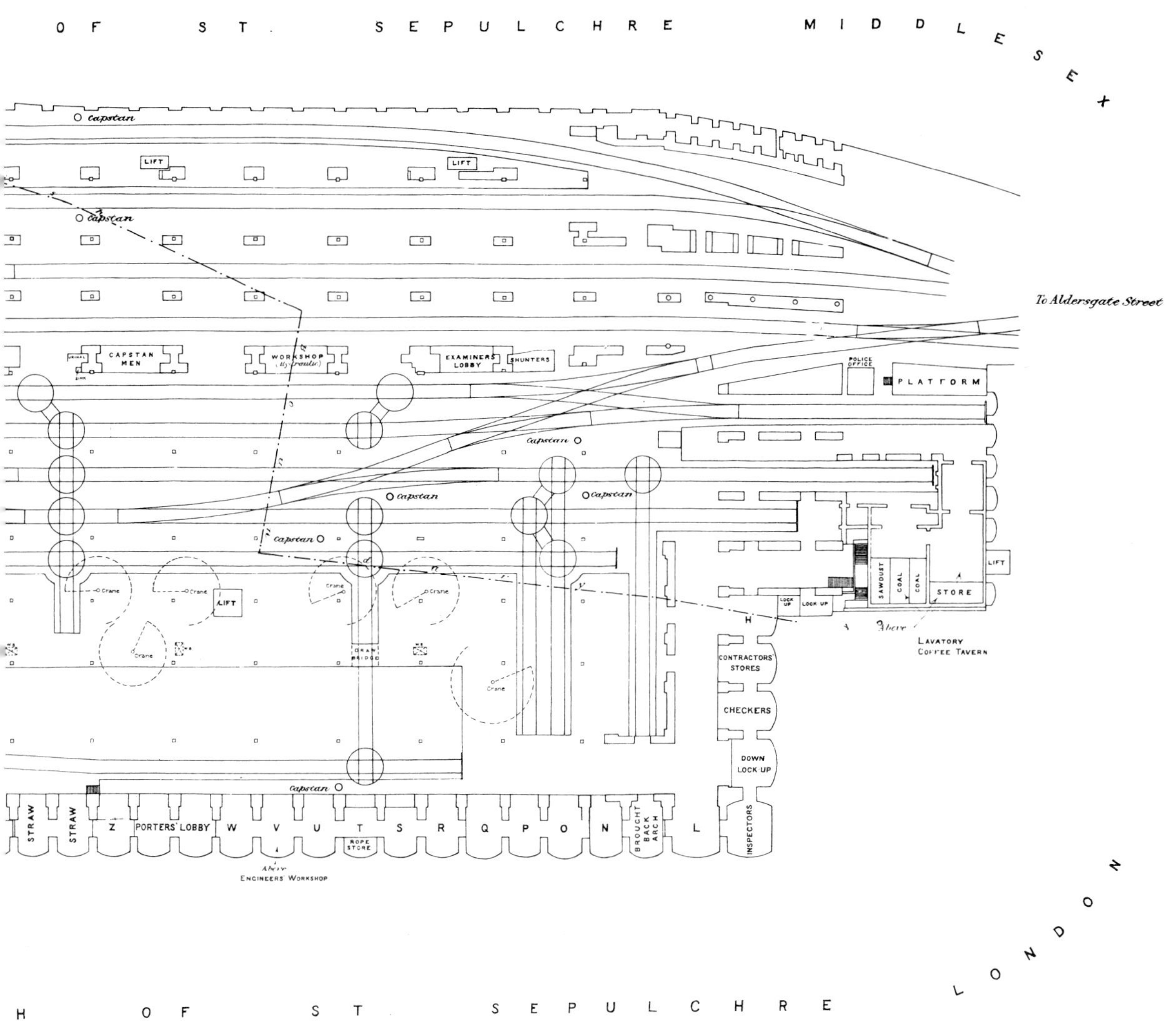

G. W. R. Smithfield Depôt.

— Scale of Feet —

Feet 10 0 50 100 150 200 250 300 Feet

An aerial view of Smithfield Central Meat Market in 1953, looking south-east towards the Thames, with St. Paul's cathedral at the top of the picture, and the Central Markets in the centre of the view. The canopies of Farringdon station can be seen at the bottom, below the right-hand end of the markets, with the ex-GNR goods depot adjacent, above and to the right, facing onto Farringdon Road. Aldersgate & Barbican station is seen at the extreme left of the picture, round the curve under the corner of the market. The GWR Smithfield depot was on the outside of this curve, under the market, and was reached by the road circling the recreation ground in the centre of the picture, immediately beyond the Central Markets. SIMMONS AEROFILMS

The corner of the end of the 1881 extension to the market buildings, looking south along to Farringdon Road at the extreme left of the picture. The diagonal covered way crossed Long Lane near the Union cold store at the King Street/Central Markets/Snow Hill triangle (just out of picture to the left). Photographed on 15th October 1938, after reconstruction work shown in the accompanying photographs. The former dining rooms on the corner under the awning in the adjacent picture were now occupied by meat wholesalers. NATIONAL RAILWAY MUSEUM

aced along which were some two dozen agon turntables. The goods platform had number of bays at right-angles to the sidigs into which wagons could be berthed sing capstans and reels (horse-powered riginally). Seventy-four wagons could be ealt with at any one time, and a further 24 ept in adjacent sidings. The roof was low; ven so, a 6-ton crane was provided, but mber, iron bars and girders, etc. longer an 18ft were not accepted, nor were furiture vans, containers, portable engines, c.

Entry by road was at the level of the acks, below the meat market, and ordiary goods were carted in the usual way a a circular access road under the market. ll other railway companies carted their eat in by road. To get meat carcasses up the market from the GWR depot, ydraulic lifts were employed; there was rovision for four, but only two were built, easuring 15ft square. The Metropolitan ailway also originally had two goods atforms, one behind the Smithfield larket Signal Box and the other squeezed etween the Circle and widened lines, oth with appropriate hydraulic cranage nd hoists. The Great Western kept such quipment up to date: new cart weighidges were installed on the circular cess road in 1935.

The reconstruction of the Snow Hill spur to Aldersgate & Barbican, March 1938, taken in the 'hole'. The decorated tower on the right is the south-western corner of the original 1869 market buildings, whilst the corner of the building with awning at centre left is the 1881 extension to the market building. The back of the Union Cold Storage Co. is seen at the right (the front of this building faces King Street). The contractor's rail-mounted crane at street level was in front of the 'Goodfare Dining Rooms'.

The installation of girders over the 'hole' to carry the roadway at the Long Lane/King Street intersection, seen on 1st April 1938. The narrow end of the Union cold store features on the left, and the 1881 building to the right. Many Smithfield-design meat barrows are seen standing round and about.

NATIONAL RAILWAY MUSEUM

ooking north along the Snow Hill spur on 29th April 1938, with the original market buildings to the right, below the girder crossing the top of he picture. The 1881 building and awnings are seen at right centre, with the roof of the diagonal covered way in the centre, going left. Snow Hill/ Iolborn Viaduct were behind the camera. The line ahead led to Farringdon station, and the tracks to the left led to the ex-GNR depot.

NATIONAL RAILWAY MUSEUM

A view into the GWR depot unde Smithfield (Aldersgate & Barbican i behind the camera, and the doubl crossover just inside the depot) on 11th January 1946. Lindsey Street (above) at the east end of the markets, wa damaged and open to the sky.
NATIONAL RAILWAY MUSEUM

Stations and Depots.	Accommodation.	Invoicing and Forwarding.
SMITHFIELD. (The Station for CITY traffic, reached over Metropolitan Railway, via Bishop's Road.)	General traffic, for delivery by cart. *See* pages 46 to 62. Traffic for Central Meat Market for delivery by hydraulic lift. The following descriptions of traffic **must not be accepted** for conveyance to Smithfield :— (*a*) Dangerous goods of any description. (*b*) Boilers and single pieces of Machinery, or any article weighing more than 6 tons. (*c*) Timber, Bar Iron, Girder Work, and similar traffic more than 18 feet long, and traffic in 6-wheeled trucks. (*d*) Furniture Vans, Portable Engines, and similar articles, on wheels. Senders tendering such traffic must be informed that there is no accommodation for it at this station, but that it can be dealt with at Paddington, Poplar, or South Lambeth. The following descriptions of traffic **must not be accepted** for conveyance to Smithfield, **except by special arrangement** :— (*a*) Traffic for which exceptional rates are in operation at Paddington, Poplar, or South Lambeth, but not at Smithfield. (*b*) Station to Station traffic. All traffic intended for through transit to Smithfield Station must be loaded in VACUUM FITTED Stock, not exceeding 16 feet in length between headstocks.	Invoice and label direct, and send invoices with Goods. The route from Bishop's Road to Smithfield is via the Metropolitan Railway. Abstract traffic as "Local."
SMITHFIELD (contd.)	The Station is situate under the Central Meat Market, with which it is connected by means of hydraulic lifts, enabling a prompt and direct delivery to be made of all meat and poultry traffic, consigned to the market via the Great Western Railway, without intermediate cartage. Being in the centre of London, it also affords to freighters a convenient depot for general traffic. The warehouse accommodation at Smithfield is not extensive, and, before dispatching large or bulky consignments, to wait order, the Agent must be communicated with. This restriction does not apply to Meat, Butter, Poultry, Eggs, or similar market traffic. Weighbridge, for Road Vehicles, is provided. Crane Power, 6 tons	

The space available for manoeuvring wagons at the cramped Smithfield underground depot was limited, so there was a complicated system of wagon turntables, capstans, and reels (with tops painted white) in a very restricted area. The Aldersgate end of the depot to the left went under Lindsey Street to the five-storey GWR warehouse (1914) that faced Hayne Street. Long Lane is behind and above in this picture taken in July 1941.
NATIONAL RAILWAY MUSEUM

The road entrance from the circular recreation ground descended from street level to the rail level of the GWR depot beneath the market. The windows on the left were of the cartage office, whilst the adjacent invoicing and other offices remained in stygian gloom! Cart weighbridges for road vehicles entering and leaving the depot were to both sides of the central wooden cabin. J. J. SMITH

Smithfield meat trains ran from Acton over the electric lines passing under Westbourne bridge, as seen here in the 1930s, with Paddington Goods yard behind. The train then entered Bishop's Road platforms and continued on the underground to Smithfield. Condensing pannier No. 9710 carried automatic clip-up apparatus for the ATC shoe when running over electric lines. The trains carried a local headcode of two lamps, one above the other, and the maximum number of vans allowed was twenty, plus a short wheelbase (Dia AA7) 'Toad'

Two views of the lifts by which the meat unloaded from the 'Mica' meat vans underground at Smithfield were taken up to the central meat market, taken in 1926; no guard rails were provided around the lift platform. The meat porter's 'uniforms' were very distinctive. A GWR checker with tripod desk can be seen in the lower picture. NATIONAL RAILWAY MUSEUM

Smithfield handled 200,000 tons of all goods annually in the first quarter of the 20th century, of which some 70,000 tons vas inwards, and of that, over 10,000 tons vent up to the market. In 1925, over one-and-a-quarter million goods consignments vere dealt with. The average weight of a ide of beef is about 3cwt, and gangs of hree or four specialist porters manhandled he meat from the railway vans to the lifts, each of which had an effective capacity of about 100–120 sides of beef per hour. The ifty vans of a Birkenhead meat train, each containing an average of ten sides, could be unshipped in around two hours using both lifts. In addition to beef, crated pigs, calves, heep, rabbits, poultry and eggs were egularly dealt with.

As well as general goods, fruit and vegetables were also taken to Smithfield goods.

Meat bought in the market for resale around the GWR system outside London

A side of beef arriving on the lift at market level. There were gates and walls around the lift at this level to isolate the hole in the floor. Pig carcasses are seen hanging on both sides.
NATIONAL RAILWAY MUSEUM

Smithfield market traders photographed in 1954, when meat rationing ended. NATIONAL RAILWAY MUSEUM

Condensing pannier No. 9702 with a goods train to Smithfield, photographed at Farringdon in 1938 passing onto the widened lines from the 'inner circle'. The train had 19 vans and a goods brake, just about the limit for Smithfield trains. J. J. SMITH

vas cut up, packed, and brought back to he underground depot for outwards rains. Between the wars, eight goods trains eft Smithfield after 7.0 p.m. with outwards raffic; the last train left at 12.48 a.m., the irst incoming meat train having already rrived at 12.8 a.m.

In 1929, Smithfield depot employed 667 eople, second only to Paddington Goods! The paperwork for goods traffic originat-ng at some of the GWR London Receiving Offices were handled at mithfield, viz; 17 Commercial Road; 65 Gresham Street; 5 Holborn Viaduct; 23 Newgate Street; 82 Queen Victoria Street; nd 11 Redcross Street. There was a Receiving Office at Smithfield (Long ane) but it dealt with passenger and arcels traffic only. With a staff of about ight, it issued tickets, etc. and handled typ-cally over 200,000 parcels per year in the 930s.

The large Great Western depot at Smithfield was unusual in that its access from the system was by means of the sub-urban station lines at Paddington (Bishop's Road) and 3¾-miles of underground, util-ising the Metropolitan line from Royal Oak.

With the exception of the meat ser-vices, Smithfield trains commenced and terminated at Acton, and in 1939 there were around 16 goods or associated light engine movements in each direction. In some respects, Smithfield was a normal goods depot, dealing with general goods for cartage, but it was with more perishable items that it became more associated. Whilst the Central Meat Market's require-ments were well known, trains also conveyed fruit and vegetables.

The bulk meat originated largely from Commonwealth and foreign ports, and was received at such docks as Birkenhead and Fishguard, although more local sup-plies were also conveyed by the Smithfield trains. There were five scheduled late-night trains from Old Oak to Smithfield, leaving at 11.0 and 11.25 pm., and 12.20, 12.40 and 1.40 am., the last of which ran only when required. On Monday mornings, the trains conveying meat left Acton instead, depart-ing at 12.35, 1.5 and 1.35 a.m., the last again conditional.

The Smithfield trains required con-densing locomotives, and 0–6–0PT Nos. 9700–10 built in 1933 were duly were duly fitted with the apparatus, to replace the old '633' class 0–6–0T (and perhaps some of the 'Metro' 2–4–0T engines) of earlier years. They performed the Smithfield duties in five turns, as well as one passenger duty.

Old Oak yards in 1936, facing east, with Old Oak Common West box to the right. Wagons were frequently tripped from the series of marshalling yards on both sides of the line to Paddington Goods, South Lambeth, Park Royal and other yards and depots by the tank engines from the adjacent shed. NATIONAL RAILWAY MUSEUM

ƆLD OAK GOODS TARGETS

ls mentioned, Old Oak Common shed was esponsible for providing the great majority of hunting power in the inner London area, vorking daily at Paddington Goods and adjacent ards, Smithfield, South Lambeth and internediate yards, depots on the old main line to lcton and Hanwell, and along the new line to ark Royal and Greenford. In addition, the hed worked local goods trips that extended urther outwards along the various routes. eyond, Southall shed provided engines for rentford and a few other main line and branch ards and depots in the outer area, though with ncursions onto the West London line. Examples of Old Oak turns over the West ondon line for 1939 are shown here.

GOODS TARGETS, WEST LONDON LINE - Examples, 1939

No.2				
SX	4/30 Old Oak	Lillie Bridge	5/29	Engine Attached
SX	7/35 Lillie Bridge	South Lambeth	7/50	Lt Eng
SX	8/30 South Lambeth	Old Oak	9/5	
D	1.10 Old Oak	Hammersmith	1.50	(via Paddington Pcls line)
D	3.20 Hammersmith	Kensington	3.52	Coal
D	4.10 Kensington	Old Oak	4.25	
No.3				
MO	2.50 Acton	South Lambeth	3.30	
MO	4.5 South Lambeth	Old Oak	4.40	
MO	5.30 Old Oak	South Lambeth	6.5	
MX	6.28 Acton	South Lambeth	7.8	
D	7.50 South Lambeth	Old Oak	9.15	
D	12/26 Kensington	South Lambeth	12/45	Lt Eng
D	1/55 South Lambeth	Old Oak	2/32	
No.4				
MO	1.20 Old Oak	South Lambeth	1.50	
MX	2.45 Old Oak	South Lambeth	3.35	
	SL No.1 Shunting Engine			
SO	9/15 South Lambeth	Acton		Stale No.1 SL Shunt Eng
SX	11/0 South Lambeth	Old Oak	11/33	
No.5				
MX	3.52 Acton	South Lambeth	4.30	
MX	5.0 South Lambeth	Old Oak	5.35	
SX	7.50 Old Oak	Shepherd's Bush	8.5	
SX	9.28 Shepherd's Bush	Old Oak	9.38	E & V
SX	10.40 Old Oak	Shepherd's Bush	10.50	
SX	2/5 Shepherd's Bush	Old Oak	2/15	
D	4/50 Old Oak	Chelsea Docks	5/50	
SO	6/25 Chelsea Docks	Shepherd's Bush	6/50	
SO	7/54 Shepherd's Bush	Old Oak	8/5	
SX	6/50 Chelsea Docks	Old Oak	7/10	
SX	9/10 Old Oak	South Lambeth	9/45	
MSX	2.30 South Lambeth	Old Oak	3.15	Stale SL No.1 Shunting Eng
No.6				
SX	4/30 Old Oak	South Lambeth	5/8	
SX	6/10 South Lambeth	Old Oak	6/45	
D	7/15 Old Oak	South Lambeth	7/42	E & V (SX); Lt Eng (SO)
SO	8/30 South Lambeth	Old Oak	9/5	
SX	9/15 South Lambeth	Acton		
No.7				
SO	11.50 Old Oak	Warwick Rd	12/10	
SO	5/55 Warwick Rd	Old Oak	6/32	
SX	3/50 Old Oak	Warwick Rd	4/5	
SX	10/20 Warwick Rd	Old Oak	10/48	
No.9				
SO	7.50 Old Oak	Shepherd's Bush	8.5	
SO	9.28 Shepherd's Bush	Old Oak	9.38	E & V
D	4/25 Old Oak	Shepherd's Bush	4/35	
SO	5/30 Shepherd's Bush	Old Oak	5/45	
SX	10/25 Shepherd's Bush	Old Oak	10/37	
No.10				
D	4/15 Hanwell Bridge	South Lambeth	5/30	
D	7/50 South Lambeth	Old Oak	8/25	
No.12				
D	6.20 Old Oak	Chelsea Docks	6.45	
D	7.20 Chelsea Docks	Old Oak	7.50	
No.15				
SX	8/35 Old Oak	South Lambeth	9/5	Lt Eng
SX	9/55 South Lambeth	Old Oak	10/30	
SO	8/35 Old Oak	South Lambeth	9/5	
SO	SL No.3 Shunting Engine			
Sun	4.10 South Lambeth	Old Oak	4.45	Lt Eng

SHEPHERD'S BUSH (UXBRIDGE ROAD)

Uxbridge Road depot came into being as a result of the development of 'Inland Coal Depots' on the line by Robert Stephenson, who had taken over the construction of the West London line as Engineer in the early 1840s. Depots of the Great Western and London & North Western companies were located alongside each other on the west side of the line, just to the north of the Uxbridge Road, with the Great Western yard initially comprising three sidings with wagon turntables on the outside (western) edge of the site. The yard was further extended to the west with three additional groups of tracks (but no turntables) by the Great War.

In 1939, there were three movements daily in each direction between Old Oak Common and Shepherd's Bush (Uxbridge Road) depot, running via North Pole Jct. to join the West London route, leaving again some ¾-mile later for the depot a the junction on the south side of th Hammersmith & City line viaduct. I addition to the transits, the target engine spent some time shunting the depot. Th primary traffic was coal, coke and miner als, but 'station to station' goods were als dealt with. There were facilities fo handling furniture containers from th trains.

The GWR section of Shepherd' Bush mileage yard, located a littl to the north of Uxbridge Road looking north on 19th June 1947 Access to the site, which containe both LMS and Great Wester yards (the latter to the west), wa from the West London line. Th J. Harrold & Co. coal office is see on the left, one of a number of coa merchants using the yard. Th structure to the left was the end o the walkway from Shepherds Bus (Uxbridge Road) station (at botton right of OS map), built in 1910 fo the Japan-British Exhibition a nearby White City. The Central lin train shed was located behind th walkway.
NATIONAL RAILWAY MUSEUM

A view of the Great Western yard looking south, showing the angle part of the Uxbridge Road statio walkway (bottom of OS map) under which the sidings ended. Th backs of houses in Tadmor Stree can be seen beyond, through th supports. As may be seen, th primary function of the yard wa for mileage traffic, including th usual mineral, coal and coke, bu also station to station consignments and furniture vans.
NATIONAL RAILWAY MUSEUM

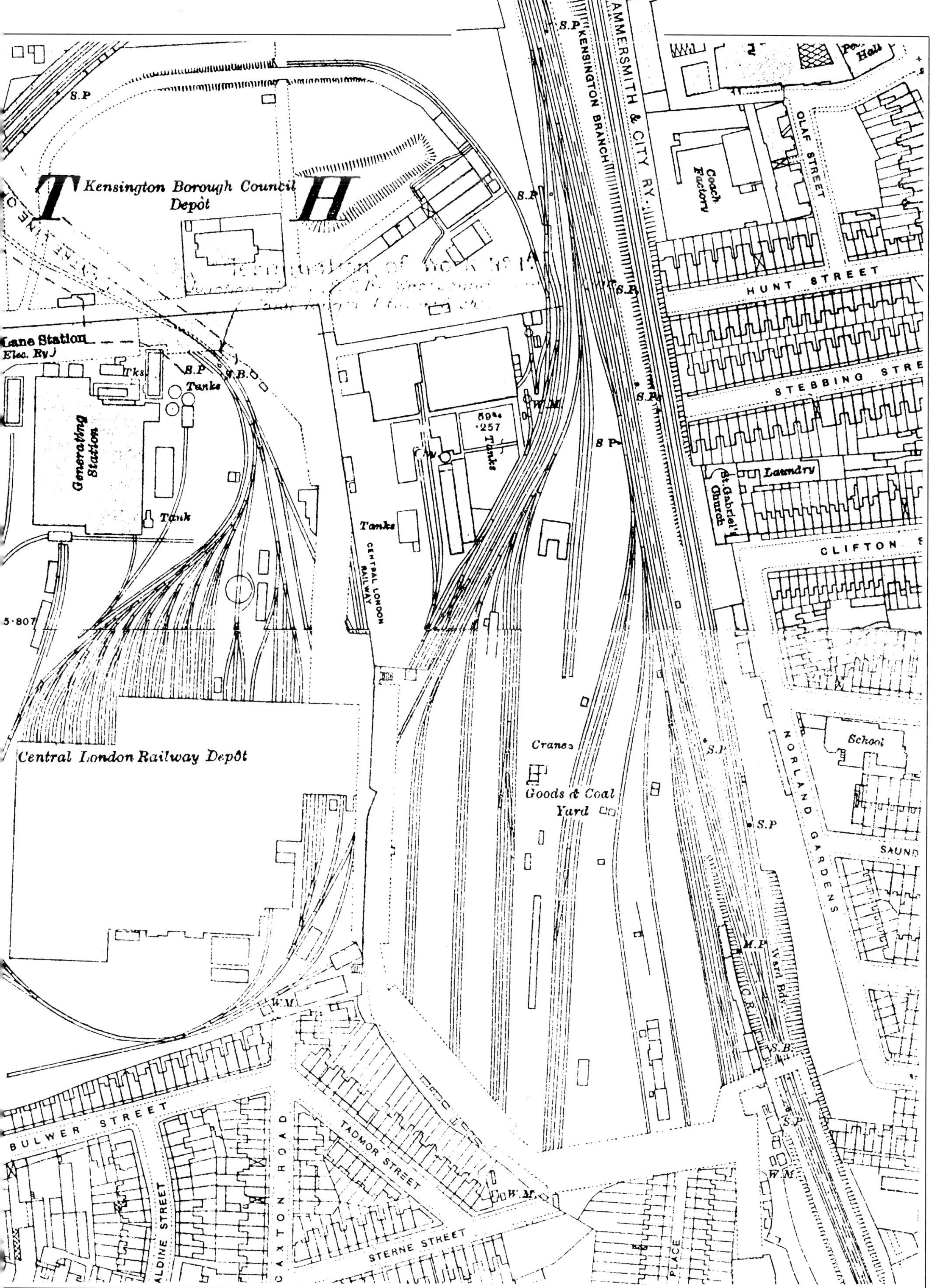

Taken from 25-inch Ordnance Survey for 1914. Crown copyright reserved.

An aerial view of Hammersmith H&C station (centre) in 1931, looking east, showing the busy Broadway to its right. The Great Western coal yard is seen to the west (near side) of the

HAMMERSMITH

nother Great Western coal depot in the ea was to be found at Hammersmith. he Hammersmith & City line from its rminus (behind King Street West) was pened in June 1864, and was vested in e Great Western and Metropolitan mpanies jointly three years later. A nall yard was built to the west of the sta- on platforms, in which two tracks (with agon turntables) served the coal depot.

To serve this yard, a single train left ld Oak in 1939 at 1.10 a.m., with a aximum load of 35 wagons between o brake vans, running via the Up oods line as far as Ladbroke Grove, and e Up Carriage line thence into ddington Parcels line. There, the engine n round its train, and set off again along e Down Main and the Crystal Palace op onto the Hammersmith & City line. is route was taken to the northern end Hammersmith (H & C) station, where a connection served the depot. Coal, coke and minerals were the main traffics, but 'station to station' goods were also handled. Having spent some ninety minutes working the yard, the return working left at 3.20 a.m. for Kensington, on H & C metals via Latimer Road and Uxbridge Road Junctions, and the West London thence into Kensington. The train left Kensington (Addison Rd.) at 4.10 a.m. via North Pole Jct. to Old Oak Common. It was necessary for this service to have a locomotive with trigger cock apparatus, and in later years a '2251' engine was so fitted.

The frontage of the Hammersmith H&C station in Beadon Road, the coal yard being immediately to its left. An interesting Great Western and Metropolitan (the owning companies) intertwined monogram is seen on the left-hand end of the canopy.
LENS OF SUTTON

Looking south from the GWR signal box into the H&C terminus, with the coal yard on the right. The H&C arrived at Hammersmith in 1863, and the coal depot is shown on maps of the early 1870s. Also on the early maps is a westwards connection from the footbridge, across the northern part of the coal yard, to the L&SW station on the Kensington & Richmond line, situated on The Grove, which was closed in 1916. Nevertheless, the footbridge extension is still to be seen in the 1931 aerial view, though it was no longer present here.
L. E. COPELAND

Looking north from the signal cabin at Hammersmith, showing the exit from the coal yard to the left, joining the H&C lines, with a Great Western goods signal controlling outwards movements. The carriage sheds to the right were originally built jointly by the GW and the H&C, and the electric rolling stock seen dates from 1938/39.
L. E. COPELAND

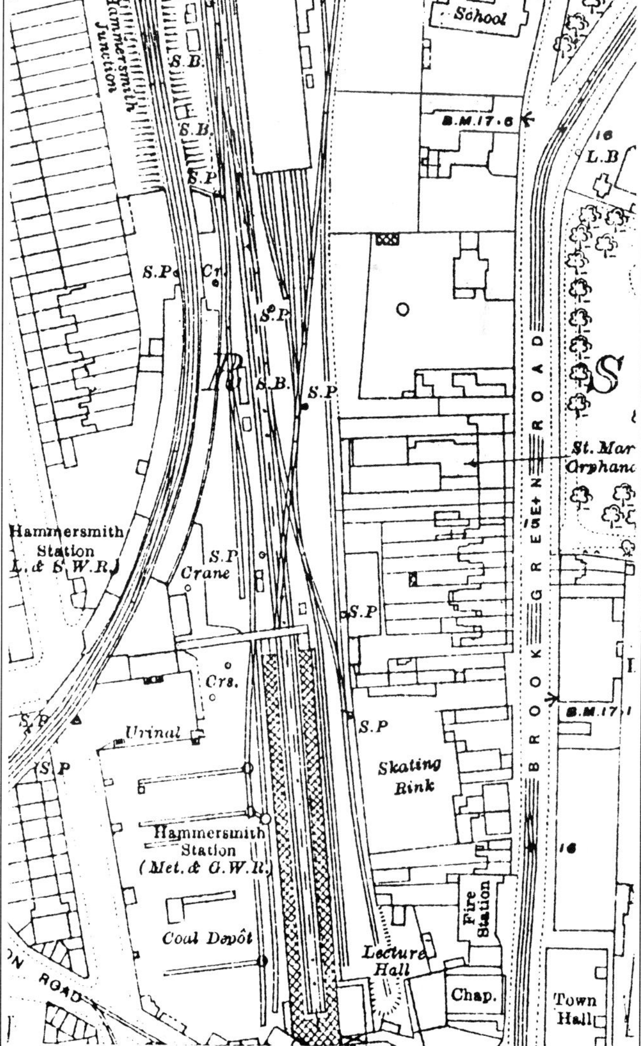

Taken from 25-inch Ordnance Survey for 1920.
Crown copyright reserved.

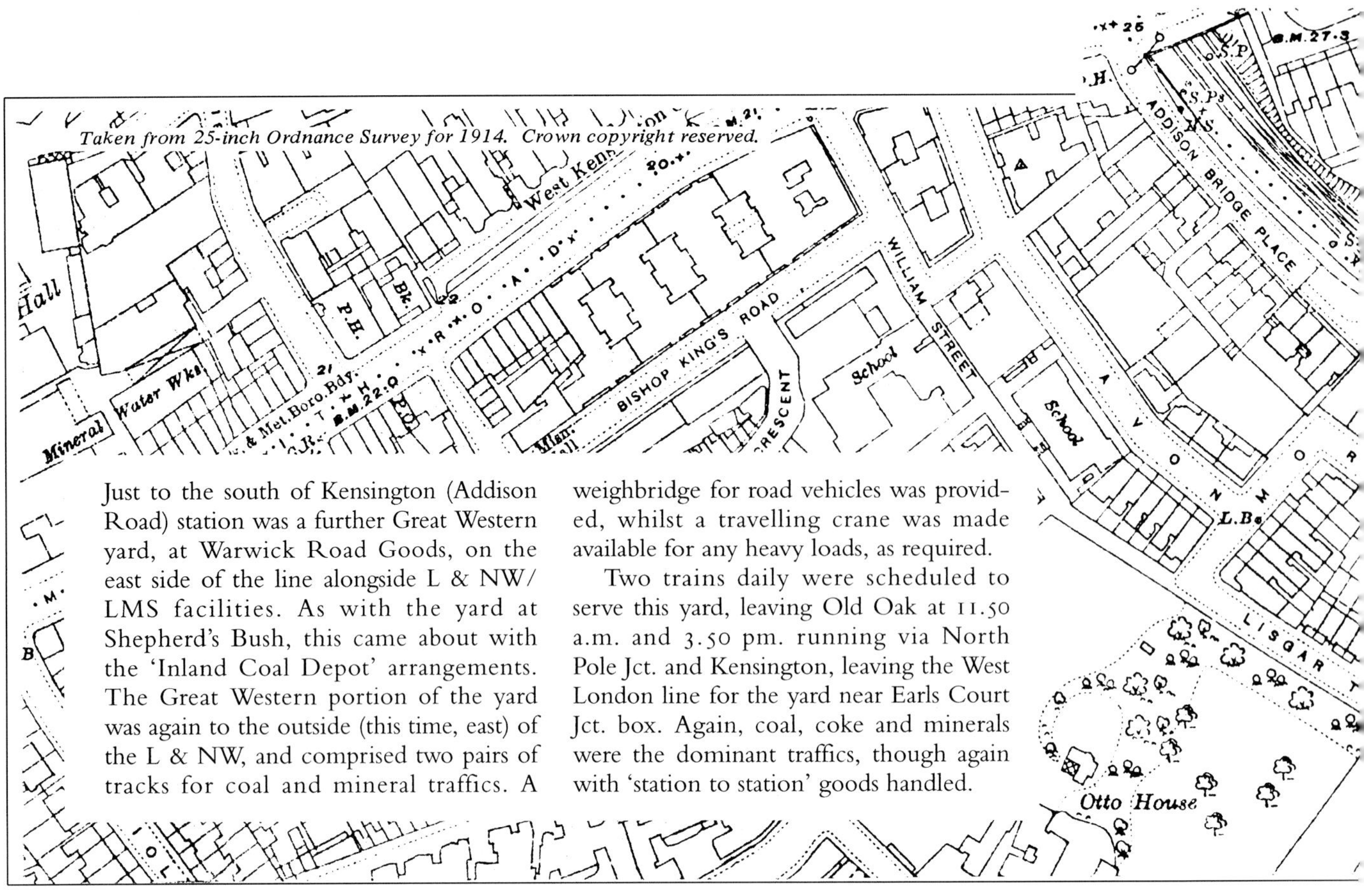

Taken from 25-inch Ordnance Survey for 1914. Crown copyright reserved.

Just to the south of Kensington (Addison Road) station was a further Great Western yard, at Warwick Road Goods, on the east side of the line alongside L & NW/ LMS facilities. As with the yard at Shepherd's Bush, this came about with the 'Inland Coal Depot' arrangements. The Great Western portion of the yard was again to the outside (this time, east) of the L & NW, and comprised two pairs of tracks for coal and mineral traffics. A weighbridge for road vehicles was provided, whilst a travelling crane was made available for any heavy loads, as required.

Two trains daily were scheduled to serve this yard, leaving Old Oak at 11.50 a.m. and 3.50 pm. running via North Pole Jct. and Kensington, leaving the West London line for the yard near Earls Court Jct. box. Again, coal, coke and minerals were the dominant traffics, though again with 'station to station' goods handled.

KENSINGTON (WARWICK ROAD)

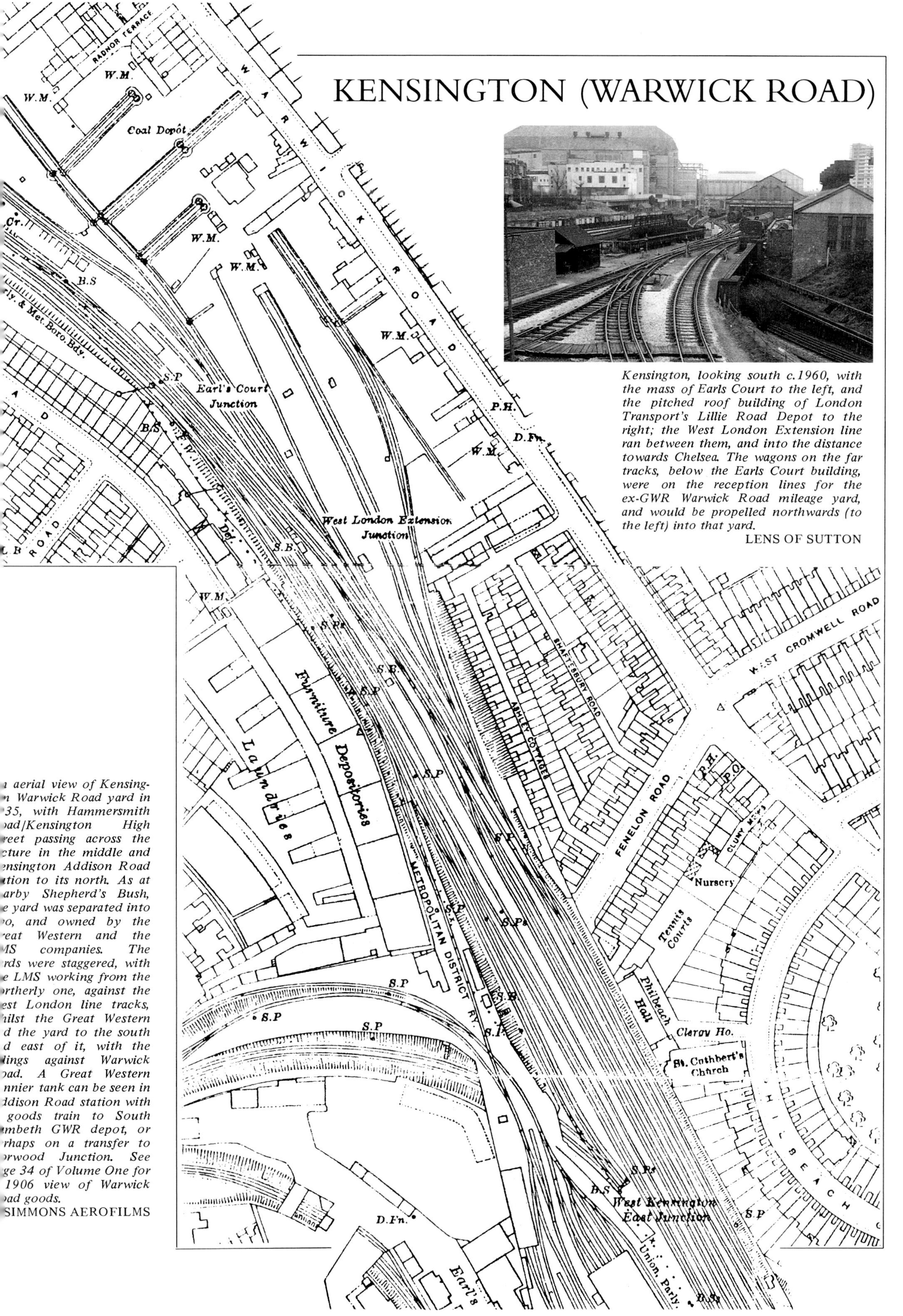

Kensington, looking south c.1960, with the mass of Earls Court to the left, and the pitched roof building of London Transport's Lillie Road Depot to the right; the West London Extension line ran between them, and into the distance towards Chelsea. The wagons on the far tracks, below the Earls Court building, were on the reception lines for the ex-GWR Warwick Road mileage yard, and would be propelled northwards (to the left) into that yard.
LENS OF SUTTON

ı aerial view of Kensing-ı Warwick Road yard in ʼ35, with Hammersmith ɔad/Kensington High ɾeet passing across the cture in the middle and ɛnsington Addison Road ıtion to its north. As at arby Shepherd's Bush, e yard was separated into ɔo, and owned by the ɾeat Western and the MS companies. The rds were staggered, with e LMS working from the ɔrtherly one, against the ɛst London line tracks, ıilst the Great Western d the yard to the south d east of it, with the lings against Warwick ɔad. A Great Western nnier tank can be seen in ddison Road station with goods train to South mbeth GWR depot, or rhaps on a transfer to ɔrwood Junction. See ge 34 of Volume One for 1906 view of Warwick ɔad goods.
SIMMONS AEROFILMS

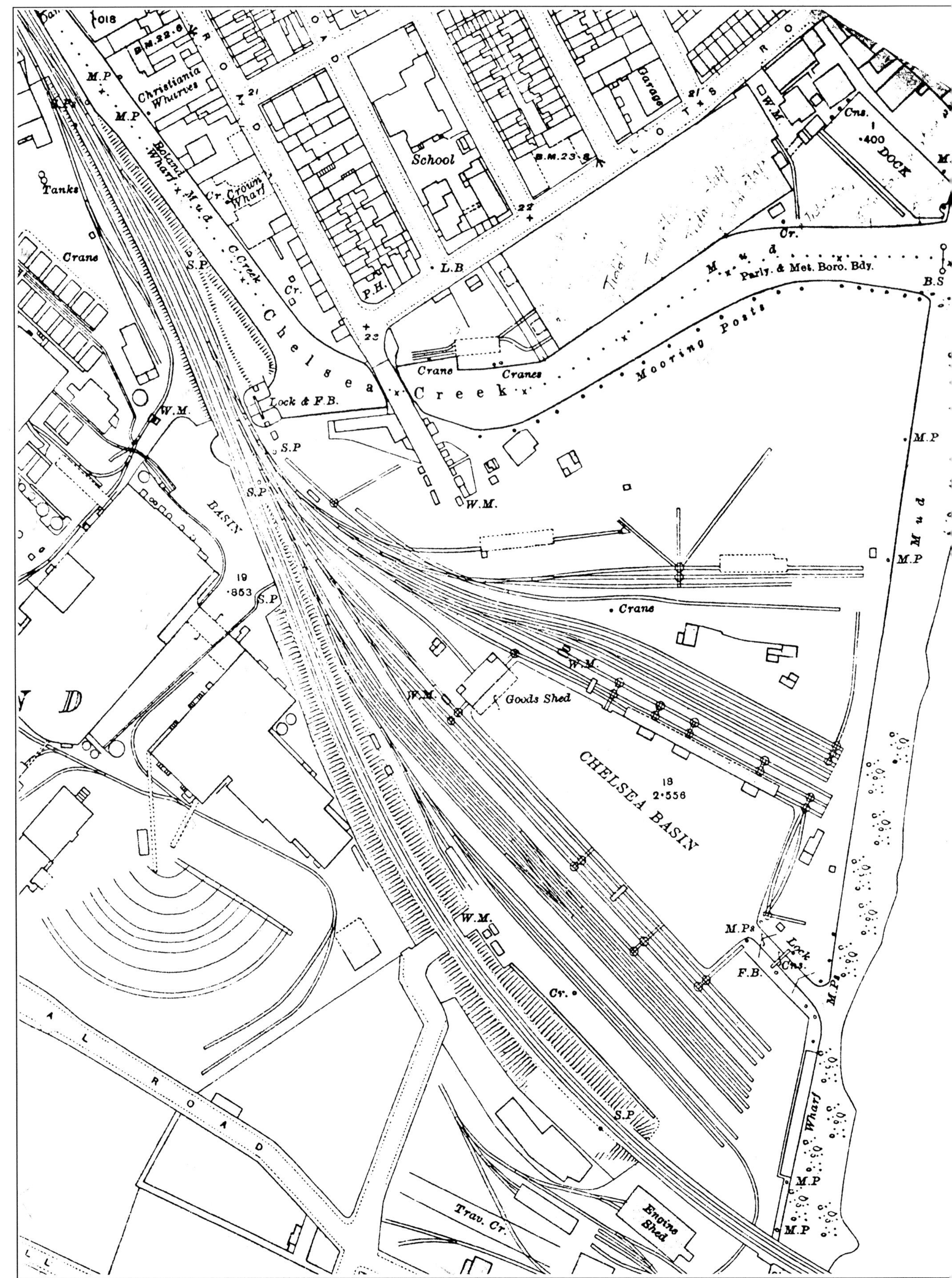

Taken from 25-inch Ordnance Survey. Crown copyright reserved.

HELSEA BASIN

urther to the south, along the West ondon Extension line, the quite extenve Chelsea Docks (or Basin) yard was tuated on the north-eastern side of the ne, on the west bank of the River hames. The West London Extension ne (onwards from Kensington) opened April 1863, and by the 1890s Chelsea asin had grown into a depot of some gnificance, located to all four sides of the nall dock. There were around a dozen tracks to each of the longer sides of the Basin, with two goods sheds adjacent to the water for transfer purposes.

Old Oak Common ran two trains daily to Chelsea in 1939, one leaving at 6.20 a.m. and the other at 4.50 p.m., again via North Pole Jct. The trains took the usual 'station to station', coal, coke and mineral traffic, but also any consignments destined for shipment by barge on the Thames. In addition, the yard served the many industrial companies in the vicinity, including Shell Mex; Macfarlane, Lang; Morgan Crucible; and Price's Patent Candle companies. The final service from Chelsea back to Old Oak on Saturdays also called at Warwick Road (when required) and Shepherd's Bush en route.

River operations at Chelsea will be covered in the *Docks* volume of this series.

Chelsea Basin in the 1930s, looking north along the Thames, with the West London Extension line crossing from left to right (Battersea New Bridge to the right), and Chelsea Basin Goods (another Joint depot) beyond it, fanning out towards the river. The sidings were divided to each side of the basin, with transfer sheds at the north-western end and on the north-eastern quay (facing the camera). The entrance to the basin was at its right-hand end, connecting to the river by means of a lock. Lots Road (LPTB) power station is seen beyond the basin, with Chelsea creek running in front and around it to the left. Part of the extensive Sand's End Gas Works features on the left. SIMMONS AEROFILMS

SOUTH LAMBETH

In addition to these depots, there was the major goods yard at South Lambeth, which stood as a large depot in its own right, handling over 335,000 tons per annum from 1928 to 1938. Building work began in 1911 on the 12½-acre site of abandoned reservoirs near Battersea Park Road, formerly belonging to the Southwark & Vauxhall Waterworks; that company had subsequently been absorbed into the Metropolitan Water Board, from whom the land was bought. The depot (as originally planned) was opened in January 1913, and was the only GWR depot in London built south of the Thames. South Lambeth was reached from Old Oak Common (North Pole Junction, Wormwood Scrubs) over the tracks of the WLR and WLER, and then from Stewart's Lane Junction over the SE & CR. Being within an area already criss-crossed with the constituent railways of the later Southern Railway (it stood just to the south of the Grosvenor Road bridge, on the tracks from Victoria), it competed with Nine Elms (L & SWR) and Bricklayers Arms (SE & CR) as regards cartage. Thus, not only did it do its intended job of relieving the increasing congestion at Paddington before WWI, and eliminating much of the expensive cartage between Paddington and the South London area, but it also attracted a large amount of new goods traffic from the area bounded by the Thames in the north, Deptford in the east to Putney in the west. Indeed, many firms whose works were outside this area brought their goods to the depot to take advantage of the GWR's quick transit of goods. The Great Western's cartage fleet itself at South Lambeth covered some 1,500 miles daily in C&D work.

The original goods shed and warehouse consisted of a three-storey reinforced concrete building 400ft long by 80ft wide, together with a basement extending under the building. The usable floor area per level was some 28,000 sq. ft. Stabling was provided for 94 horses in a two-storey building, the first time a GWR stable had been constructed of ferro-concrete. Two platforms extended the length of the building, and beyond it for another 70ft. There were three roads in the shed that could each accept 24 wagons, with a wagon traverser from the central track (for empty wagons) to the platform roads. It was the first 'modern' goods shed design on the GWR, with the platforms (25ft and 16ft wide

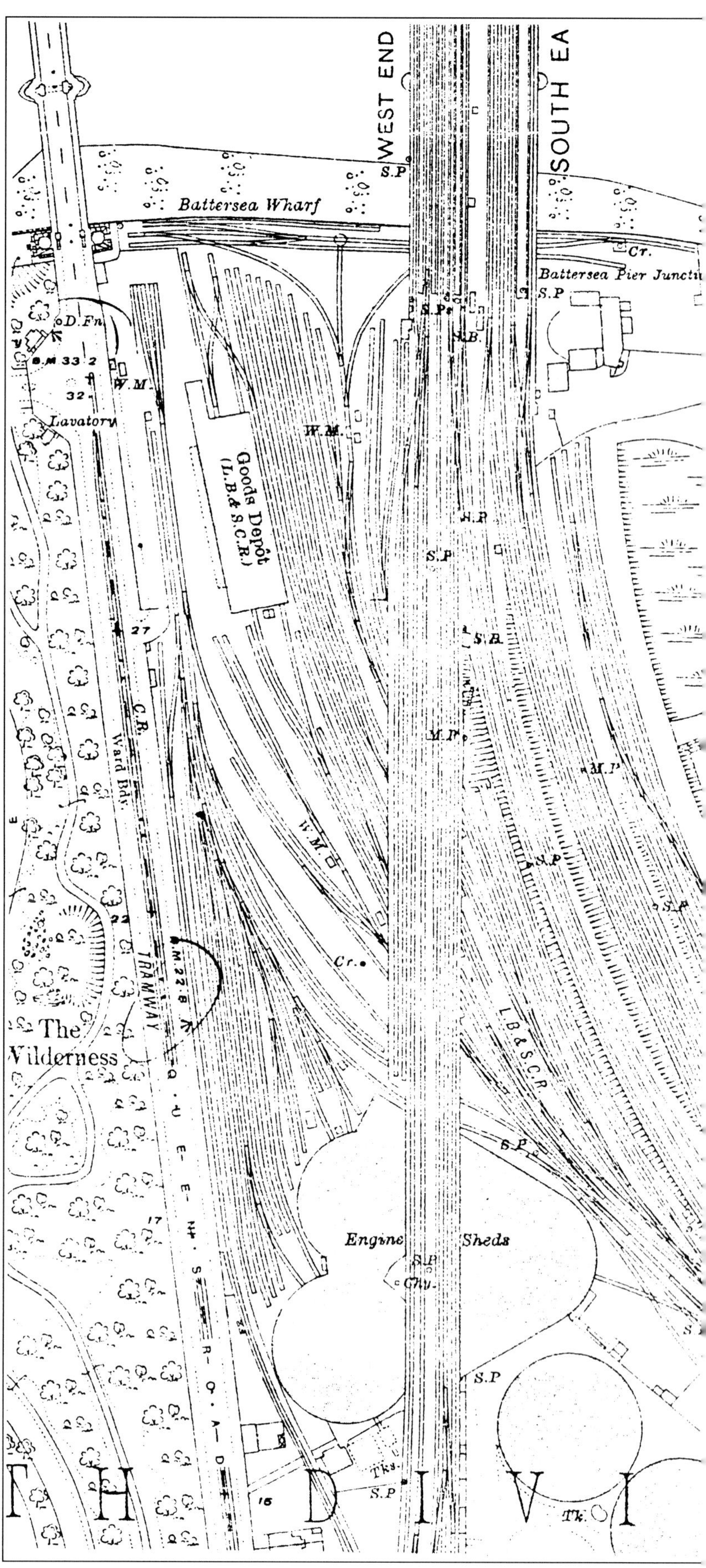

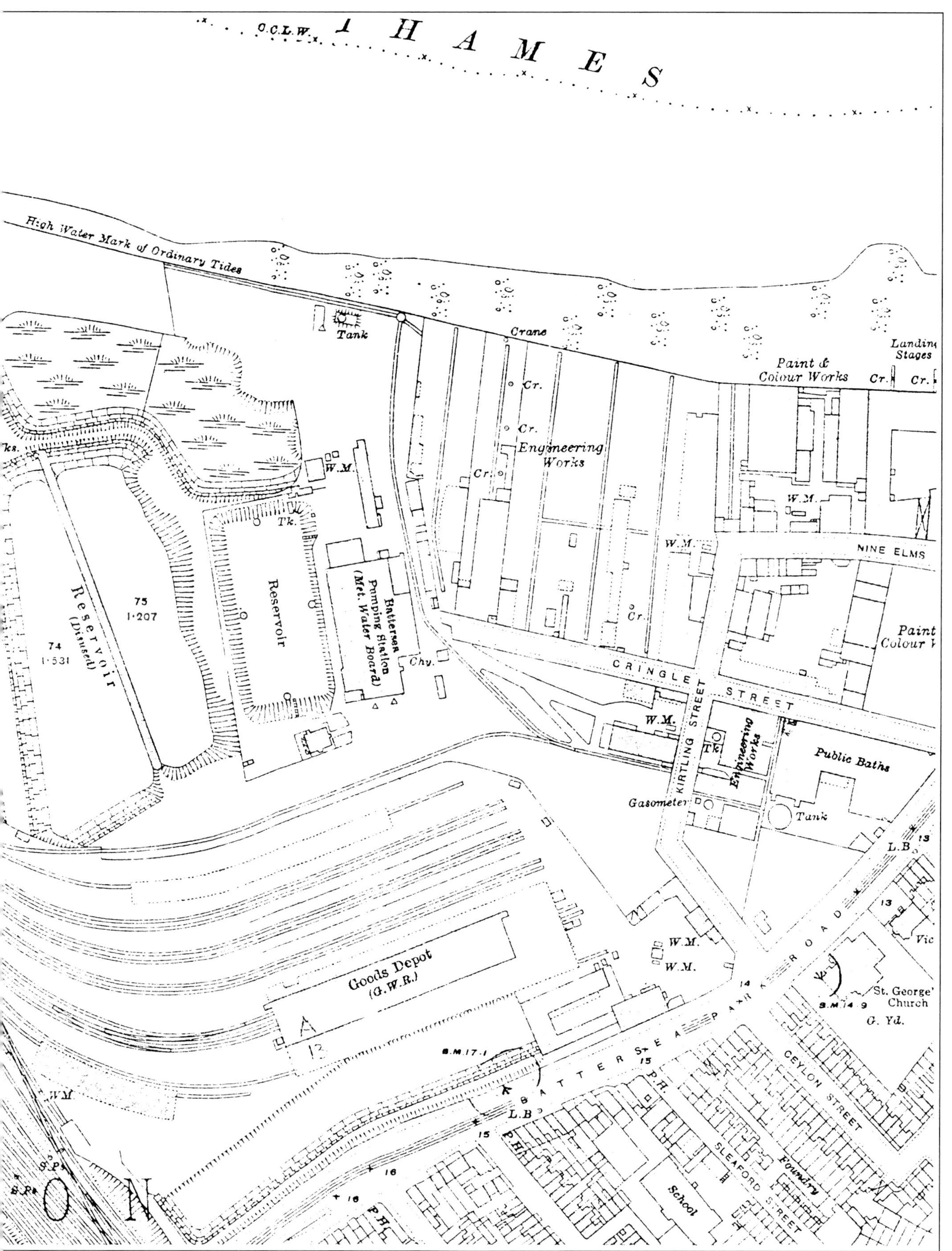

Taken from 25-inch Ordnance Survey for 1914. Crown copyright reserved.

South Lambeth goods warehouse and yard, photographed in March 1924 from Kirtling Street, looking west towards the LB&SC lines. The prominent roof lettering facing the yard proclaimed 'GWR', 'Cornish Riviera', 'Birmingham 2 Hours', and finally 'South Lambeth Goods Station' along the bottom row. The layout of the depot was as opened in 1913, and shown on the OS map. A Babcock & Wilcox electric gantry crane spanned the centre tracks of the mileage yard, with the covered goods shed and warehouse on the right. One of the

espectively) free of fixed cranes and other ›bstructions common in older types of hed, all lifting being performed by a 1-ton ravelling underhung overhead electric rane. There was also an electrically-vorked bridge between the two platforms vhich slid beneath the platforms during hunting. All the openings to the platform ›n the north front were fitted with Kinnear patent roller shutters, each 19ft igh by 23ft 9ins wide; roller shutters were tted on various other buildings too, such s the motor lorry garage, straw store, van heet shed, manure shoots, etc. This was the irst use of roller shutters on GW goods uildings.

The main feature of the open yard was he (then) modern travelling electric antry crane (by Babcock & Wilcox) with span of 51ft 6in; this enabled two sidings vith a capacity of 24 wagons each to be ealt with without any shunting being ecessary. There were two gears on the rane, lifting 10 and 35 tons respectively. 'he mileage sidings accommodated over 00 wagons, with the goods shed lines 114 vagons. The goods offices, parcels receiv-ıg depot, etc, fronted on to Battersea Park

The interior of the original three-road goods shed, South Lambeth, in 1929 showing electric overhead underslung cranes, with plate 'Babcock & Wilcox Makers London & Renfrew Load not to exceed 1 ton' on the gantry. A second crane behind was loading a long crate into an open wagon.

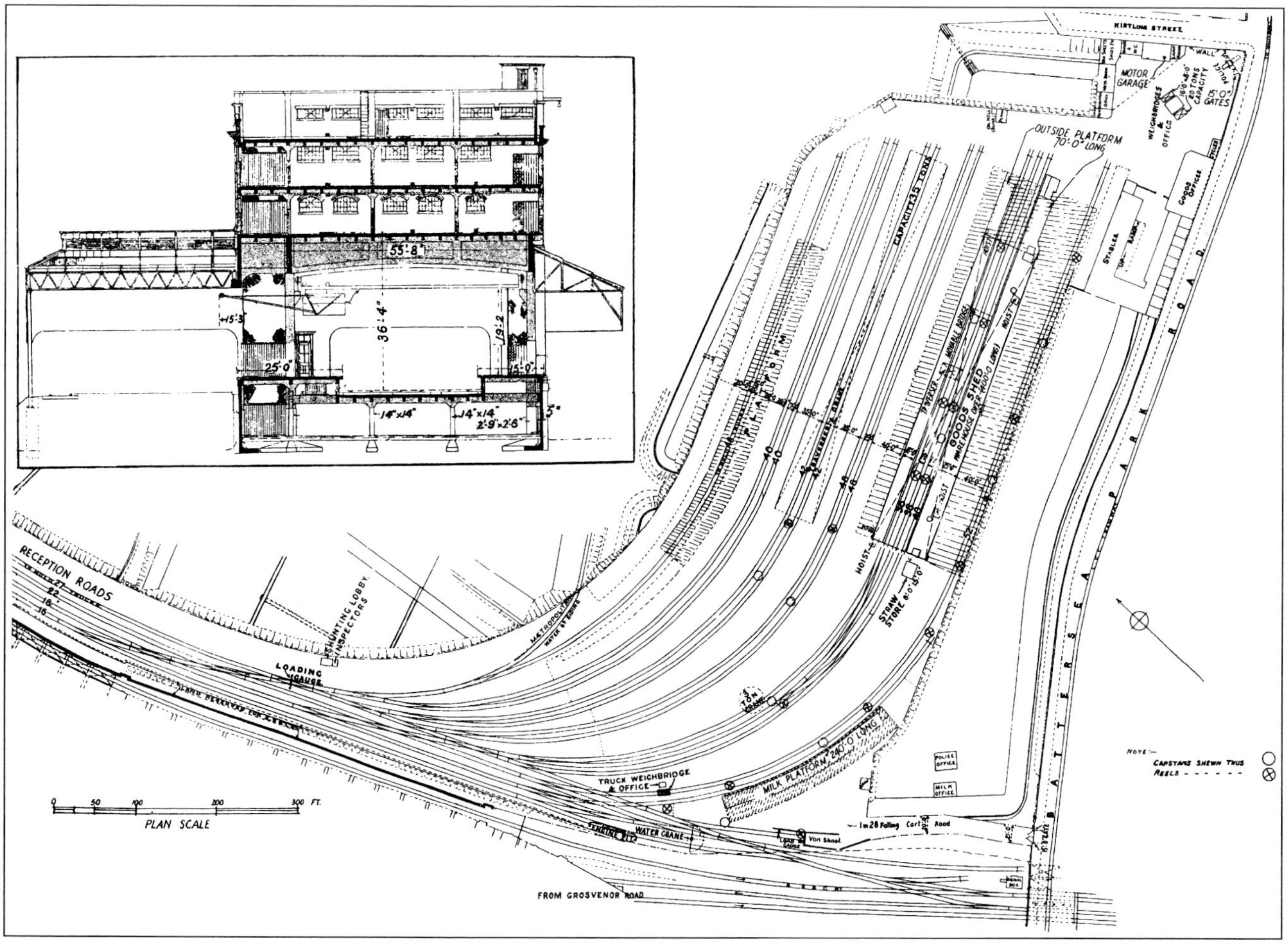

Great Western Railway goods depot, South Lambeth. Plan of the original layout and, inset, a sectional elevation of the goods warehouse.
RAILWAY GAZETTE

A view of the original milk platform that opened soon after work began in 1911 on the site at South Lambeth. The rest of the yard had still to be constructed; no sidings had been laid beyond the milk platform, and the warehouse had yet to be erected. A separate cartage exit for milk traffic was up the road on the right, and out through a gate in Battersea Park Road. Contemporary records indicate a thriving milk traffic from Wiltshire (and surrounding counties), with the midnight train from Southall to South Lambeth conveying an average of ten 6-wheel 'Siphons' for Clapham Junction, and fourteen for South Lambeth. The track alongside the rising road above the point lever was the end-loading line. In the foreground, the

NATIONAL RAILWAY MUSEUM

.d. In 1926, 590 people were employed y the GW at South Lambeth, with 128 orse-drawn and 45 motor vehicles.

Traffic increased so much in the years ter WWI that, in 1929, an additional oods shed with upper and basement arehousing of similar construction to the ld was built in the space between the riginal shed and Battersea Park Road. here were two wide, 400ft-long plat-rms, again served by an underhung aversing jib crane which served the plat-rms, tracks and cartways. This time, stead of the sliding bridges of 1913, ounter-balanced lifting bridges (by then stalled at Paddington and Bristol) half ay down their length permitted trolley-g between platforms.

Both sides of the new shed had road-ays, that on the north side being beneath e original covered way of the older uilding. The cartway on the south was anked by a siding in the open for direct ading from rail to road (and vice-versa), which was protected by a cantilever roof from the side of the new shed. The main entrance yard to the depot was opened out to give freer movement by road into the goods sheds, mileage yard and 'empties' shed. Two Pooley 20-ton cart weighbridges were installed, and soon after opening over 800 weighings per day were being made.

The improved entrance layout was achieved by knocking down the old offices, and building improved offices for invoicing, abstracting and other clerical work. An item of staff interest was that there were in London numerous 'shipping clerks', paid weekly and not on the estab-lishment; they were often on night work,

New buildings backing on to the boundary wall of the South Lambeth site near Kirtling Street, in course of construction in the summer of 1927, preparatory to improving the cartage entrance; this was on the corner of Battersea Park Road and Kirtling Street.
NATIONAL RAILWAY MUSEUM

Construction of the awning for road motors on the south side of the new warehouse, April 1929. The new structure was located to the south of the existing shed, and 400ft in length. Its construction involved the filling-in of a remaining part of one of the old Southwark & Vauxhall Water Co. reservoirs, on the site of which South Lambeth Goods was built. The contract was carried out by Holliday & Greenwood, whose board can be seen prominently displayed on the roof. The sidings in the foreground from the original milk platform were realigned since the new warehouse was built on undeveloped land.
NATIONAL RAILWAY MUSEUM

An empty lorry reversed into the loading bay for demountable flats. There was a similar (and contemporary) installation at Birkenhead.
NATIONAL RAILWAY MUSEUM

A close-up view, showing the lorry backed in, and the load being slid across on rollers; this system allowed the loads to be 'pre-packed', and minimised the time that the lorry occupied the bay.
NATIONAL RAILWAY MUSEUM

The Bay into which the motor lorry backed to pick up or drop off a demountable flat, with the guide rails on the ground to line up the vehicle, and the roller girders mounted on jacks that carried the load above the lorry's platform. United Glass products in crates were warehoused at South Lambeth for distribution, and a consignment for delivery can be seen on the platform at the rear.
NATIONAL RAILWAY MUSEUM

r awkward turns, continuously. In these ffices at South Lambeth during the 1930s, he whole of the Accounts department was 1 the hands of two women, with virtually ll women clerks under them, working a ystem of repetitive drudgery. The paper-work for goods traffic from the Receiving)ffices at 141 High Street, Borough and 83 Westminster Bridge (closed in 1918) vas handled at South Lambeth. There was Receiving Office at South Lambeth, pened in 1928, but it did not deal with oods traffic.

A special feature in the 1929 rebuilding vas the installation of a framework along 1e extent of the roadside of the platforms that loaded 'demountable flats' could be ut on and taken off motor lorries. The amework extended from the platform a istance equal to the average length of a orry, with a height equal to the height of 1e chassis. In the middle was a bay into hich a lorry could back, and flats could e slid by hand (they were on roller bear-ngs) on or off the lorry; this enabled a ery quick turn around for the vehicles. 'he concept of demountable flats was developed by the Great Western's Road Traffic Department, superintended by F.C.A. Coventry, following earlier experi-ments with the Rendell system. The idea was novel, but was overtaken by the intro-duction of the 'mechanical horse' in the early 1930s (both aspects will be covered in our *Cartage* volume).

Many of the trains from South Lambeth conveyed traffic for the fast goods trains to South Wales, the Midlands and the West Country, and was taken by pilot trips

The interior of the new 1929 shed at South Lambeth, showing the two-road, two-platform arrangement with a 20-cwt overhead underslung travelling electric crane, and a balancing platform bridge for trolleying across platforms. A further line was added to the left, alongside the internal roadway.

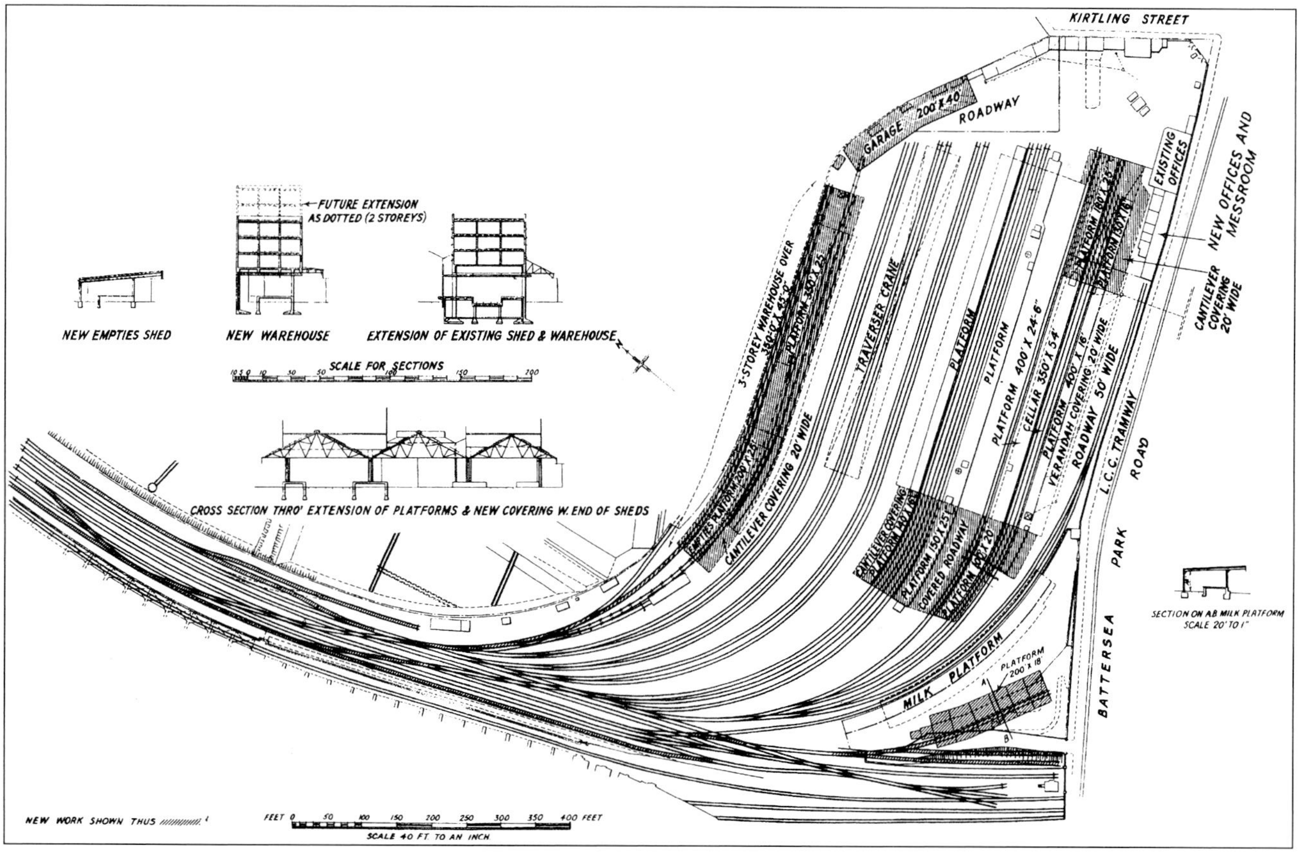

Plan of the new layout at South Lambeth, showing completed extensions and those which were to be put in hand. RAILWAY GAZETTE

The west ends of the two South Lambeth goods sheds in 1929, looking east into the depot from the entrance tracks. The original building features on the left, and the new building with two floors above tracks at this end, on the right; the three lines can be seen entering the old shed, the one intermediate line alongside the internal roadway, and two into the new shed. There was a second new warehouse with four storeys on the far (north) side of the depot, not to be confused with this one.

One of the manufacturers using South Lambeth for distribution was Nestlés, whose products were stored at the warehouse in 1932. Read the advertising puff on the boxes! NATIONAL RAILWAY MUSEUM

The new warehouse (opened in 1929), with four floors above the platform tracks, on the northern boundary of the South Lambeth site is seen here, looking north. The gantry crane of the original yard layout is seen below, with the rail exit to the left.

The rear extension to the new 1929 three-storey shed/warehouse (the one adjacent to the original building), built in 1932, with three floors above tracks at this end (only two at the other end — see page 168). The road entrance to the depot was behind, and to the left of, the camera. The invoicing offices and the mess room were to the left. The awning arrangement that joined the original shed/warehouse to the new can be seen to the right, with the internal roadway between the two on the extreme right.

NATIONAL RAILWAY MUSEUM

A view of the 1932 extension, south side, looking east towards the road entrance and cart weighbridges (seen through the end of the awning on the right). The track in the bottom right-hand corner ran along the Battersea Park Road boundary, and was the end of the realigned siding from the original milk platform. A photograph taken from further back, before the extension was built, is on page 165.

NATIONAL RAILWAY MUSEUM

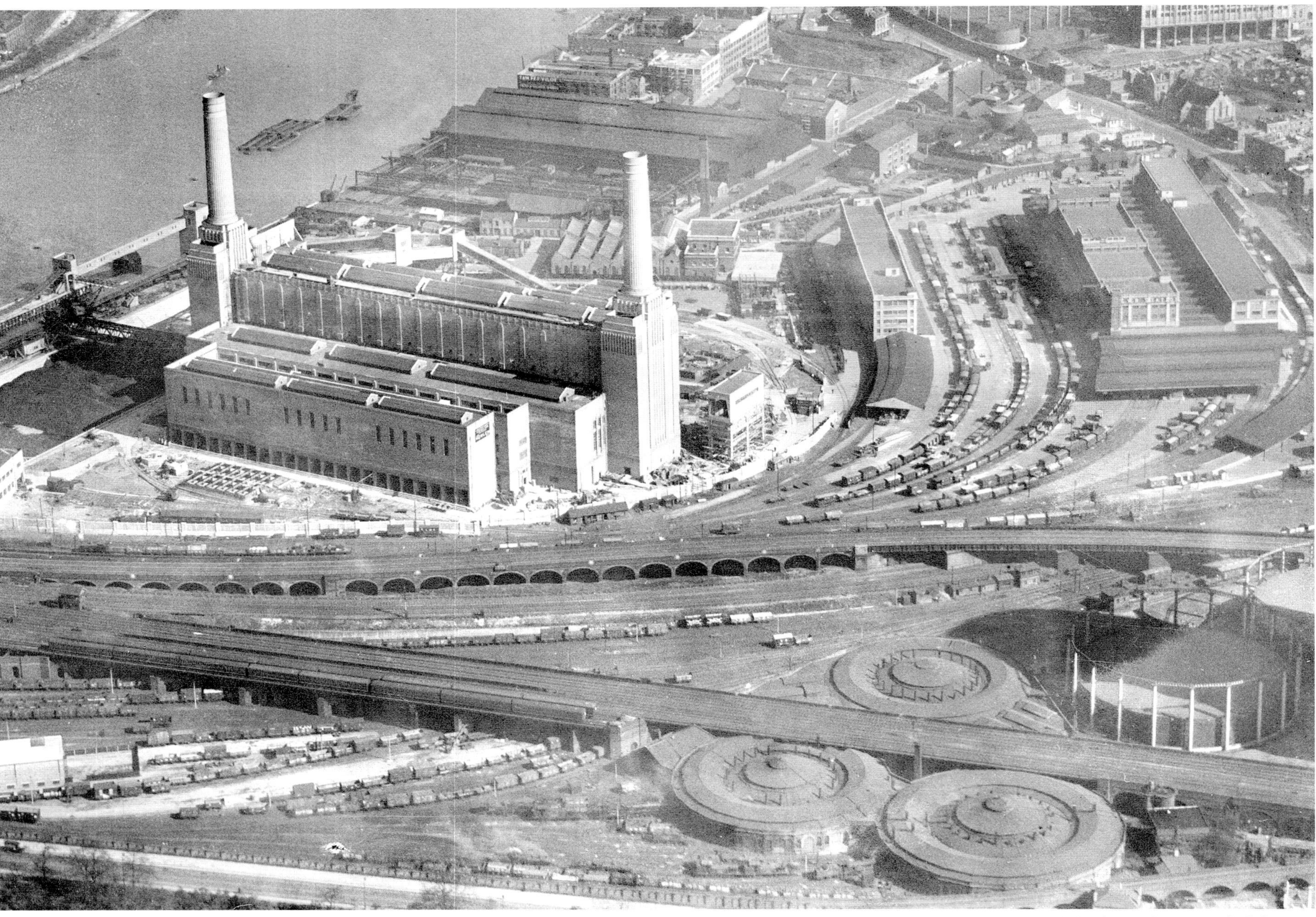

An aerial view of South Lambeth depot in 1933, looking east, clearly showing the layout of the yard. The four-storey warehouse on the northern edge of the site can be seen to the left, then the mileage yard to its right, and the original building with the new 1929 shed/warehouse joined by canopies on the right of the site. The two sheds had platform and canopy extensions on their fronts now, whilst the new milk platform canopy can be seen curving to the left in front of them. Another new, small shed was located to the right of the milk platform, just out of view here. Battersea Park Road ran to the right of the site. Other landmarks include the new Battersea power station on the left (with only two chimneys, as built).

'57XXs' and '97XXs' were employed on shunting turns and local goods/transfer services in the London area from 1929, with over eighty of the classes allocated to Old Oak at nationalisation. Amongst their duties were the South Lambeth turns, which involved both transfer and shunting work at that depot. Here, Old Oak's '97XX' No. 9701 was passing Chelsea & Fulham box with a transfer from South Lambeth to Old Oak on 24th August 1957. The three-lamp SR code indicates a Hither Green, Stewarts Lane, Norwood or South Lambeth to Old Oak service. Lots Road (LPTB) power station can be seen to the rear with Chelsea Basin beyond the train. PAMLIN PRINTS

about 14 per day) to Acton or Old Oak Common for remarshalling. When traffic was heavy, the train would be double-eaded because of a steeply-curving gradi-nt that was encountered within 250 yards of leaving the depot. The start had to be a risk one! When the Battersea Power tation was built nearby in 1931, the depot was used to receive the large electrical nachinery being installed, and all the uilding materials.

In addition to all the usual merchandise assing through a goods depot, South ambeth dealt with fresh milk on a large cale, with from 2,000 to 3,000 churns eing handled daily between the two world wars from four train loads. A sepa-ate 240ft long milk platform had been rovided at the 1913 opening, and the olume had increased so much that the 929 additions to the depot included the engthening of the original milk platform, nd the provision of a second, both com-letely roofed-over. Milk was handled in he south-western corner of the site, and it ad its own separate entrance from Battersea Park Road. A GWR working document noted that 70ft vehicles would not clear the milk platform at South Lambeth, and that they should not there-fore be loaded to that point.

A feature of both large goods sheds at South Lambeth was the warehousing in the upper storeys and basement. In 1913 the first floor of the original building had been allocated to the storage of tinplate, glass, iron, hardware, etc; the second for blankets, carpets, drapery, etc; and the base-ment for bacon, butter and general provi-sions. A great deal of space in the 1929 building was let out to private firms (for glass bottle storage in particular) who used the railway to distribute their goods.

South Lambeth depot was situated near to the south bank of the Thames, to the east of the lines leading into Victoria sta-tion. Again, this was reached from Old Oak and other parts of the system via North Pole Jct. and the West London lines as far as Longhedge, Clapham, and thence by former South Eastern & Chatham metals around to the site (later, near Battersea Power station). Most of the traffic for South Lambeth was routed from the yards at Old Oak, although trains also ran through from Hanwell Bridge, Acton and Park Royal. In all, around ten trains (including light engine or engine & van movements) ran each way daily to and from the depot in 1939. The general traffic carried by the trains was destined for cartage into or out of the surrounding sub-urbs, whilst coal, coke, minerals, explosives, acids, furniture and many other commodi-ties were conveyed. Perishables were also carried on the services, as were consign-ments for or from the extensive warehous-ing on the South Lambeth site. The working of this busy depot required a 24-hour shunting engine, together with addi-tional evening shunting by train engines to prepare for the night's departures. Once this had been largely completed, the emphasis changed to inbound traffic, which continued from the early hours of the new day until the commencement of the normal working time. Even within those main flows, a few trains still ran inbound during the afternoons, and departures made in the early hours.

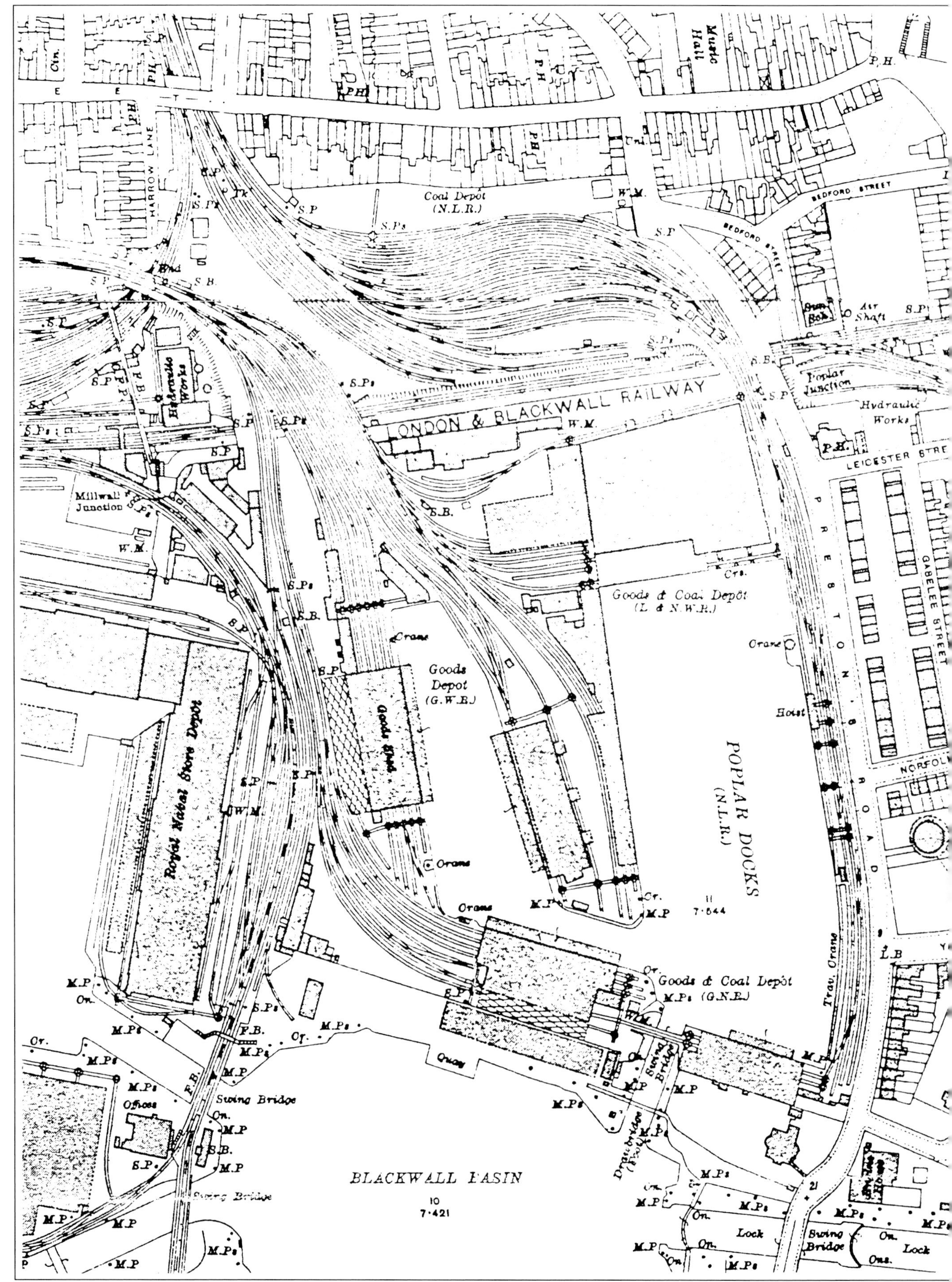

Taken from 25-inch Ordnance Survey. Crown copyright reserved.

POPLAR

The Great Western's Poplar depot dated from 1878, and was situated to the north-east of the West India Dock complex, on the north side of the River Thames. It was reached by the LMS (North London) line, with three or four departures made from Acton or Poplar daily, utilising LMS power.

Poplar depot comprised a large warehouse and five long sidings with wagon turntables at either end; about 240 wagons could be accommodated. It was situated on the west side of the small Poplar Docks, with a direct rail connection off the North London Railway's metals.

The general traffic taken was for delivery locally by cart, truck or barge, whilst 'station to station', mineral and livestock were also conveyed. Coal and coke was carried, though largely for disposal by barge, whilst facilities were provided for explosives and other dangerous materials, and also for furniture traffic. Poplar specifically collected and delivered general traffic for Limehouse, Bow and Old Ford, and was handling 300,000 tons per year before WWI, though this fell to some 100,000 tons per annum in the 1930s.

Poplar depot was badly damaged by bombing in 1940, and was closed.

A view looking eastwards across the eastern part of West India Docks in 1938, with Poplar Docks (NLR) at the far end, in the very centre of the picture. The hexagonal-shaped Blackwell Basin, with which Poplar Dock (and the West India Docks) communicated, is seen to its right, giving access to the River Thames beyond. The Great Western's Poplar Goods depot is just visible against the near quay of the U-shaped dock, with the shiny glass (saw-tooth style) canopy roof to the loading bay on the lower side of the main building. The former L&NWR, Great Northern and North London Railways also had goods and coal depots in the immediate vicinity, and these may be seen by reference to the OS map. Right: *The NLR goods warehouse at Poplar, leased to the Great Western, and viewed in 1898. The glass roof of the cartage loading bay to the left of the main building was that which shines in the adjacent aerial photo of the docks. A tank locomotive is seen shunting on the adjacent GNR lines.*
SIMMONS AEROFILMS

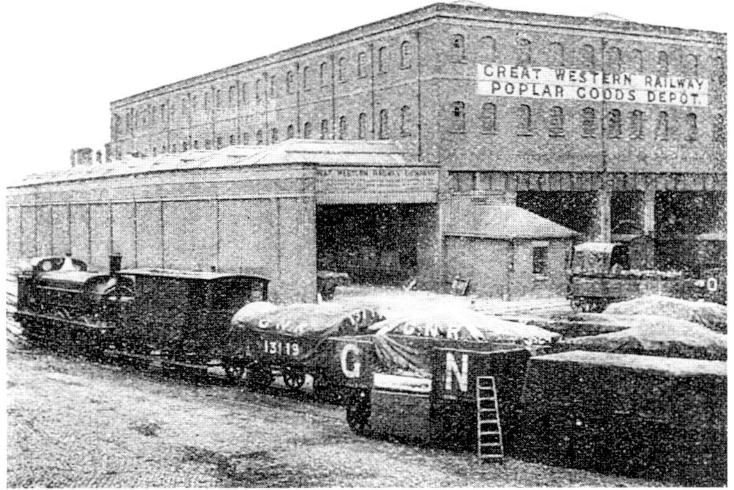

/ICTORIA & ALBERT

he main Victoria & Albert depot dated ɔm 1902. It was located near the north-estern corner of the Royal Albert Dock, ıd was reached by rail from the Great 'estern main line over the North ondon, Great Eastern and Port uthority lines. About 150 wagons could ≥ stabled at V & A. As well as docks traf-c, it dealt with general traffic for arking, East Ham, Woolwich, Ilford and ɛighbouring suburbs, which was carted ,/ GWR road vehicles. Before WWI, some 200,000 tons of goods passed through the depot each year, falling to 125,000 tons in the 1930s.

There was also the 'Waterside Depot' at the V & A (Victoria Dock), which was actually inside the docks, and handled traffic of all kinds from firms having waterside premises on the Lower Thames and on the River Medway, no charge being made for use of the GWR's wharf.

A 12-ton crane was provided at the V & A goods station, and another of 7-tons capacity at the waterside depot (hence, no single article weighing more than 7 tons could be accepted for barging). In 1925, a total of 213 men were employed by the GWR at this goods depot, which was also provided with over 70 horse-drawn and 34 motor vehicles.

Dock working at Poplar and V&A docks will be covered in the *Docks* volume of this series.

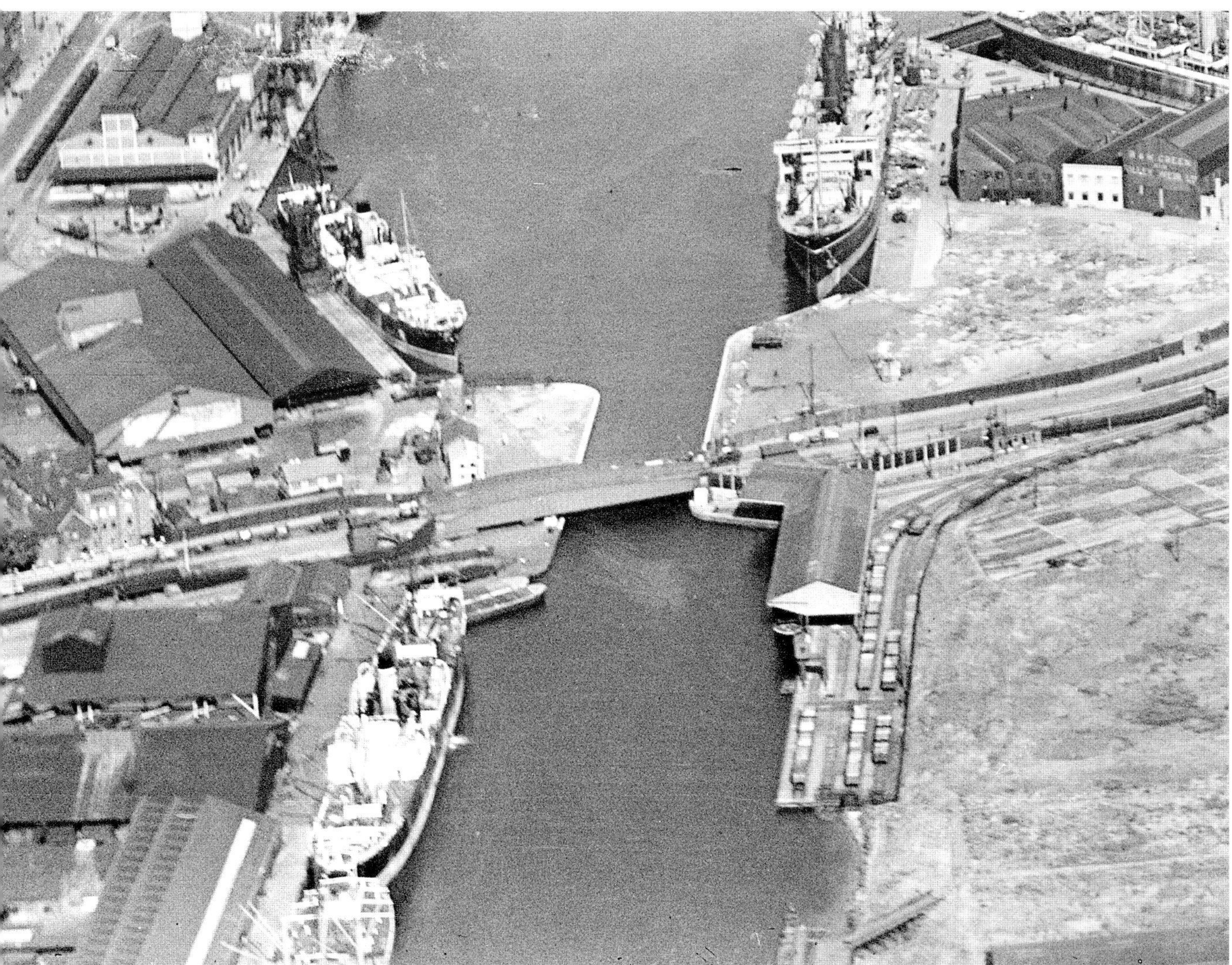

ːft: *A view eastwards along the axis of the Royal Victoria and oyal Albert Docks towards the river and the Gallions Reach ›rtion of the Thames in May 1934. Most of the Victoria Dock was ›low and behind the camera, below the swing bridge at the bottom ' the picture. The Albert Dock is seen running up the middle of the :ture, with the Albert Basin at the top, against the river. The King ›orge V Dock features at top right. Both of the two GWR depots the V&A Docks are shown, the terminal depot proper at lower ·ft, to the left of a loop of track that ran around the site, with its ileage yard running up the picture on the extreme left, parallel to e docks cut. The Waterside depot (for barge traffic) is seen on the 'ctoria Dock, immediately to the right of the swing bridge at e bottom right of the picture, with a 'kinked' awning.*

Above: *A close-up of Waterside depot, at bottom right, in July 1930, with a barge just visible under the canopy. The space on the left dock wall of the connecting waterway was left for the road-rail bridge to swing safely out of the way to allow shipping to pass between the two docks. Notice the number of barges alongside ocean-going ships for over-side loading and unloading. Both dry docks (upper right) had ships in for repair.*

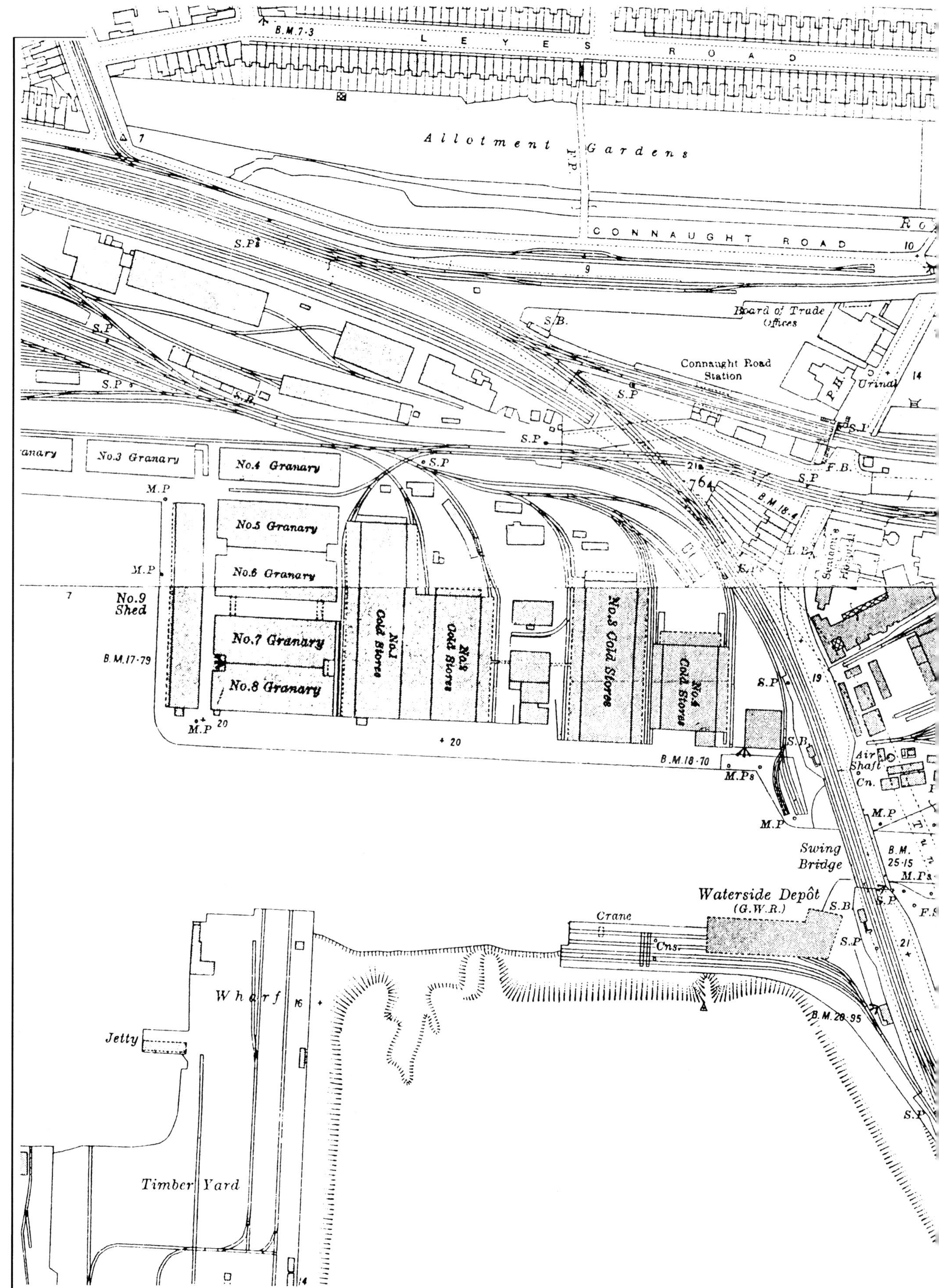

Taken from 25-inch Ordnance Survey for 1914. Crown copyright reserved.